LEAD LIKE JESUS
DAILY DEVOTIONAL

Lead Like Jesus Daily Devotional

©2012 The Center for Faithwalk Leadership dba Lead Like Jesus

Published by The Center for Faithwalk Leadership dba Lead Like Jesus
3506 Professional Circle, Augusta, GA 30907
800.383.6890
LeadLikeJesus.com

Unless otherwise noted, Scripture quotations are taken from the HOLY BIBLE,
NEW INTERNATIONAL VERSION®. NIV®. ©1973, 1978, 1984 by International Bible
Society. Used by permission of Zondervan. All rights reserved.

Scripture quotations marked NLT are taken from the Holy Bible, New
Living Translation, © 1996, 2004. Used by permission of Tyndale
House Publishers, Inc., Wheaton, Illinois 60189. All rights reserved.

ISBN-13: 9781612914503

Printed in the United States of America

Dear Reader,

It is with great joy that I invite you to a daily connection with our Heavenly Father through the pages of this book. We are deeply grateful for Debbie Piper, Lead Like Jesus Master Facilitator, whose written words are truly the overflow of her heart and an invitation to yours.

We believe that effective leadership begins on the inside with the heart. We also believe the only way to have a healthy heart is by creating time and space to connect with the Father as Jesus did while He was on earth. Through the pages of this book, there are reminders of what God's Word has to say about a specific topic, insights for application, and prayers especially for your life.

Remember that our desire is to help you create a habit of connecting with the Father. It isn't just about how many Scripture verses you memorize (although it is a helpful thing to do) or checking off your "daily devotion." In fact, spending time reading this book or setting aside space to be with God is not about you improving who you are at all. Reading these devotions daily will not provide a ladder to get up to God; He has already come down to you. These devotions are thoughtful reflections to remind you that we have been redeemed today and forever by His grace. The space we create for God to speak and act in our lives will remind us of His great one-way love for us in that "while we were still sinners, Christ died for us" (Romans 5:8). His love for us grows love in us, and then **from** us! It is as we soak in His unconditional love, the antidote for our pride and fear, that our hearts become healthy and we find freedom to lead, love, and live boldly in service to others.

I pray that out of His glorious riches He may strengthen you with power through His Spirit in your inner being, so that Christ may dwell in your hearts through faith. And I pray that you, being rooted and established in love, may have power, together with all the saints, to grasp how wide and long and high and deep is the love of Christ, and to know this love that surpasses knowledge—that you may be filled to the measure of all the fullness of God.
(Ephesians 3:16-19)

Amen!

Praying for you,

Phyllis H. Hendry
President & CEO
Lead Like Jesus

DEBBIE PIPER HAS BEEN DEVELOPING AND EQUIPPING LEADERS SINCE 1986.

An experienced leadership coach, author, consultant and speaker, Debbie is gifted at connecting people and ideas. She serves leaders, churches, organizations, and corporations, helping to create results-based strategies that align people with their personal strengths, one another, and organizational goals.

As a coach, Debbie helps leaders discover creative solutions and design effective next steps. As a facilitator and speaker, her presentations are marked by creativity, interaction, and insight customized for the needs of participants.

Debbie has been a Lead Like Jesus facilitator since August 2007 and a master trainer since 2011. Debbie works with the Florida Baptist Convention to spread the Lead Like Jesus message to churches, ministry leaders, and pastors throughout Florida.

Debbie's writing credits include a book, curriculum, small group studies, several devotional series, and creative development pieces for organizations and corporations. She is also the author of the 2011, 2012, and 2013 *Lead Like Jesus Devotions* included in this book.

Find out more about Debbie online at **WWW.DEBBIEPIPERCONSULTING.COM**.

 # A DIFFERENT WAY

JESUS CALLED THEM TOGETHER AND SAID, "YOU KNOW THAT THE RULERS OF THE GENTILES LORD IT OVER THEM, AND THEIR HIGH OFFICIALS EXERCISE AUTHORITY OVER THEM. NOT SO WITH YOU. INSTEAD, WHOEVER WANTS TO BECOME GREAT AMONG YOU MUST BE YOUR SERVANT..."
MATTHEW 20:25-26

Looking at the world around us, it is easy to assume that the only way to lead is to look out for ourselves. Looking at Jesus offers a different perspective. We hear His words, "Not so with you." We see Him wash His disciples' feet. His words and actions model a new way of leadership. Whose model of leadership are you following?

PRAYER
Lord, I want my life to be different. I choose to follow You. I want to model my life after Your life, not after the world. Help me learn what that means. Show me how I can serve others today. In Jesus' Name, Amen.

_____
_____
_____
_____
_____
_____
_____
_____

 A FRESH START

BECAUSE OF THE LORD'S GREAT LOVE WE ARE NOT CONSUMED, FOR HIS COMPASSIONS NEVER FAIL. THEY ARE NEW EVERY MORNING; GREAT IS YOUR FAITHFULNESS.
LAMENTATIONS 3:22-23

Each morning gives us a fresh start, a new opportunity to take the tendency to edge God out and exchange it for a perspective of exalting God only. Each morning gives us a chance to reflect and regroup, to breathe deeply of God and renew our energy for the day ahead. The newness of each day reflects God's ongoing work of grace, grace that frees us from the past and offers a way forward. Grace offers God's presence and power at the point of your need. Where do you need a fresh start?

PRAYER
Lord, thank You for fresh starts. Thank You for Your grace, poured out through the cross and through the Spirit. Thank You that Jesus comes to me and invites me to move forward. Help me to move forward into this day as one who extends grace to others so that they, too, can have fresh starts. In Jesus' Name, Amen.

_____

_____

_____

_____

_____

_____

_____

_____

 A LEADER'S PRAYER

**...GOD SAID, "ASK FOR WHATEVER YOU WANT ME TO GIVE YOU."
SOLOMON ANSWERED, "... I AM ONLY A LITTLE CHILD AND DO NOT
KNOW HOW TO CARRY OUT MY DUTIES.... SO GIVE YOUR SERVANT A
DISCERNING HEART TO GOVERN YOUR PEOPLE AND TO DISTINGUISH
BETWEEN RIGHT AND WRONG."**
1 KINGS 3:5-9

What is your greatest need as a leader? Your answer to that question
might vary day by day, depending on the challenge you're currently facing.
It's easy to focus on externals, like "If only that person would do something
differently" or "If only these circumstances would change." When God
offered to give Solomon anything he asked for, Solomon wisely focused on
himself. He admitted that he was dependent on God, and humbly asked
God to give him the discernment to lead well.

PRAYER
*God, what a privilege it is to be used by You to influence others. I want my
influence to count. I humbly admit that I need You to show me how to lead
well. Please give me the discernment I need to lead Your people. In Jesus'
Name, Amen.*

_____

_____

_____

_____

_____

_____

_____

_____

A NEW WAY OF LEADING: LOVE

SO NOW I AM GIVING YOU A NEW COMMANDMENT: LOVE EACH OTHER. JUST AS I HAVE LOVED YOU, YOU SHOULD LOVE EACH OTHER. YOUR LOVE FOR ONE ANOTHER WILL PROVE TO THE WORLD THAT YOU ARE MY DISCIPLES.
JOHN 13:34-35 (NLT)

After washing His disciples' feet, Jesus gave them a new command: "Love one another." No longer was love for others to be defined by the Old Testament teaching of loving our neighbors as we love ourselves; Jesus' love for us is now the standard by which true love is measured. Jesus had already demonstrated His humility and selfless nature throughout His life and ministry, and He was about to go to the cross to give up His life so that others could live. What does obedience to His command to love one another look like in your life today?

PRAYER
Jesus, I can't obey Your command to love in my own strength. Give me a new heart and a new spirit; transform my thinking about love. Open my eyes to how You want me to love the people in my life. Transform me into a person who loves others like You love me. In Your Name, Amen.

_____

_____

_____

_____

_____

_____

_____

_____

 A TRANSFORMED LIFE

AND WE, WHO WITH UNVEILED FACES ALL REFLECT THE LORD'S GLORY, ARE BEING TRANSFORMED INTO HIS LIKENESS WITH EVER-INCREASING GLORY, WHICH COMES FROM THE LORD, WHO IS THE SPIRIT.
2 CORINTHIANS 3:18

Simon Peter and Andrew and James and John, are two sets of brothers who heard Jesus' call. From being competitors in business, they found themselves transformed into followers of Jesus, and eventually into ministry partners. Jesus has a way of taking us on life-transforming journeys, and nothing is left untouched: personality, business, or relationships. What part of your life does He want to transform today?

PRAYER

Jesus, I hear Your call. I don't know what all it will mean in my life, but I want to respond. And I want You to start Your transformational work right here where You find me. Transform my character, my relationships, and my daily work. I want to look, speak, and act like You. In Your Name, Amen.

_____

_____

_____

_____

_____

_____

_____

_____

_____

 AN AUDIENCE OF ONE

WORK HARD AND CHEERFULLY AT WHATEVER YOU DO, AS THOUGH YOU WERE WORKING FOR THE LORD RATHER THAN FOR PEOPLE. REMEMBER THAT THE LORD WILL GIVE YOU AN INHERITANCE AS YOUR REWARD, AND THE MASTER YOU ARE SERVING IS CHRIST.
COLOSSIANS 3:23-24 (NLT)

Whom do you serve? Is it hard to come up with a list? Or is the list of names that comes to mind overwhelming? When all is said and done, each of us serves only one person. Allow your mind today to focus on serving and pleasing God. As His servant, move into each situation with a conscious awareness of His presence, listening for His voice to direct you.

PRAYER
Jesus, just like You kept Your eyes and ears tuned to the Father's voice, I want to move through this day listening for Your direction and seeing others through Your eyes. Whatever I do, I want to focus on pleasing You above all others this day. In Jesus' Name, Amen.

_____
_____
_____
_____
_____
_____
_____
_____
_____

CREATIVE CONFLICT

GOD HAS GIVEN GIFTS TO EACH OF YOU FROM HIS GREAT VARIETY OF SPIRITUAL GIFTS. MANAGE THEM WELL SO THAT GOD'S GENEROSITY CAN FLOW THROUGH YOU.
1 PETER 4:10 (NLT)

Conflict is the natural result of differing perspectives and personalities. Yet conflict doesn't need to be destructive. When we as team members serve the goal rather than our own egos, conflict can actually be constructive. As we humbly bring our best thinking to the table and invite others to do the same, new insights and solutions can emerge, resulting in increased creativity and synergy. Where can you use conflict as a springboard to creativity?

PRAYER
Lord, thank You that in Your wisdom You call people with differing points of view to serve together to accomplish team-sized goals. Help me to humbly offer the best of what I have to give, to graciously receive the best that others give, and to work toward creative results that reflect the power of collaboration. In Jesus' Name, Amen.

_____

_____

_____

_____

_____

_____

_____

_____

DEFINING SUCCESS

JOHN REPLIED, "GOD IN HEAVEN APPOINTS EACH PERSON'S WORK. YOU YOURSELVES KNOW HOW PLAINLY I TOLD YOU THAT I AM NOT THE MESSIAH. I AM HERE TO PREPARE THE WAY FOR HIM—THAT IS ALL. THE BRIDE WILL GO WHERE THE BRIDEGROOM IS. A BRIDEGROOM'S FRIEND REJOICES WITH HIM. I AM THE BRIDEGROOM'S FRIEND, AND I AM FILLED WITH JOY AT HIS SUCCESS. HE MUST BECOME GREATER AND GREATER, AND I MUST BECOME LESS AND LESS.
JOHN 3:27-30 (NLT)

How do you define success? Is it about receiving personal rewards and recognition? John the Baptist's followers became upset when Jesus began to eclipse John in the public eye. John quickly reminded them that his life mission was to point other people to Jesus, not to make a name for himself. John knew what God had called him to do. What has God called you to do?

PRAYER

Lord, my life is not my own. You created me for Your purposes. Forgive me when I get off-track. Refocus me on what You want me to do, and help me point others to You through my life. In Jesus' Name, Amen.

 DAY BY DAY

AT DAYBREAK JESUS WENT OUT TO A SOLITARY PLACE. THE PEOPLE WERE LOOKING FOR HIM AND WHEN THEY CAME TO WHERE HE WAS, THEY TRIED TO KEEP HIM FROM LEAVING THEM.
LUKE 4:42

Everyone seems to have an agenda for our lives—bosses, team leaders, clients, co-workers, friends, our children. Even Jesus had to work to maintain His focus in the midst of training followers, meeting needs, public speaking, demanding crowds, and a busy travel schedule. How did Jesus maintain His focus? He regularly made time to get away with His Father to talk things over. How do you maintain your focus?

PRAYER
Jesus, if You needed to take time with God to stay focused, then I know I need to make a point of spending time with God, too. Thank You for this reminder today. Help me to keep time with You at the top of my priorities. In Jesus' Name, Amen.

_____
_____
_____
_____
_____
_____
_____
_____

FIRST THINGS FIRST

WE LOVE BECAUSE HE FIRST LOVED US.
1 JOHN 4:19

Our love for others increases as we come to know and experience God's love for us. What do you know of God's love? Do you know that God loves you? Do you believe that He loves you? Believing implies confidence, satisfaction, and resting in God's love for you. As you believe—have confidence in, are satisfied by, rest in—as you come to trust His redemptive love for you, you will find yourself passing on God's unconditional love to those around you.

PRAYER
God, I need Your love. I need You. Let Your love heal and restore me, and give me confidence and courage to live this day. I am grateful that Your love for me never wavers, that it doesn't depend on my performance or circumstances. Thank You for reminding me that I can trust You and Your love to transform me into someone who loves like Jesus. Help me to drink deeply of Your love so that I overflow with love for others, like Jesus did. In Jesus' Name, Amen.

 FREE TO SERVE

FOR YOU HAVE BEEN CALLED TO LIVE IN FREEDOM—NOT FREEDOM TO SATISFY YOUR SINFUL NATURE, BUT FREEDOM TO SERVE ONE ANOTHER IN LOVE.
GALATIANS 5:13 (NLT)

Free time, free giveaways, buy one/get one free, free to choose... freedom in large and small things is a big deal to most of us. Scripture tells us that we are free in Christ; but what are we free to do? How do we use our freedom? Jesus used His freedom to serve us. How do you use the freedom you have in Christ?

PRAYER

Lord, thank You for the freedom I have in Christ Jesus. I am humbled that He used His freedom to benefit me and others. Reshape my perspective on freedom, especially the freedom I have in Christ. Transform me so that I live for the benefit of others and not just for myself. I ask this in the Name of Jesus, who died for me so that I might be free from condemnation. In Jesus' Name, Amen.

_____
_____
_____
_____
_____
_____
_____
_____
_____

 INVESTING IN DEVELOPING OTHERS

YOU HAVE HEARD ME TEACH MANY THINGS THAT HAVE BEEN CONFIRMED BY MANY RELIABLE WITNESSES. TEACH THESE GREAT TRUTHS TO TRUSTWORTHY PEOPLE WHO ARE ABLE TO PASS THEM ON TO OTHERS.
2 TIMOTHY 2:2 (NLT)

Paul's letters throughout the New Testament reflect his commitment to developing leaders in local churches. His ministry wasn't about making a name for himself; it was about bringing the good news of Jesus Christ to people and establishing functioning local churches. Servant leaders focus on calling forth and developing the gifts of others, not on drawing attention to themselves. They call others to follow in Jesus' footsteps as servant leaders. Who can and will you invest in today?

PRAYER
Father, open my eyes to those whom I can invest in today. I want my influence in their lives to point to You and to Jesus as their role model for life and leadership. Remove the things in me that would keep them from being drawn to You through my example. In Jesus' Name, Amen.

_____
_____
_____
_____
_____
_____
_____
_____
_____

 LASTING IMPACT

EVEN CHILDREN ARE KNOWN BY THE WAY THEY ACT, WHETHER THEIR CONDUCT IS PURE AND RIGHT.
PROVERBS 20:11 (NLT)

Day-to-day interactions with others offer rich opportunities for us to influence the thinking, behavior, and development of people. As we invest in relationships with family, friends, and co-workers, we can create a legacy of servant leadership. How do your values shape your interactions with those closest to you? How will they know God better because of you today?

PRAYER

Lord, I want my actions to reveal that I am Your child. I want people who know me to be drawn to You because of my life. How will they see You in me today? How can I reflect You more clearly? Make me aware of the power of my words and actions, Lord, I pray. In Jesus' Name, Amen.

_____

_____

_____

_____

_____

_____

_____

_____

_____

 LOVE IS...

LOVE IS PATIENT, LOVE IS KIND. IT DOES NOT ENVY, IT DOES NOT BOAST, IT IS NOT PROUD. IT IS NOT RUDE, IT IS NOT SELF-SEEKING, IT IS NOT EASILY ANGERED, IT KEEPS NO RECORD OF WRONGS. LOVE DOES NOT DELIGHT IN EVIL BUT REJOICES WITH THE TRUTH. IT ALWAYS PROTECTS, ALWAYS TRUSTS, ALWAYS HOPES, ALWAYS PERSEVERES.
1 CORINTHIANS 13:4-7

Sometimes we make relationships harder than they need to be. Sometimes we allow cultural definitions of love to overshadow God's definition of love. God defines love as action taken in the best interest of the one who is loved. Paul spells out some of these actions in 1 Corinthians 13:4-7. How do these qualities describe you and your relationships with others?

PRAYER
Thank You, God, for loving me like this; and thank You, Jesus, for modeling this kind of love. I know that through Your Spirit I have the ability to love others like You love me. As I go through this day, remind me to love others with the love You've poured out on me. In Jesus' Name, Amen.

_____

_____

_____

_____

_____

_____

_____

_____

MODELING SERVICE

JESUS KNEW THAT THE FATHER HAD PUT ALL THINGS UNDER HIS POWER, AND THAT HE HAD COME FROM GOD AND WAS RETURNING TO GOD; SO HE GOT UP FROM THE MEAL, TOOK OFF HIS OUTER CLOTHING, AND WRAPPED A TOWEL AROUND HIS WAIST. AFTER THAT, HE POURED WATER INTO A BASIN AND BEGAN TO WASH HIS DISCIPLES' FEET, DRYING THEM WITH THE TOWEL THAT WAS WRAPPED AROUND HIM.

JOHN 13:3-5

Jesus used every available means to help His disciples understand servant leadership. When their hearts and minds still couldn't grasp it, He showed them what it looked like. The simplest acts, performed with love and respect, can open our eyes to profound truth. This clear demonstration of servanthood was burned into the hearts and memories of the disciples. What opportunities will you use to model servant leadership today?

PRAYER

Lord Jesus, I am humbled at Your willingness to wash Your disciples' feet. Forgive me for thinking that some things are beneath me. Open my eyes to ways that I can serve others with love and respect. Remind me that my actions and attitudes have a profound impact on those I love and lead. In Your Name, Amen.

⟳ PRAYER THAT CHANGES THINGS

AND PRAY IN THE SPIRIT ON ALL OCCASIONS WITH ALL KINDS OF PRAYERS AND REQUESTS. WITH THIS IN MIND, BE ALERT AND ALWAYS KEEP ON PRAYING FOR ALL THE SAINTS.
EPHESIANS 6:18

How is prayer impacting your relationships with those you lead? What insights is God giving you about how to love and serve others? Talking with God (not just *at* God) about the people in our lives helps us to build and maintain healthy relationships with them. What if your prayer today was for God to help you see others as He sees them and love them as He loves them? Try it.

PRAYER
Father, I lift up to You the people in my life—my family members, my co-workers, and my friends. As I name them before You now, give me Your heart for them. I know that Jesus died for each one of them, to bring them forgiveness, reconciliation with You, and wholeness in exchange for their brokenness. In Jesus' Name, Amen.

_____

_____

_____

_____

_____

_____

_____

_____

RESULTS OR RELATIONSHIPS

WE LOVED YOU SO MUCH THAT WE GAVE YOU NOT ONLY GOD'S GOOD NEWS BUT OUR OWN LIVES, TOO. DON'T YOU REMEMBER, DEAR BROTHERS AND SISTERS, HOW HARD WE WORKED AMONG YOU? NIGHT AND DAY WE TOILED TO EARN A LIVING SO THAT OUR EXPENSES WOULD NOT BE A BURDEN TO ANYONE THERE AS WE PREACHED GOD'S GOOD NEWS AMONG YOU.
1 THESSALONIANS 2:8-9 (NLT)

How do you deal with the tension between results and relationship in your leadership? Are there times when your desire to see something accomplished means that you are willing to sacrifice relationship? As servant leaders, we understand that developing people is best accomplished through relationship. No more using others to satisfy our need to prove ourselves. Paul followed Jesus' example, investing relationally in the lives of others in order to help them realize their God-given potential and accomplish God-given goals. What about you?

PRAYER
Jesus, thank You for inviting me into relationship with You as well as inviting me to be part of Your purposes in the world. Show me how to develop caring relationships with those I lead. In Your Name, Amen.

_____

_____

_____

_____

_____

_____

_____

_____

_____

SPIRITUAL FRIENDSHIPS

AND LET US CONSIDER HOW WE MAY SPUR ONE ANOTHER ON TOWARD LOVE AND GOOD DEEDS.
HEBREWS 10:24

Jesus dug deep into relationships with people. Mary, Martha, and Lazarus were close friends, as were Peter, James, and John. As closely connected to the Father as He was, Jesus still needed relationships with people during His lifetime on earth. If Jesus needed friends, it makes sense that we need friends. Friends to encourage us, offer us comfort, pray for us, challenge us, and hold us accountable. Who do you count among your closest friends? What are you doing to cultivate spiritual friends to journey with you through life?

PRAYER
Jesus, I need friends to walk with me in life, friends who point me toward You. Open my eyes to the people You've placed around me, and help me to develop trusting relationships with them. Make me into a friend who spurs others on toward love and good deeds. Show me how I can be that kind of friend today. In Your Name, Amen.

_____

_____

_____

_____

_____

_____

_____

_____

_____

THE HEART OF THE MATTER

ABOVE ALL ELSE, GUARD YOUR HEART, FOR IT IS THE WELLSPRING OF LIFE.
PROVERBS 4:23

Solid relationships are the basis for teams and families that are able to weather the challenges of living and working together. Each of us has experienced times when our contributions have been welcomed by others, as well as times when they've been rejected. Truth be told, we've probably also experienced times when we've hardened our hearts against other people and rejected them. What helps you keep your heart open to others in the midst of the ups and downs of life?

PRAYER

Jesus, I'm amazed at how You were able to handle whatever life threw at You—temptation, bickering disciples, the death of a friend, even popularity—and use it to reveal God's purposes. Help me walk securely in my relationship with You and to be a contributor in the settings in which You've placed me. Keep my heart open to God and to the needs of others. In Your Name, Amen.

THE INNER AND OUTER LIFE

BUT SOMEONE WILL SAY, "YOU HAVE FAITH; I HAVE DEEDS." SHOW ME YOUR FAITH WITHOUT DEEDS, AND I WILL SHOW YOU MY FAITH BY WHAT I DO.
JAMES 2:18

Mary and Martha were sisters, born and raised in the same family. Yet they each had distinct personalities and behaviors. While both were drawn to Jesus, Mary's longing was to listen to His teaching, while Martha's devotion ultimately expressed itself in practical service. For centuries, they have served as examples of the inner life of devotion and the outer expression of service. Which end of the spectrum are you most drawn to? What are you doing to make sure that your service for Jesus is fed by a growing devotion to Him?

PRAYER

Jesus, thank You for creating me so that my spiritual life is nurtured both by my relationship with You and by serving in Your name. I want my outward service to reflect my inner devotion to You, just like Your life was an expression of Your intimate relationship with Your Father. In Your Name, Amen.

_____

_____

_____

_____

_____

_____

_____

_____

_____

 THEY TOOK NOTE

WHEN THEY SAW THE COURAGE OF PETER AND JOHN AND REALIZED THAT THEY WERE UNSCHOOLED, ORDINARY MEN, THEY WERE ASTONISHED AND THEY TOOK NOTE THAT THESE MEN HAD BEEN WITH JESUS.
ACTS 4:13

When others look at you, what do they see? Is there anything about your leadership that says you are different? Different from the world around you? Different from who you used to be? Jesus has a way of taking ordinary people on a journey that transforms them into men and women who live with courage and compassion. What will others take note of in your life today?

PRAYER

Jesus, You know where I was when You and I started this transformational journey. I'm so glad You didn't just leave me there. Keep transforming me - that's my prayer. I want others to know that I have been with You. In Your Name, Amen.

TREASURES NEW AND OLD

HE SAID TO THEM, "THEREFORE EVERY TEACHER OF THE LAW WHO HAS BEEN INSTRUCTED ABOUT THE KINGDOM OF HEAVEN IS LIKE THE OWNER OF A HOUSE WHO BRINGS OUT OF HIS STOREROOM NEW TREASURES AS WELL AS OLD."
MATTHEW 13:52

Sometimes ministry opportunities arise unexpectedly. A phone call to a colleague, friend or family member turns out to be God's sovereign timing, and you discover that God has placed you in a unique position to speak into their life. Where do you find words of wisdom, comfort, and encouragement? Jesus often spoke in parables, helping people find spiritual truth through everyday examples. He was so familiar with Scripture that He could speak God's truth in any situation. What about you?

PRAYER
Lord, I want to be prepared for any ministry opportunity that You send my way today. Help me to listen to what You are saying to me in Scripture, not just settle for reading the words. I want to add fresh insight to the truth You've already revealed to me, so that I will have Your word to offer to others today. In Jesus' Name, Amen.

_____

_____

_____

_____

_____

_____

_____

_____

_____

WHEN A LEADER FAILS

IF WE CONFESS OUR SINS, HE IS FAITHFUL AND JUST AND WILL FORGIVE US OUR SINS AND PURIFY US FROM ALL UNRIGHTEOUSNESS.
1 JOHN 1:9

As servant leaders, we are not immune to failure or temptation, nor to giving into temptation. The question is not if we will succumb to temptation, but how we respond when we fail, when we do give in. Writing to first century believers, John offers a promise that still holds true today. Accepting responsibility is the first step in receiving God's forgiveness, a forgiveness that is ours when we simply and humbly acknowledge our shortcomings to Him. His forgiveness offers us the path forward. Will you take the first step?

PRAYER

God, thank You for offering me a way forward. Thank You that Your forgiveness is just as powerful and cleansing today as it was the day I first received it. You know my most recent failure. I acknowledge that I need Your forgiveness and Your cleansing in order to move ahead. Show me the way forward, I ask in Jesus' Name, Amen.

WHEN A LEADER QUESTIONS

WHEN JOHN HEARD IN PRISON WHAT CHRIST WAS DOING, HE SENT HIS DISCIPLES TO ASK HIM, "ARE YOU THE ONE WHO WAS TO COME, OR SHOULD WE EXPECT SOMEONE ELSE?"
MATTHEW 11:2-3

There are times in our journeys as servant leaders when we find ourselves unsure, confused. Circumstances or results aren't what we expected, and doubt and questions fill our minds. Instead of allowing our confusion to drive us away from God, we can follow John the Baptist's example and take our questions to Jesus. Where are you struggling in your ability to serve as Jesus did? What difference could it make to bring those questions to Jesus instead of struggling with them on your own?

PRAYER
Jesus, You know the circumstances in my life that cause me to wonder if I'm really making any difference as a leader. Thank You that I don't have to hide these doubts from You, that I can bring my questions to You. Thank You for being the One who is the difference-maker in my life and in the lives of those I care for. In Your Name, Amen.

WHERE THE SPIRIT LEADS

AFTER PAUL HAD SEEN THE VISION, WE GOT READY AT ONCE TO LEAVE FOR MACEDONIA, CONCLUDING THAT GOD HAD CALLED US TO PREACH THE GOSPEL TO THEM.
ACTS 16:10

In Acts 16:6-14, Paul had mapped out his ministry plan, but Jesus kept closing the doors for him. By staying tuned in to the Spirit's direction, Paul found a group of women that God had prepared to hear his message. As leaders, we have to keep our hearts and minds focused on God's purposes and direction, for our families, our work, our ministry. Sometimes that involves closed doors; sometimes it involves unexpected invitations. Always, it involves staying open to the Spirit's leading. How is God using circumstances to guide you toward His purposes? How are you responding?

PRAYER

Lord, I want to respond as well to the closed doors in my life as to the unexpected invitations You give me. Most of all, I want my life to reflect my faith in You to those I journey with and those to whom You send me. May my attitudes reflect my trust and confidence in You. In Jesus' Name, Amen.

_____

_____

_____

_____

_____

_____

_____

_____

_____

A HELP OR A HINDRANCE

DAVID FASTENED ON HIS SWORD OVER THE TUNIC AND TRIED WALKING AROUND, BECAUSE HE WAS NOT USED TO THEM. "I CANNOT GO IN THESE," HE SAID TO SAUL, "BECAUSE I AM NOT USED TO THEM." SO HE TOOK THEM OFF.

1 SAMUEL 17:39

King Saul was impressed with David's courage and wanted to help by providing him with the best that he could offer. But Saul's equipment was matched to his own skill set and turned out to be a hindrance to David. Saul had to accept that there were other ways of accomplishing the task than how he might approach it. Are you willing to allow others to lead according to how God has designed them, even if it might be different from you?

PRAYER

Lord, I'm grateful for the ways You work in my life, the things You've taught me, and the gifts You've given me. Sometimes I think You work in everyone else's life exactly like You do in mine. Help me to give others the freedom to develop their gifts and lead using the insight and experience You've given them, and help me to support them in ways that matter. In Jesus' Name, Amen.

 A NEW CREATION

SO WE HAVE STOPPED EVALUATING OTHERS BY WHAT THE WORLD THINKS ABOUT THEM. ONCE I MISTAKENLY THOUGHT OF CHRIST THAT WAY, AS THOUGH HE WERE MERELY A HUMAN BEING. HOW DIFFERENTLY I THINK ABOUT HIM NOW! WHAT THIS MEANS IS THAT THOSE WHO BECOME CHRISTIANS BECOME NEW PERSONS. THEY ARE NOT THE SAME ANYMORE, FOR THE OLD LIFE IS GONE. A NEW LIFE HAS BEGUN!
2 CORINTHIANS 5:16-17 (NLT)

Jesus transforms our future. Saul, persecutor of Christians, was transformed into Paul, Christian leader and teacher. Thomas, doubting as he once did, turned into an evangelist. Peter, denier of Christ, became a preacher. Don't allow your past to define your future or limit what God wants to accomplish through you. Dare to live humbly and confidently based on your new identity in Christ. Who in your life needs to hear this message today?

PRAYER
Jesus, thank You that my future doesn't need to be limited by my past. I want my life today to reflect my new identity in You. Show me the people in my life who need to hear this message today. Let my life and example encourage others to dare to attempt great things for You. In Your Name, Amen.

💜 AN INSIDE PERSPECTIVE

MAY THE WORDS OF MY MOUTH AND THE MEDITATION OF MY HEART BE PLEASING IN YOUR SIGHT, O LORD, MY ROCK AND MY REDEEMER.
PSALM 19:14

Depending on the circumstances in which we find ourselves, we may appear overly confident to those around us or they may judge us as woefully inadequate to the situation. When God looks at your heart, does He see a heart that is humbly dependent upon Him? This is the kind of person God is looking for, the kind of person God uses, the kind of person who can influence others. What does God see as He looks at your heart today?

PRAYER

Lord, when You look at my heart, what do You see? Which of my words have been pleasing to You? What am I meditating on? Does it please You? Search me, Lord. Know me. Forgive me. Shape me. Make me pleasing in Your sight. You are my Rock and my Redeemer. In Jesus' Name, Amen.

APPEARANCES CAN BE DECEIVING

BUT THE LORD SAID TO SAMUEL, "DON'T JUDGE BY HIS APPEARANCE OR HEIGHT, FOR I HAVE REJECTED HIM. THE LORD DOESN'T MAKE DECISIONS THE WAY YOU DO! PEOPLE JUDGE BY OUTWARD APPEARANCE, BUT THE LORD LOOKS AT A PERSON'S THOUGHTS AND INTENTIONS."
1 SAMUEL 16:7 (NLT)

It is a common thing to judge others based on outward appearances and first impressions. Common, but not spiritual. The prophet Samuel had a similar experience when he first saw God's anointed king, David. He saw a boy, unimpressive, unskilled at kingly duties and leading a nation. God saw a faithful, teachable heart in both Samuel and David. These were the qualities that God was looking for in a leader for His people. What do you look for when you look at others? Who around you shows evidence of a faithful, teachable heart?

PRAYER

Lord, let me see others through Your eyes, through spiritual eyes. Give me eyes that see beyond appearances, beyond skill sets, beyond personality. Help me to see what You see, spiritual qualities that combine to create potential servant leaders. Help me to recognize and invest in emerging leaders. In Jesus' Name, Amen.

♥ AUTHENTIC LEADERSHIP

THAT WHICH WAS FROM THE BEGINNING, WHICH WE HAVE HEARD, WHICH WE HAVE SEEN WITH OUR EYES, WHICH WE HAVE LOOKED AT AND OUR HANDS HAVE TOUCHED--THIS WE PROCLAIM CONCERNING THE WORD OF LIFE.

1 JOHN 1:1

Jesus' first disciples proclaimed a message based on their personal relationship with Jesus. We have that same privilege. If our lives and leadership are not based on an intimate, experiential knowledge of Jesus, our words will sound empty, and we will not be able to sustain a lifestyle of servant leadership. Who do you know Jesus to be? Have you heard Him speak to you? Have you seen Him at work? What can you tell others about Him?

PRAYER

Jesus, I want my life and leadership to flow from my relationship with You. I want to see you, to hear You, to touch You. I want to share with others the life that You have given me. In Your Name, Amen.

_____

_____

_____

_____

_____

_____

_____

_____

BLESSED ARE THE PEACEMAKERS

BLESSED ARE THE PEACEMAKERS, FOR THEY WILL BE CALLED SONS OF GOD.
MATTHEW 5:9

Jonathan, heir apparent to the throne of Israel, was caught between his father Saul and his best friend. Threatened by David's success and popularity, Saul was convinced that David was trying to steal the throne. Jonathan risked his father's wrath, his own future, even his life, to plead David's case and reconcile Saul and David. Do you instigate conflict or work to achieve peace? When conflict grows heated, are you willing to take a stand for what is right? Are you known as a peacemaker?

PRAYER

Lord, it can be hard to avoid being caught up in conflict. There are so many things I don't want to be known as: an instigator, a conflict avoider, or someone who takes sides. Instead, I'd like to be called a peacemaker, following in Jonathan's (and Jesus') footsteps. Show me how I can live as a peacemaker today. In Jesus' Name, Amen.

 CHRIST IN ME

I HAVE BEEN CRUCIFIED WITH CHRIST AND I NO LONGER LIVE, BUT CHRIST LIVES IN ME. THE LIFE I LIVE IN THE BODY, I LIVE BY FAITH IN THE SON OF GOD, WHO LOVED ME AND GAVE HIMSELF FOR ME.
GALATIANS 2:20

To turn from a lifestyle of Edging God Out to one of Exalting God only requires dying to self. It is not accomplished by simply learning new external behaviors or erasing existing behaviors. We need to come to the point of surrendering all that we are to God, to be used for His purposes. The lives that we live are lived in the power of the Holy Spirit, as if Christ Himself were living through us. Where do you need to die to yourself and allow Christ to live through you?

PRAYER
Jesus, I am grateful that the Christian life is not a self-improvement program. I thank You that through Your sacrifice I can die to myself, and through Your resurrection I can rise to live in the power of the Spirit. Remake me in Your image. Empower me by Your Spirit. Transform my heart and mind so that I live, think, and act like You. In Your Name, Amen.

_____

_____

_____

_____

_____

_____

_____

_____

_____

COMPELLED BY LOVE

FOR CHRIST'S LOVE COMPELS US, BECAUSE WE ARE CONVINCED THAT ONE DIED FOR ALL, AND THEREFORE ALL DIED. AND HE DIED FOR ALL, THAT THOSE WHO LIVE SHOULD NO LONGER LIVE FOR THEMSELVES BUT FOR HIM WHO DIED FOR THEM AND WAS RAISED AGAIN.
2 CORINTHIANS 5:14-15

What compels your leadership? Making a name for yourself? Making a difference in the world of business? A desire to serve others? Or is it the love of Christ? The early followers of Jesus found that they couldn't live like they had before they came into contact with Jesus. They were changed by His love, changed by knowing Him. And they wanted others to experience the power of His love, the life change that knowing Him could bring. What about the people you will influence today? What difference will Christ's love for you make in how you treat them?

PRAYER

Jesus, thank You for loving me unconditionally, wholeheartedly, from the depths of Your being. Your love is changing my life. Your love is changing my leadership. Make me a leader who is compelled by Your love. In Your Name, Amen.

 FACING THE FACTS

YET HE [ABRAHAM] DID NOT WAVER THROUGH UNBELIEF REGARDING THE PROMISE OF GOD, BUT WAS STRENGTHENED IN HIS FAITH AND GAVE GLORY TO GOD, BEING FULLY PERSUADED THAT GOD HAD POWER TO DO WHAT HE HAD PROMISED.
ROMANS 4:20-21

Abraham faced the facts that at his and Sarah's advanced ages, it was impossible to have a son. But he didn't stop at the facts, and he didn't let the facts stop him. As leaders, there are times when we will be called to trust God in the face of overwhelming odds. That's when leaders are needed. That's when faith makes a difference. That's when God gets the glory. What impossible situation are you facing?

PRAYER

God, I believe that You can and will accomplish what You want to accomplish, regardless of the facts as I see them. I choose to trust You and Your power. I choose to focus on Your promises. Help me to point others to Your presence as together we move into the future You have in store for us. In Jesus' Name, Amen.

_____

_____

_____

_____

_____

_____

_____

_____

_____

 HIDE OR SEEK

"WHAT WAS IT HE SAID TO YOU?" ELI ASKED. "DO NOT HIDE IT FROM ME. MAY GOD DEAL WITH YOU, BE IT EVER SO SEVERELY, IF YOU HIDE FROM ME ANYTHING HE TOLD YOU." SO SAMUEL TOLD HIM EVERYTHING, HIDING NOTHING FROM HIM. THEN ELI SAID, "HE IS THE LORD; LET HIM DO WHAT IS GOOD IN HIS EYES."
1 SAMUEL 3:17-18

Eli knew that Samuel had been given a message from the Lord. He was determined to hear what God said, even if it was bad news. How important is it to you to get God's perspective on your life? Do you hide from it? Or do you seek it out?

PRAYER

Lord, I want to be like Eli, actively seeking Your perspective on my life through Scripture and godly friends, acknowledging Your right to do what You think is best and accepting Your way, even if it is difficult to hear. I trust that all You do flows from Your justice and loving kindness. In Jesus' Name, Amen.

_____
_____
_____
_____
_____
_____
_____
_____

LIKE SHEEP WITHOUT A SHEPHERD

WHEN HE SAW THE CROWDS, HE HAD COMPASSION ON THEM, BECAUSE THEY WERE HARASSED AND HELPLESS, LIKE SHEEP WITHOUT A SHEPHERD.
MATTHEW 9:36

Jesus knows people, not only because He created them, but because He was one of us. He has walked in our paths, understood our stresses, struggled with our temptations, and is intimately acquainted with our needs. He came to earth because He loves us. He taught that loving others is a natural overflow of our love for God. He sends us to love people who desperately need to be loved, even if they cannot articulate that need. How are you following in His footsteps?

PRAYER

Jesus, help me to see people through Your eyes today. Help me to interact with them at the level of their need. Help me to provide the guidance and encouragement they need. Help me to be a good shepherd of those within my care. In Your Name, Amen.

 # ONE THING

ONE THING I ASK OF THE LORD, THIS IS WHAT I SEEK: THAT I MAY DWELL IN THE HOUSE OF THE LORD ALL THE DAYS OF MY LIFE, TO GAZE UPON THE BEAUTY OF THE LORD AND TO SEEK HIM IN HIS TEMPLE.
PSALM 27:4

Many things vie for our attention in life—family, work, community, entertainment, success, even ministry. In the midst of your life's demands, where is Jesus? It's possible to lose focus on our relationship with Him even though He has promised to be with us always. Is He the One you seek? Are you attuned to His presence?

PRAYER

Jesus, I confess that many things pull at me and cause me to lose sight of Your presence in my life. But that isn't how I want it to be. In these quiet moments now, tune my heart to Your presence. Thank You for the invitation to seek You and know You. Let me worship You with my life today. In Your Name, Amen.

_____

_____

_____

_____

_____

_____

_____

_____

OVERCOMING EVIL WITH GOOD

DO NOT BE OVERCOME BY EVIL, BUT OVERCOME EVIL WITH GOOD.
ROMANS 12:21

Jesus forgave those who crucified Him in the midst of the pain they were causing Him. Does that thought stop you dead in your tracks? Not afterward, but in the midst of what was going on, Jesus was able to pray for those who were causing His pain. He calls us to follow in His footsteps, denying our urges for justification or retaliation. He calls us to pray for those who cause us pain and to continue to act in the best interests of those who cause us stress.

PRAYER

Jesus, Your example of praying for those who crucified You humbles me. This is not a natural response for me. You know those whom I struggle to love and serve. Give me Your perspective and change my heart for them. Teach me to pray for them in the same way that You are praying for them. In Your Name, Amen.

_____

_____

_____

_____

_____

_____

_____

_____

_____

 PAST AND PRESENT

"THE LORD WHO DELIVERED ME FROM THE PAW OF THE LION AND THE PAW OF THE BEAR WILL DELIVER ME FROM THE HAND OF THIS PHILISTINE." SAUL SAID TO DAVID, "GO, AND THE LORD BE WITH YOU."
1 SAMUEL 17:37

When David came up against a new challenge, one that caused others to cower in fear, he looked at it through his past experiences with God. David knew that he could depend on God to be as reliable in the present as He had been in the past. He knew that he could fight this new battle using the strength and skill God gave him. What past experiences with God give you strength and courage as you face today's challenges?

PRAYER

Lord, thank You for the ways You have worked in my life in the past. Thank You that I can depend on Your presence and guidance as I move into the future. I want to move confidently toward the challenges and opportunities this day holds. In Jesus' Name, Amen.

_____

_____

_____

_____

_____

_____

_____

_____

PUTTING IT INTO PRACTICE

THEREFORE EVERYONE WHO HEARS THESE WORDS OF MINE AND PUTS THEM INTO PRACTICE IS LIKE A WISE MAN WHO BUILT HIS HOUSE ON THE ROCK.
MATTHEW 7:24

Lead Like Jesus helps us understand how to put servant leadership into practice. Spending time focusing on leadership principles is a good practice for leaders, just as spending time focusing on Scripture is for followers of Christ. Just reading words and gaining new insight doesn't change things, though; it is in when we put those insights into practice that we see real change occur. How will you put into practice the things that God is teaching you about servant leadership?

PRAYER
Jesus, thank You for this time to focus on how to be a better servant leader. When I listen to You speak, I am sitting at the feet of the greatest servant leader of all time. Because You lived as a servant leader, my life is different today. Help me to make a difference in someone's life today by putting Your words into practice. In Your Name, Amen.

_____

_____

_____

_____

_____

_____

_____

_____

RECOGNIZING GOD'S CALL

THE LORD CALLED SAMUEL A THIRD TIME, AND SAMUEL GOT UP AND WENT TO ELI AND SAID, "HERE I AM; YOU CALLED ME." THEN ELI REALIZED THAT THE LORD WAS CALLING THE BOY. SO ELI TOLD SAMUEL, "GO AND LIE DOWN, AND IF HE CALLS YOU, SAY, 'SPEAK, LORD, FOR YOUR SERVANT IS LISTENING.'" SO SAMUEL WENT AND LAY DOWN IN HIS PLACE.
1 SAMUEL 3:8-9

As servant leaders, one of the privileges we have is coming alongside others to help them recognize God's call on their lives. Just like Samuel was not able to recognize that it was the Lord who was calling him, sometimes people may have a difficult time recognizing God's voice when He calls them. As we develop trusting relationships, we can help people reflect on their circumstances and see God's hand. Are you able to recognize God's activity in others' lives?

PRAYER
Lord, I realize that in order to point others to You, I must first know Your voice. Keep me close to You today, my heart tuned to Your voice and my eyes open to Your ways. Help me to be known as a person who will point others to God. Thank You for allowing me the privilege of pointing others to You. In Jesus' Name, Amen.

↻ ROOTED AND ESTABLISHED

AND I PRAY THAT YOU, BEING ROOTED AND ESTABLISHED IN LOVE, MAY HAVE POWER, TOGETHER WITH ALL THE SAINTS, TO GRASP HOW WIDE AND LONG AND HIGH AND DEEP IS THE LOVE OF CHRIST, AND TO KNOW THIS LOVE THAT SURPASSES KNOWLEDGE—THAT YOU MAY BE FILLED TO THE MEASURE OF ALL THE FULLNESS OF GOD.
EPHESIANS 3:17-19

The only sure foundation for servant leadership is love. Power and knowledge are poor substitutes for being grounded in the immeasurable and unconditional love of God. Leading without love sets the stage for the potential misuse of both power and knowledge. Jesus' love provides the foundation and creates the atmosphere for serving others. How fully have you grasped Christ's love? What difference does His love make in your life and leadership?

PRAYER
Jesus, thank You that love compelled You to come for us and that love characterizes Your interaction with us. I confess that there are times when I am tempted to lead from power and knowledge, instead of serving from an awareness of Your love for me and others. Overwhelm me with a deep awareness of Your love, I pray, Amen.

THE POWER OF VISION

"FOR THE SON OF MAN CAME TO SEEK AND TO SAVE WHAT WAS LOST."
LUKE 19:10

Jesus knew why He was on the earth. In many ways, God's vision for our lives matches His vision for Jesus' life. The sphere of influence, in both time and location, is unique for each of us, as is the specific call and gifting He provides for us. Jesus came to die on the cross to provide reconciliation with the Father for us. Only He could do that. What is God's call on your life? How has He gifted you to fulfill His vision to reach others? How will you live out of that call today?

PRAYER

Jesus, I am so grateful that You organized Your life around God's call to seek and save those who were lost, including me. As I live today, help me to live in line with God's purposes for me. I want to serve others in such a way that they are drawn to the Father through You. In Your Name, Amen.

 TRANSFORMATION

**"COME, FOLLOW ME," JESUS SAID, "AND I WILL MAKE YOU FISHERS OF MEN."
AT ONCE THEY LEFT THEIR NETS AND FOLLOWED HIM.**
MATTHEW 4:19-20

The call to follow Jesus is a call to transformation. He does not leave us as
He finds us. What great news! He leaves no area of our lives untouched:
family relationships, friendships, our perspective on life, work, leadership,
and the world in which we live, all are fair game. Jesus doesn't come to
justify our current lives; He comes to call us to real life. Are you ready to
trade in your life to find real life? Are you ready to follow Him?

PRAYER

*Jesus, I hear You call me to follow You. I don't know all the places You will
take me, but I'm beginning to believe that You are a trustworthy guide.
I want to follow You today. In Your Name, Amen.*

_____

_____

_____

_____

_____

_____

_____

_____

 # TRUE LIFE

NOW THIS IS ETERNAL LIFE: THAT THEY MAY KNOW YOU, THE ONLY TRUE GOD, AND JESUS CHRIST, WHOM YOU HAVE SENT.
JOHN 17:3

In Jesus' prayer before heading to the cross, He was clear that life is all about knowing God and knowing Jesus. True life is centered on relationship with God, and that relationship comes through knowing Jesus. Our spheres of influence may or may not offer us opportunities to speak directly to people's spiritual needs. Yet true servant leadership reflects the heart and nature of God to those we serve. How will others experience God's love, interest, and enabling through your leadership today?

PRAYER

Jesus, I am so grateful that Your life brought me life. I want my life today to reflect Your Spirit. I want to be a life-giving force in the lives of others. Help me to live so that when others find out I am Yours, they will know You more truly. In Your Name, Amen.

_____
_____
_____
_____
_____
_____
_____
_____
_____

↻ TRUTH TELLERS

**THEN DAVID SAID TO NATHAN, "I HAVE SINNED AGAINST THE LORD."
NATHAN REPLIED, "THE LORD HAS TAKEN AWAY YOUR SIN. YOU ARE
NOT GOING TO DIE."**
2 SAMUEL 12:13

Friends and associates play a variety of roles in our lives. Although we may not admit it, the truth tellers in our lives are every bit as important as the encouragers and supporters. David had a long-standing relationship with the prophet Nathan. When David sinned with Bathsheba, God sent Nathan to confront him about his sin. David responded with confession and repentance. Who are the truth tellers in your life? How do you respond when God sends them to speak into your life?

PRAYER

Lord, I confess that there are times I get off track as a leader. Help me to find people that I can trust to be truth tellers and to develop trusting relationships with them. Keep my ears open so that I hear Your Spirit speaking to me through others. In Jesus' Name, Amen.

_____
_____
_____
_____
_____
_____
_____
_____

 UNEXPECTED ENCOUNTERS

**PREACH THE WORD; BE PREPARED IN SEASON AND OUT OF SEASON;
CORRECT, REBUKE AND ENCOURAGE—WITH GREAT PATIENCE AND
CAREFUL INSTRUCTION.**
2 TIMOTHY 4:2

Acts 8 records Philip's unexpected encounter with a high official of
Ethiopia. When Philip left home that morning, he had no idea that he
would be talking with an important foreign government official later that
day. Philip's journey started with being in tune with the Spirit and obeying
God's direction. Where will God take you today? Whose life will intersect
yours? What spiritual opportunities might God bring your way? Will you
be ready for the opportunities when they come?

PRAYER

*Lord, I don't know all that this day holds. I want to be alert to the
opportunities You bring my way, opportunities to serve, to teach, to
influence others. Make me a person like Philip who hears and obeys
and is used by You. In Jesus' Name, Amen.*

WHEN A LEADER GETS DISCOURAGED

WAIT FOR THE LORD; BE STRONG AND TAKE HEART AND WAIT FOR THE LORD.

PSALM 27:14

What do you do when you get discouraged? Do you run toward God or away from Him? Jesus knew it would be hard for us, just as it was for Him. He asks us to stick with Him, to keep our focus on Him. Scripture after Scripture encourages us to trust in the Lord. Making a difference in the lives of others doesn't happen overnight. It's a daily commitment, a lifestyle. Do you let your discouragement separate you from God? Don't quit. Stay with God.

PRAYER

Lord, You know where I've been discouraged lately. You know the struggles I am facing. I need You to strengthen my heart as I wait on You to act. Keep me focused on You, Jesus. Thank You for knowing my need and loving me. Thank You for strengthening me through Your Spirit. In Jesus' Name, Amen.

_____

_____

_____

_____

_____

_____

_____

_____

_____

 WHEN FEAR STRIKES

FOR GOD DID NOT GIVE US A SPIRIT OF TIMIDITY, BUT A SPIRIT OF POWER, OF LOVE AND OF SELF-DISCIPLINE.
2 TIMOTHY 1:7

When fear strikes and you find yourself intimidated—intimidated by other's gifts, intimidated by the situation in which you find yourself—turn your attention to God. He is the One who places you in the circumstances where He wants to use you. You don't need to be someone else. You don't need to depend on your own abilities. Choose to trust in God's sovereign timing and placement of you. Depend on His Spirit to empower you. Step by step, be who God has called you to be in each situation and allow Him to use you.

PRAYER

God, thank You that You are always with me and that Your Spirit is more than adequate to equip me for anything I will face today. You know the people and situations that intimidate me. I choose to be confident in You. Display your power and love through me today, I pray. In Jesus' Name, Amen.

YOU HAVE HEARD, BUT I TELL YOU

"YOU HAVE HEARD THAT IT WAS SAID, 'LOVE YOUR NEIGHBOR AND HATE YOUR ENEMY.' BUT I TELL YOU: LOVE YOUR ENEMIES AND PRAY FOR THOSE WHO PERSECUTE YOU."
MATTHEW 5:43-44

The Jewish leaders of Jesus' day knew the words of the commandments, but they missed God's intent. As servant leaders, do we find ourselves talking the talk of servant leadership but focusing exclusively on external behaviors? Or do we understand that at the very core of His being, Jesus was a servant? Jesus longed to help people experience the love of God through His life. This internal focus will sustain us when things are difficult. It gives life to our words and actions, and to our leadership. It is the only thing that really matters.

PRAYER
Jesus, thank You for coming to bring God's truth to life through Your life. Help me to do the same today. I don't want to be externally focused, I want to be internally motivated to serve others. May I be a leader who overflows with Your Spirit of serving others today. In Your Name, Amen.

_____

_____

_____

_____

_____

_____

_____

_____

_____

A LIFESTYLE OF PRAYER

"O LORD, LET YOUR EAR BE ATTENTIVE TO THE PRAYER OF THIS YOUR SERVANT AND TO THE PRAYER OF YOUR SERVANTS WHO DELIGHT IN REVERING YOUR NAME."
NEHEMIAH 1:11

Nehemiah's leadership legacy includes his habit of prayer. Persistent, passionate, humble prayer; prayer that stems from a heart broken over the condition of the world; prayer that produces a resolve to be used by God; prayer in the moment of need. Nehemiah's lifestyle of prayer produced discernment, courage, and boldness. Nehemiah didn't depend on his position of proximity to the king to bring success; he depended on intimate connection to God. What does your leadership depend on?

PRAYER
Lord, I want my heart to be broken by the things that break Your heart. I want to become more dependent on You, not on the position I have or the people I know. Help me develop a lifestyle of prayer that produces spiritual discernment and keeps me ready to respond with God-given confidence. In Jesus' Name, Amen.

♥ A LIVING SACRIFICE

AND SO, DEAR BROTHERS AND SISTERS, I PLEAD WITH YOU TO GIVE YOUR BODIES TO GOD BECAUSE OF ALL HE HAS DONE FOR YOU. LET THEM BE A LIVING AND HOLY SACRIFICE—THE KIND HE WILL FIND ACCEPTABLE. THIS IS TRULY THE WAY TO WORSHIP HIM.
ROMANS 12:1 (NLT)

Jesus is our example of a living sacrifice. He lived His whole life as an act of worship, pouring Himself out on our behalf as an expression of His love for His Father. His devotion wasn't restricted to His private relationship with God; it permeated every hour of every day. What difference does God's mercy make in how you live? How will your life today reflect your devotion to God?

PRAYER
God, forgive me for the times when I've failed to live my life in light of the mercy You've shown me. Don't let me rest on my accomplishments or live a self-satisfied life; don't let me take for granted all that Jesus did for me on the cross. Let me live my life today as Jesus did, as an act of worship. In Jesus' Name, Amen.

A NEW WAY OF LEADING: COMMUNITY

NOW THAT I, YOUR LORD AND TEACHER, HAVE WASHED YOUR FEET, YOU ALSO SHOULD WASH ONE ANOTHER'S FEET. I HAVE SET YOU AN EXAMPLE THAT YOU SHOULD DO AS I HAVE DONE FOR YOU."
JOHN 13:14-15

Jesus lived life with His disciples as one of them. He didn't exalt Himself, even though He was God; He simply lived in relationship with His disciples and pursued God's call on His life. Knowing that He was there to serve them allowed Him to teach, lead, and correct them as needed, all within the context of a deep and selfless love for them. He wants us to do the same, to pour ourselves out for others at their point of need, as He did.

PRAYER

Jesus, I see You wash Your disciples' feet. I hear You call me to follow Your example. Help me to serve those I lead today, meeting them at their point of need, and serving them without regard to position. May my leadership create true community, a community that reflects Your presence and example. In Your Name, Amen.

↻ A NEW WAY OF LIVING: UNITY

"MY PRAYER IS NOT FOR THEM ALONE. I PRAY ALSO FOR THOSE WHO WILL BELIEVE IN ME THROUGH THEIR MESSAGE, THAT ALL OF THEM MAY BE ONE, FATHER, JUST AS YOU ARE IN ME AND I AM IN YOU. MAY THEY ALSO BE IN US SO THAT THE WORLD MAY BELIEVE THAT YOU HAVE SENT ME."
JOHN 17: 20-21

Jesus prayed for His disciples before going to the cross, and He prayed for us, too. He asked God for our lives and our unity to be a witness to the world. What does your life, your leadership, your family, your relationships with others say to the world? How does your impact in the lives of others reflect the Spirit of Jesus? How can you promote unity with other believers?

PRAYER
Jesus, I want my life to be a living reflection of You. Let me live this day deeply rooted in Your love and truth, focused on loving others as You love me. In Your Name, Amen.

A NEW WAY OF THINKING: TRUST

BUT JESUS IMMEDIATELY SAID TO THEM: "TAKE COURAGE! IT IS I. DON'T BE AFRAID."
MATTHEW 14:27

In the middle of the storm, Peter was sure of one thing: He would take his chance with Jesus rather than stick with man-made solutions. Can you imagine that night? The darkness, the sound of the waves crashing, the disbelief of seeing Jesus doing what common sense told Peter could not be done? Yet Peter recognized Jesus' voice, and his only thought was, "I've got to get to Jesus." Trust in Jesus replaced terror; confidence in Christ birthed courage. How is your relationship with Jesus changing how you think and live?

PRAYER

Jesus, You know the circumstances and relationships in my life where I'm feeling caught in a storm, uncertain of how to make it through safely. I find such confidence in the thought that You come to me in the midst of these storms, urging me to take courage in Your presence. Hold out Your hand to me, Lord, and help me walk on water with You. I want my life and leadership to reflect my trust in You. In Your Name, Amen.

 A ROAD MAP TO CHANGE

THEREFORE, SINCE WE ARE SURROUNDED BY SUCH A GREAT CLOUD OF WITNESSES, LET US THROW OFF EVERYTHING THAT HINDERS AND THE SIN THAT SO EASILY ENTANGLES, AND LET US RUN WITH PERSEVERANCE THE RACE MARKED OUT FOR US.
HEBREWS 12:1

How do you respond to personal failure? The 12 Steps of Leading Like Jesus offer a path forward for those of us who can admit that we struggle with failure as servant leaders. This admission is like the "You are here" symbol on a map. Once we know our starting point, we can begin the journey to a lifestyle of Christ-like servant leadership. Where are you on the journey? What is your next step today?

PRAYER

God, I admit that I am not the servant leader I'd like to be. I want to follow Jesus' example of servant leadership in my day-to-day life. Thank You that I can confess this to You, leave my failure behind, and move forward right from where I find myself today. Help me to use the 12 Steps as a pathway to becoming a Christ-like servant leader. In Jesus' Name, Amen.

_____

_____

_____

_____

_____

_____

_____

_____

_____

 # A WAY FORWARD

FORGET THE FORMER THINGS; DO NOT DWELL ON THE PAST. SEE, I AM DOING A NEW THING! NOW IT SPRINGS UP; DO YOU NOT PERCEIVE IT? I AM MAKING A WAY IN THE DESERT AND STREAMS IN THE WASTELAND."
ISAIAH 43:18-19

The first three steps of leading like Jesus are foundational to the servant journey. Step One involves confessing that there is room for growth in our leadership. Step Two is a step of hope as we realize that God offers the possibility of transformation. Step Three is a step of choice as we decide to yield our leadership to God, being willing for Him to change us into Christ-like servant leaders. Which step will you take today?

PRAYER

Lord Jesus, thank You for making a way for me. I confess that I have not lived up to Your example of being a servant leader. Thank You that there is hope for me, that You can transform me and show me the way forward. I choose today to make You my role model and my life's leader. Make me like You, Lord, Amen.

_____

_____

_____

_____

_____

_____

_____

BETTER TOGETHER

PLANS FAIL FOR LACK OF COUNSEL, BUT WITH MANY ADVISERS THEY SUCCEED. A MAN FINDS JOY IN GIVING AN APT REPLY—AND HOW GOOD IS A TIMELY WORD.
PROVERBS 15:22-23

The early chapters of Acts record a time of God-given opportunity, resulting in a time of growth that brought the early church both internal and external challenges. As they moved forward, they continued to seek God's guidance together, and they engaged in collaborative dialogue. How will you collaborate with God and others today to achieve His purposes together?

PRAYER

Lord, today I want to listen to You and to those around me. Infuse me with Your wisdom and help me bring timely wisdom to my discussions with others. Give me ears to hear You speaking through my family, friends, and co-workers. Help us together to achieve greater things than we could separately. In Jesus' Name, Amen.

_____

_____

_____

_____

_____

_____

_____

_____

 CHRIST-LIKE HUMILITY

YOUR ATTITUDE SHOULD BE THE SAME AS THAT OF CHRIST JESUS: WHO, BEING IN VERY NATURE GOD, DID NOT CONSIDER EQUALITY WITH GOD SOMETHING TO BE GRASPED, BUT MADE HIMSELF NOTHING, TAKING THE VERY NATURE OF A SERVANT, BEING MADE IN HUMAN LIKENESS. AND BEING FOUND IN APPEARANCE AS A MAN, HE HUMBLED HIMSELF AND BECAME OBEDIENT TO DEATH—EVEN DEATH ON A CROSS!
PHILIPPIANS 2:5-7

Sometimes people mistake humility for weakness. Jesus' life shows us that humility requires great strength and that a humble life reflects God-given courage. Strength and courage come from an unshakable confidence in God. Knowing who we are in relationship to God frees us to humbly serve God's purposes with our lives. Does your life reflect Christ-like humility?

PRAYER

Jesus, I am humbled at Your willingness to serve us. You know the prideful places in my heart, the places that fight the thought of humbling myself. Thank You that knowing this, You still love me and You forgive me. I humble myself before You and ask that Your example of humility would permeate my life today. In Your Name, Amen.

COME TO A QUIET PLACE

THE APOSTLES GATHERED AROUND JESUS AND REPORTED TO HIM ALL THEY HAD DONE AND TAUGHT. THEN, BECAUSE SO MANY PEOPLE WERE COMING AND GOING THAT THEY DID NOT EVEN HAVE A CHANCE TO EAT, HE SAID TO THEM, "COME WITH ME BY YOURSELVES TO A QUIET PLACE AND GET SOME REST." SO THEY WENT AWAY BY THEMSELVES IN A BOAT TO A SOLITARY PLACE.
MARK 6:30-32

Jesus knew about the demands of leadership. People followed Him day and night, searching for Him in the middle of His prayer time, hijacking His attempts to get away and rejuvenate. In the midst of all the hustle and bustle, He invited His disciples to get away with Him to a quiet place. He still invites His disciples to get away with Him. What is your response?

PRAYER
Jesus, I hear You calling me to come spend time with You. Thank You for wanting time with me in the midst of all the demands and cares of the world. Here I am, Lord, Amen.

_____

_____

_____

_____

_____

_____

_____

_____

# COMING ALONGSIDE

**FOR EVEN THE SON OF MAN DID NOT COME TO BE SERVED,
BUT TO SERVE, AND TO GIVE HIS LIFE AS A RANSOM FOR MANY."**
MARK 10:45

Jesus lived a life characterized by coming alongside people who needed spiritual, emotional, mental, and physical help. He did not make a point of aligning Himself with reigning power structures; instead He purposely chose to help those who couldn't help themselves. What motivates your leadership? Are you willing to let God place you where He needs you most?

PRAYER

Jesus, I am humbled and grateful when I think of Your heart for us. Thank You that you still choose to come alongside those who are hurting and need help. Search my heart and cleanse me from any motives that do not reflect Your example. Place me where You need me so that I can help others. Give me Your heart for others, I ask, Amen.

FACING CRITICISM

BUT PETER AND JOHN REPLIED, "JUDGE FOR YOURSELVES WHETHER IT IS RIGHT IN GOD'S SIGHT TO OBEY YOU RATHER THAN GOD. FOR WE CANNOT HELP SPEAKING ABOUT WHAT WE HAVE SEEN AND HEARD."
ACTS 4:19-20

Christ-like leaders are not exempt from being criticized, even when our actions as parents, friends, or colleagues spring from a desire to help others. There will be times when we need to respond to the criticism, and times when God directs us to stay silent. Follow Jesus' example and live so that when you are criticized, you are criticized for obeying God and helping others.

PRAYER

Jesus, You are an example to me in all things, even in knowing how to handle criticism. You know the ways I am tempted to respond to criticism, whether it is undeserved or has a basis in fact. Help me listen to Your voice above all else and to respond with humility and obedience to Your correction, especially when others criticize me unjustly. In Your Name, Amen.

_____

_____

_____

_____

_____

_____

_____

_____

_____

 # GOD FIRST

BUT BE SURE TO FEAR THE LORD AND SERVE HIM FAITHFULLY WITH ALL YOUR HEART; CONSIDER WHAT GREAT THINGS HE HAS DONE FOR YOU.
1 SAMUEL 12:24

Whom do you seek to please, love, and fear? When the people of Israel chose their first king, Samuel charged them to keep their eyes on pleasing God, not on their new king. It is easy to get our eyes off of God and onto those around us, losing focus about who we are truly serving. When we serve God first, we will serve others well, both those to whom we are accountable and those for whom we are responsible.

PRAYER

Lord, help me to see You more clearly than those around me so that I serve You above all others. You have done great things for me, and You deserve the best I can give. I want to fear You above all others and serve You faithfully with all my heart. In Jesus' Name, Amen.

JUST PASSING THROUGH

TEACH US TO NUMBER OUR DAYS ARIGHT, THAT WE MAY GAIN A HEART OF WISDOM.
PSALM 90:12

What is your approach to life? Are you "just passing through," moving quickly toward the future, passing by opportunities to engage with the world around you? Are you mired in today's pressures, unable to lift your head and see the future that beckons? We see Jesus moving though His days with purpose yet simultaneously open to the possibilities and people that He encounters. What can you learn from His approach to life?

PRAYER
Thank You, Jesus, for giving me this day. Thank You for the opportunity to live it for You. Make me a blessing to those around me. Make my heart beat in time with Yours, so that I can bring Your perspective to each situation in which I find myself. In Your Name, Amen.

_____

_____

_____

_____

_____

_____

_____

_____

_____

# LEADING FORWARD

AND DAVID SHEPHERDED THEM WITH INTEGRITY OF HEART; WITH SKILLFUL HANDS HE LED THEM.
PSALM 78:72

Character matters, and so do leadership skills. The transformational journey that begins in a leader's heart works its way out in how a leader relates to those around him or her. Leaders who have a heart for God want to touch other people's lives in significant ways. They aren't satisfied with just getting by. Leading like Jesus involves developing a greater heart for God and others and becoming increasingly skilled at connecting with and developing those around them. How will you grow as a leader today?

PRAYER

Lord, I want to be a leader who is wise in how I interact with people. I want to keep my focus on how I can grow as a leader, today, and every day. I know this day will offer new opportunities to lead like Jesus. Don't let me settle for yesterday's leadership patterns. Help me seize the opportunities You give me to grow as a leader today. In Jesus' Name, Amen.

_____
_____
_____
_____
_____
_____
_____
_____

LEADING UNDER THE INFLUENCE

I HAVE BEEN CRUCIFIED WITH CHRIST AND I NO LONGER LIVE, BUT CHRIST LIVES IN ME. THE LIFE I LIVE IN THE BODY, I LIVE BY FAITH IN THE SON OF GOD, WHO LOVED ME AND GAVE HIMSELF FOR ME.
GALATIANS 2:20

Under whose leadership do you lead? Do you lead under the influence of those you seek to please and those you fear? Or do you lead under the influence of those you are committed to serve and those you love? Out of those you are committed to love and serve, does Jesus have first place? Only as Jesus has first place in your heart and lives through you will others assume their proper place in your life.

PRAYER

Jesus, I want You to live in me so that I am free to live for You. I know this servant life can only be lived by the power of Your Spirit. Help me to keep focused on my relationship with You so that my relationships with others honor You. In Your Name, Amen.

 # MAKE EVERY EFFORT

MAKE EVERY EFFORT TO LIVE IN PEACE WITH ALL MEN AND TO BE HOLY. WITHOUT HOLINESS, NO ONE WILL SEE THE LORD.
HEBREWS 12:14

Comparison, competition, and strife are clear signs that we are leading out of pride or fear. When we live in humility and confidence in the Lord, we have an awareness that we are set apart to serve His purposes. When we are confident in who we are in Christ, we are free to focus on what is best for others, not just ourselves. What marks your life and leadership? How clearly will others see the Lord through you today?

PRAYER

Lord, I want other people to see You through me today. I know I'll have opportunities to choose between leading out of pride and fear or humility and confidence. I want to make every effort to live in a way that reflects Your presence in my life. In Jesus' Name, Amen.

MAKING YOUR VOICE HEARD

DO NOT LET ANY UNWHOLESOME TALK COME OUT OF YOUR MOUTHS, BUT ONLY WHAT IS HELPFUL FOR BUILDING OTHERS UP ACCORDING TO THEIR NEEDS, THAT IT MAY BENEFIT THOSE WHO LISTEN.
EPHESIANS 4:29

What keeps your voice from being heard by those around you? Are you living a life of integrity and compassion? Do you consider the perspectives of others and how they might hear your words before you speak? Are you speaking in such a way that your words build up those who hear them? Sharing your thoughts so that you are able to influence others is an art, not a science. How can you improve your communication with others?

PRAYER
Lord, I want the things I say to benefit those who hear me. Help me to listen to those I come in contact with, discern their needs, and speak words that encourage and strengthen them. Help me know when to listen and when to speak. May my words convey Jesus' love, wisdom, and character and build up the people with whom I interact today. In Jesus' Name, Amen.

PERSPECTIVE

One of the challenges of the apprentice stage of leadership is not having a broad enough perspective to accurately assess success and failure. Did your efforts succeed because of natural talent or systems already in place? What precipitated failure, lack of planning, bad timing, or undeveloped skills? Were the results typical and repeatable? What lessons can you learn to set yourself up for greater success in the future? This is where an apprentice needs an established, experienced leader to provide insight, perspective, praise, and correction. Who can you talk with in order to gain a better perspective on your leadership?

PRAYER

Lord, I want to be open to the wisdom of others today. Especially in the areas where I am learning how to lead, where I have new and untried tasks, give me the humility to ask, listen, and learn from those who have more experience and wisdom than I do. In Jesus' Name, Amen.

_____
_____
_____
_____
_____
_____
_____
_____

🗣 POINT OF VIEW

SEND FORTH YOUR LIGHT AND YOUR TRUTH, LET THEM GUIDE ME; LET THEM BRING ME TO YOUR HOLY MOUNTAIN, TO THE PLACE WHERE YOU DWELL.
PSALM 43:3

The world is full of voices that clamor for attention. Servant leaders need to be able to discern God's voice in the midst of the noise surrounding them. Developing a biblical perspective, a godly perspective, is an intentional process. How do you recognize God's voice? How can you saturate your mind with God's truth so that your leadership perspective increasingly reflects God's wisdom?

PRAYER

God, thank You for the Scriptures that incorporate Your light and truth. Thank You for Jesus, who reveals Your light and truth through His words and life. Give light to my eyes so that I can see Your truth, and tune my ears to hear Your voice as You speak to me through the Scriptures and through Your Spirit. Shape my thinking so that I reflect Your perspective. In Jesus' Name, Amen.

_____

_____

_____

_____

_____

_____

_____

_____

_____

↻ REFRESHING YOUR SOUL

HOW PRECIOUS IS YOUR UNFAILING LOVE, O GOD! ALL HUMANITY FINDS SHELTER IN THE SHADOW OF YOUR WINGS. YOU FEED THEM FROM THE ABUNDANCE OF YOUR OWN HOUSE, LETTING THEM DRINK FROM YOUR RIVER OF DELIGHTS. FOR YOU ARE THE FOUNTAIN OF LIFE, THE LIGHT BY WHICH WE SEE.
PSALM 36:7-9 (NLT)

The demands of servant leadership left even Jesus depleted at times. He frequently retreated to find refreshment, drawing apart to spend time with His Father, His disciples, and His close friends. He offered living water to the crowds at the Feast of the Tabernacles and to the Samaritan woman, water that would quench thirst and refresh weary souls. What or who do you turn to when you are weary? How do you find rest and refreshment for your soul?

PRAYER
Jesus, thank You for Your example of drawing away to find rest and refreshment in the midst of leadership demands. Thank You, too, for offering us living water, and for the hope and encouragement of the words of Scripture. Today refresh my soul, quench my thirst, give me strength so I can lead like You. In Your Name, Amen.

REMEMBER YOUR LEADERS

REMEMBER YOUR LEADERS, WHO SPOKE THE WORD OF GOD TO YOU. CONSIDER THE OUTCOME OF THEIR WAY OF LIFE AND IMITATE THEIR FAITH.
HEBREWS 13:7

Who invested in you to make you the leader you are today? What difference has their example made in your life? Where would you be without their influence? What values shaped their leadership? What leadership principles did you learn from them? What qualities of their faith and lives do you want to emulate in your life and leadership? How will you reflect their influence today as you interact with others? Live today in such a way that others will be blessed by having known you.

PRAYER

Lord, thank You for the men and women You have placed in my life through the years. Thank You for the life lessons and leadership lessons I have learned and am learning from them. Help me to live a life that others can imitate. In Jesus' Name, Amen.

RESISTING DISCOURAGEMENT

LET US FIX OUR EYES ON JESUS, THE AUTHOR AND PERFECTER OF OUR FAITH, WHO FOR THE JOY SET BEFORE HIM ENDURED THE CROSS, SCORNING ITS SHAME, AND SAT DOWN AT THE RIGHT HAND OF THE THRONE OF GOD. CONSIDER HIM WHO ENDURED SUCH OPPOSITION FROM SINFUL MEN, SO THAT YOU WILL NOT GROW WEARY AND LOSE HEART.
HEBREWS 12:2-3

As leaders, we need a biblical perspective on opposition to keep us from becoming discouraged. Jesus endured opposition, so opposition does not necessarily mean that we are out of the will of God. Opposition can mean that we are right where God needs us to be. Where are you struggling with discouragement? What does God want to accomplish in and through you as you focus on Him and persevere?

PRAYER
Jesus, I'm so grateful that You kept Your eyes fixed on God's purposes as You faced the cross. I want to focus on You as I face the challenges in my life. Fill my mind with Your truth, help me to see things as You see them, and give me strength to endure. In Your Name, Amen.

SET YOUR MIND

SINCE, THEN, YOU HAVE BEEN RAISED WITH CHRIST, SET YOUR HEARTS ON THINGS ABOVE, WHERE CHRIST IS SEATED AT THE RIGHT HAND OF GOD. SET YOUR MINDS ON THINGS ABOVE, NOT ON EARTHLY THINGS.
COLOSSIANS 3:1-2

Trying to lead like Jesus can be challenging. Developing people is a long process. Teams face challenges in real time. Organizations change only as the individuals within them change. From a human perspective, leading requires constant attention to an ever-changing landscape. Leaders who follow Jesus take time to get an eternal perspective on their leadership. Where do you need to get an eternal perspective? What difference might an eternal perspective make in your leadership?

PRAYER
Jesus, thank You that You offer me an eternal perspective on the situations I face. Remind me today to seek Your face and Your perspective so that I keep my focus on exalting God in each situation and relationship. I want my heart and my mind to reflect Yours. In Jesus' Name, Amen.

TRANSFORMED THINKING

DO NOT CONFORM ANY LONGER TO THE PATTERN OF THIS WORLD, BUT BE TRANSFORMED BY THE RENEWING OF YOUR MIND. THEN YOU WILL BE ABLE TO TEST AND APPROVE WHAT GOD'S WILL IS—HIS GOOD, PLEASING AND PERFECT WILL.

ROMANS 12:2

The work of transformation begins in the heart and then moves to the mind. As our thought patterns are transformed to reflect the mind of Christ, we begin to gain an eternal perspective. This perspective is the springboard for living differently right where we are. We begin to realize that there is a different way to look at things—God's way. There is a different way to respond—as Jesus did. There is a new way to live— under the influence of the Spirit.

PRAYER

God, show me where I have been settling for conforming to the world's pattern of thinking, living, and leading. Bring to my mind Your perspective, Your truth, about my life and my leadership. Remind me of Jesus' example and teaching. Breathe on me, Holy Spirit, and live through me. Let my mind and my life reflect Your presence. In Jesus' Name, Amen.

_____

_____

_____

_____

_____

_____

_____

_____

 A JOB WELL DONE

I HAVE BROUGHT YOU GLORY ON EARTH BY COMPLETING THE WORK YOU GAVE ME TO DO.

JOHN 17:4

What criteria do you use to evaluate yourself as a leader? John 17 records Jesus' prayer as He assessed His season of leadership. He evaluated His personal focus on His God-given mission, His responsibility to teach His disciples what they needed to know to be successful, having protected them while they were under His leadership and prepared them for the future. How would you assess your leadership using these same criteria?

PRAYER

Holy Spirit, help me to evaluate my leadership as Jesus did, and to be more concerned with how I influence others than I am with worldly success. Show me where You want to redirect me. May others be more fulfilled because of my influence in their lives. Most of all, I want to be found faithful to Your call. In Jesus' Name, Amen.

_____

_____

_____

_____

_____

_____

_____

_____

_____

A LEADER WHO STRENGTHENS OTHERS

TWO PEOPLE ARE BETTER OFF THAN ONE, FOR THEY CAN HELP EACH OTHER SUCCEED. IF ONE PERSON FALLS, THE OTHER CAN REACH OUT AND HELP. BUT SOMEONE WHO FALLS ALONE IS IN REAL TROUBLE. ... A PERSON STANDING ALONE CAN BE ATTACKED AND DEFEATED, BUT TWO CAN STAND BACK-TO-BACK AND CONQUER. THREE ARE EVEN BETTER, FOR A TRIPLE-BRAIDED CORD IS NOT EASILY BROKEN.
ECCLESIASTES 4:9-12 (NLT)

Deborah gave her life in service to God and His people. Her wisdom and discernment brought stability during a time of oppression. When the time came for God to move on behalf of His people, God's chosen leader would not move forward without Deborah at his side. Are you a leader who serves with God-given wisdom and discernment? Are others able to depend on you, knowing that You have God's purposes in mind and will stand beside them to see God's plan accomplished?

PRAYER
Lord, I want to be a friend and leader whom others can depend on to point them to You. Show me how You want to use me to bring stability and strengthen those around me, so that together we accomplish Your purposes. In Jesus' Name, Amen.

ADVICE OR WISDOM

BUT THE WISDOM THAT COMES FROM HEAVEN IS FIRST OF ALL PURE; THEN PEACE-LOVING, CONSIDERATE, SUBMISSIVE, FULL OF MERCY AND GOOD FRUIT, IMPARTIAL AND SINCERE.
JAMES 3:17

Many people give advice, while others are sources of wisdom. How can you tell one from the other? Advice typically comes in the form of opinion and reflects the viewpoint of the person offering it. Wisdom, the kind of wisdom that Jesus exhibited in His life, has the ring of God's truth about it, an overarching truth that transcends human understanding. Even His enemies marveled at Jesus' selfless, God-centered wisdom. Do you give advice or offer godly wisdom?

PRAYER

Jesus, thank You for offering me Your eternal perspective and wisdom through Scripture and Your Spirit. I don't want to offer people temporary fixes or self-serving opinions. I want Your wisdom to shape my perspective and my words today. In Your Name, Amen.

_____

_____

_____

_____

_____

_____

_____

_____

 # BROKEN BREAD

"DO NOT OFFER THE PARTS OF YOUR BODY TO SIN, AS INSTRUMENTS OF WICKEDNESS, BUT RATHER OFFER YOURSELVES TO GOD, AS THOSE WHO HAVE BEEN BROUGHT FROM DEATH TO LIFE; AND OFFER THE PARTS OF YOUR BODY TO HIM AS INSTRUMENTS OF RIGHTEOUSNESS."
ROMANS 6:13

Where do you see yourself in the story of Jesus feeding thousands with just a few fish and loaves of bread? Are you part of the hungry crowd? Are you one of the disciples, helpless to know what to do, then amazed at seeing Jesus' solution? Are you the little boy, having brought enough for yourself, willingly offering what you have? Or do you relate to Jesus, asking God to bless and multiply limited resources to care for needy people? Offer yourself to serve others today in Jesus' Name. Ask God to use you to make a difference.

PRAYER
Jesus, I am amazed at what You can do when we offer ourselves and what we have to You. Thank You for including me in the miracle of serving others. In Jesus' Name, Amen.

 EXAMINATION

TEST ME, O LORD, AND TRY ME, EXAMINE MY HEART AND MY MIND;
PSALM 26:2

Leading like Jesus is a daily commitment. On this lifelong journey, each day begins with a mindset focused on serving others and ends with an opportunity to reflect on how we have done. Asking God to examine our motives, to search our hearts and minds, keeps pride from taking root in our hearts and allows God to continually shape us as servant leaders. What does God want to reveal to you about your heart and mind today?

PRAYER
God, show me what You know about my heart and mind. Show me where I am on this journey and where You want to take me. Give me hope and courage that I can become the person and leader You want me to be. I know I can trust You to tell me the truth and to shape me into a Christ-like servant leader. In Jesus' Name, Amen.

FACING OPPOSITION

NOW MY HEART IS TROUBLED, AND WHAT SHALL I SAY? 'FATHER, SAVE ME FROM THIS HOUR'? NO, IT WAS FOR THIS VERY REASON I CAME TO THIS HOUR. FATHER, GLORIFY YOUR NAME!" THEN A VOICE CAME FROM HEAVEN, I HAVE GLORIFIED IT, AND WILL GLORIFY IT AGAIN."
JOHN 12:27-28

Jesus faced opposition as He tried to influence the existing leadership system. Where did He find the stamina to keep going? He kept His eyes on the goal and maintained a close relationship with the Father. He evaluated changes and the energy it would take to accomplish them in light of how the results would accomplish God's purposes. What changes are you facing today? How can you respond so that God's purposes are accomplished in your life and in the lives of those around you?

PRAYER
Father, it helps me to hear Jesus' words when His heart was troubled. Sometimes my heart is troubled, too, as a leader; yet Jesus' words teach me to look to You and step forward in faith to lead. Keep me focused on accomplishing Your purposes, no matter what circumstances I am facing. In Jesus' Name, Amen.

GETTING WISDOM

IF YOU NEED WISDOM, ASK OUR GENEROUS GOD, AND HE WILL GIVE IT TO YOU. HE WILL NOT REBUKE YOU FOR ASKING. BUT WHEN YOU ASK HIM, BE SURE THAT YOUR FAITH IS IN GOD ALONE. DO NOT WAVER, FOR A PERSON WITH DIVIDED LOYALTY IS AS UNSETTLED AS A WAVE OF THE SEA THAT IS BLOWN AND TOSSED BY THE WIND.
JAMES 1:5-6 (NLT)

How quickly do you seek God's perspective and guidance when new challenges arise? Are you committed to seeking and living in light of godly wisdom? Scripture is clear that God is in the business of revealing Himself and His wisdom to those who seek Him. Where do you need to seek His wisdom today?

PRAYER
God, I confess that at times I have made seeking Your wisdom harder than it needs to be. I run from Scripture, I hurry through my prayer time and keep my conversation with you superficial. Here is where I need Your wisdom; show me where I am trusting in someone or something other than You. I confess that I am totally dependent on You to direct me. In Jesus' Name, Amen.

BEING JESUS

NOW THAT I, YOUR LORD AND TEACHER, HAVE WASHED YOUR FEET, YOU ALSO SHOULD WASH ONE ANOTHER'S FEET. I HAVE SET YOU AN EXAMPLE THAT YOU SHOULD DO AS I HAVE DONE FOR YOU.
JOHN 13:14-15

Who has been Jesus to you? Who has come alongside you and walked with you, helping you to discover life from God's perspective? God sent Jesus, who lived with us as Emmanuel: "God with us." He walked with His disciples, teaching, guiding, loving, caring for them, and calling them to imitate Him. He continues to use men and women today to walk with and minister to people in Jesus' name. To whom will you be Jesus today?

PRAYER

Jesus, Your grace overflows to me. Thank You for showing me the way to the Father through Your words and actions. Thank You for those who were Jesus to me. Open my eyes to the people and possibilities I have today to be Jesus for others. Help me to serve them well, in Jesus' Name, Amen.

# GOD'S REQUIREMENTS FOR LEADERS

AND NOW, O ISRAEL, WHAT DOES THE LORD YOUR GOD ASK OF YOU BUT TO FEAR THE LORD YOUR GOD, TO WALK IN ALL HIS WAYS, TO LOVE HIM, TO SERVE THE LORD YOUR GOD WITH ALL YOUR HEART AND WITH ALL YOUR SOUL, AND TO OBSERVE THE LORD'S COMMANDS AND DECREES THAT I AM GIVING YOU TODAY FOR YOUR OWN GOOD?
DEUTERONOMY 10:12-13

What does God expect of you as a leader? He doesn't keep it a secret. First and foremost, He asks for your wholehearted devotion, a devotion that flows out in a life of obedience, love, and service. He looks for men and women who fear Him alone, who do what He tells them to do, and serve Him wholeheartedly. As God seeks someone for His next leadership assignment, will He find someone who meets His requirements when He looks at you?

PRAYER
Lord, I want to be a leader You can use, like Moses, like Jesus. Shape my heart and my soul to meet your standards. Help me keep first things first today, fearing, loving, and serving You, walking in Your ways and observing Your commands. Thank You for remaking me in Jesus' image. In Jesus' Name, Amen.

_____
_____
_____
_____
_____
_____
_____
_____
_____

 LAY DOWN YOUR LIFE

THIS IS MY COMMANDMENT: LOVE EACH OTHER IN THE SAME WAY I HAVE LOVED YOU. THERE IS NO GREATER LOVE THAN TO LAY DOWN ONE'S LIFE FOR ONE'S FRIENDS.
JOHN 15:12-13 (NLT)

Jesus' call to lay down our lives to serve others is very clear. He gave His life for us and to us so that we can live our lives serving others like He did. How has Jesus worked in your life? Where have you experienced life in the face of death, forgiveness instead of judgment, power where once there was weakness? How can you help others experience newfound confidence and capability in their lives and work? What would it look like to lay down your life for others today?

PRAYER
Jesus, thank You for giving Your life for us and for giving us life through Your Spirit. As You lived to serve, I want to live my life to serve. In Your Name, let me bring life, forgiveness and power to others today. Amen.

 LIVING CONGRUENTLY

**DO NOT MERELY LISTEN TO THE WORD, AND SO DECEIVE YOURSELVES.
DO WHAT IT SAYS.**

JAMES 1:22

God revealed His laws to Moses so that God's people would live in the
light of His truth in every area of their lives. He wanted His people to live
lives that showed evidence of their love relationship with Him and revealed
His character to the world. He continued to extend that call through the
prophets until it was perfectly displayed in Jesus' life. How is God's truth
purifying and shaping you? What do others know of God's character and
truth because of your life and character?

PRAYER

*God, I don't want to be divided—one person at home and another in
public. I want to live in line with Your truth, increasingly reflecting Your
character. I want to be whole, living and leading with integrity from the
inside out. Make me like Jesus, so that others see You more clearly when
they see my life. In Jesus' Name, Amen.*

_____

_____

_____

_____

_____

_____

_____

_____

_____

NAVIGATING CHANGE

AY OUR LORD JESUS CHRIST HIMSELF AND GOD OUR FATHER, WHO LOVED S AND BY HIS GRACE GAVE US ETERNAL ENCOURAGEMENT AND GOOD OPE, ENCOURAGE YOUR HEARTS AND STRENGTHEN YOU IN EVERY GOOD EED AND WORD.

THESSALONIANS 2:16-17

erving in Jesus' name frequently took the first disciples out of their omfort zone, and failures were part of the learning curve. Jesus knew nat people often feel awkward in the face of change, so He made sure o give His disciples clear direction and frequent feedback. He offers us ne same encouragement, direction, and guidance today.

RAYER

hank You, Lord, for faithfully meeting me where I am and guiding me as am becoming a servant leader. It isn't always easy or comfortable, but know that this is the path You have for me. When change is hard and I eel self-conscious, encourage and strengthen me through Your Spirit. want to keep moving forward. In Jesus' Name, Amen.

 PREPARING THE WAY

THEN MOSES SUMMONED JOSHUA AND SAID TO HIM IN THE PRESENCE OF ALL ISRAEL, "BE STRONG AND COURAGEOUS, FOR YOU MUST GO WITH THIS PEOPLE INTO THE LAND THAT THE LORD SWORE TO THEIR FOREFATHERS TO GIVE THEM, AND YOU MUST DIVIDE IT AMONG THEM AS THEIR INHERITANCE. THE LORD HIMSELF GOES BEFORE YOU AND WILL BE WITH YOU; HE WILL NEVER LEAVE YOU NOR FORSAKE YOU. DO NOT BE AFRAID; DO NOT BE DISCOURAGED."
DEUTERONOMY 31:7-8

A time of transition for leadership is a critical moment for any organization. When Moses knew that his time of leadership was drawing to a close, he took steps to fully empower Joshua as his successor by publicly affirming Joshua's call and charging him to lead God's people. How can you strengthen the leaders around you and help them to look to God as they lead?

PRAYER

Lord, help me speak words that build others up and inspire confidence in those around me. Help me to remember to affirm the leadership strengths I see in people around me and inspire them to look to You as they lead. In Jesus' Name, Amen.

_____

_____

_____

_____

_____

_____

_____

_____

_____

SALT AND LIGHT

YOU ARE THE SALT OF THE EARTH. BUT IF THE SALT LOSES ITS SALTINESS, HOW CAN IT BE MADE SALTY AGAIN? IT IS NO LONGER GOOD FOR ANYTHING, EXCEPT TO BE THROWN OUT AND TRAMPLED BY MEN. YOU ARE THE LIGHT OF THE WORLD. A CITY ON A HILL CANNOT BE HIDDEN. NEITHER DO PEOPLE LIGHT A LAMP AND PUT IT UNDER A BOWL. INSTEAD THEY PUT IT ON ITS STAND, AND IT GIVES LIGHT TO EVERYONE IN THE HOUSE. IN THE SAME WAY, LET YOUR LIGHT SHINE BEFORE MEN, THAT THEY MAY SEE YOUR GOOD DEEDS AND PRAISE YOUR FATHER IN HEAVEN.
MATTHEW 5:13-16

As we incorporate the leadership principles and practices of Jesus into our lives, we begin to model a new way to lead for those around us. Do you want to transform your world? Let Jesus infuse your leadership with His Spirit and wisdom so that you become a light that points to the Father. How is your leadership impacting your family, team, and organization so that others want to lead like Jesus?

PRAYER

Jesus, make me like salt that brings out the flavor in food, making it savory and appetizing. Change me so that my leadership reflects Your light to others. In Jesus' Name, Amen.

 SEEING CLEARLY

YOUR WORD IS A LAMP TO MY FEET AND A LIGHT FOR MY PATH.... THE UNFOLDING OF YOUR WORDS GIVES LIGHT; IT GIVES UNDERSTANDING TO THE SIMPLE.

PSALM 119:105, 130

Fear and pride distort our ability to see the world from God's perspective. When our own interests loom larger than God, our thinking becomes too narrow; focusing solely on other people can lead to worry. We need God's Spirit and His truth to bring clarity to our vision and perspective to our thinking if we are to see as He sees and lead like Jesus. What difference will seeking God's perspective make in your life today?

PRAYER

Lord, I confess that fear and pride cloud my vision. Thank You that Your words bring light and understanding when I look at the world from Your perspective. Help me to see beyond myself and see others as You see them. Most of all, help me see You in every situation, so that I can lead like Jesus. In His Name, Amen.

SELF-EXAMINATION AND CONFESSION

CONFESS YOUR SINS TO EACH OTHER AND PRAY FOR EACH OTHER SO THAT YOU MAY BE HEALED. THE EARNEST PRAYER OF A RIGHTEOUS PERSON HAS GREAT POWER AND PRODUCES WONDERFUL RESULTS.
JAMES 5:16 (NLT)

Examining our lives for evidence of how we have misused our leadership would be difficult, if not impossible, without God's forgiveness and cleansing power. This habit of ongoing self-examination can only happen within the context of trusting relationships (with both God and others) that allow us to be completely honest. What things would you choose to do differently if given a second chance? What trusted advisors has God given you to help you examine your life and leadership?

PRAYER

Lord Jesus, thank You for the forgiveness and freedom that come through confessing my leadership failures to You and to another person. Show me the people in my life who can help me be honest about who I am and how I can become a more Christ-like leader. Free me from crippling guilt, and give me the courage to take the steps of self-examination and confession. In Jesus' Name, Amen.

🗣 SHARPENING YOUR FOCUS

FOR WE ARE GOD'S WORKMANSHIP, CREATED IN CHRIST JESUS TO DO GOOD WORKS, WHICH GOD PREPARED IN ADVANCE FOR US TO DO.
EPHESIANS 2:10

How clear are you on God's mission for your life? To find out, ask yourself: "What is God's vision of the future that haunts my thoughts? How has God shaped and called me to be part of making that vision a reality?" To live with purpose is to align your answers to these questions with Jesus' values of loving God and loving others. How can you focus more intentionally on your purpose today?

PRAYER

God, as I move through this day, I want Jesus' values of loving You and loving others to characterize my life. I want to live in light of Your vision for my life, fulfilling Your calling and using the gifts and talents You've given me for Your purposes. Thank You for creating me to be part of Your plan. In Jesus' Name, Amen.

↻ SUSTAINING FRIENDSHIPS

I LONG TO SEE YOU SO THAT I MAY IMPART TO YOU SOME SPIRITUAL GIFT TO MAKE YOU STRONG—THAT IS, THAT YOU AND I MAY BE MUTUALLY ENCOURAGED BY EACH OTHER'S FAITH.
ROMANS 1:11-12

How did leaders in the Bible cope with the demands of leadership? One way was to cultivate spiritual friendships and partnerships. David had Jonathan. Esther had Mordecai. Moses had his father-in-law, Aaron, Miriam, and Joshua. Jesus had Peter, James, John, Mary, Martha, and Lazarus. Paul had Barnabas, Luke, and Timothy. How do you encourage one another in faith? What can you do to help one another focus on leading like Jesus today?

PRAYER

Lord, I want to be an encouragement to others who are seeking to lead like Jesus, and I need their encouragement. Help me prioritize and cultivate relationships with like-minded leaders. Show me how we can encourage one another. In Jesus' Name, Amen.

♥ TAKING PRIDE IN YOUR STRENGTHS

**THEREFORE, MY DEAR FRIENDS, AS YOU HAVE ALWAYS OBEYED—
NOT ONLY IN MY PRESENCE, BUT NOW MUCH MORE IN MY ABSENCE—
CONTINUE TO WORK OUT YOUR SALVATION WITH FEAR AND TREMBLING,
FOR IT IS GOD WHO WORKS IN YOU TO WILL AND TO ACT ACCORDING
TO HIS GOOD PURPOSE.**
PHILIPPIANS 2:12-13

What are your strengths as a leader? Has God gifted you with a charismatic presence, inspiring words, exceptional physical skills and abilities, or insight into people? How do you keep the right perspective on your gifts so that you don't fall victim to pride? Remember that God is the One who created you with strengths and gifts to be used to serve others. Discover your strengths; more importantly, get to know the God who made you and humbly use the gifts He gives you for His purposes.

PRAYER
Creator God, thank You for the strengths and gifts You placed within me. Thank You for working in and through me to accomplish Your purposes. Use me to bring value to the world and specifically to others. Help me to remember that all I am and all I can do comes from You. In Jesus' Name, Amen.

THE GREATEST IS LOVE

AND NOW THESE THREE REMAIN: FAITH, HOPE AND LOVE. BUT THE GREATEST OF THESE IS LOVE.
1 CORINTHIANS 13:13

What characteristics do you look for in leaders? Christians in Corinth were caught up in the comparison game, ranking people with certain gifts as more spiritual, more honored than others. Paul's response to them cut through their bickering to focus on the one characteristic that outshines all others: love. From God's perspective, love is the indispensable characteristic of a leader. Without it, nothing else matters. Is love the defining characteristic of your leadership?

PRAYER

Lord, do You see love growing in me? When all is said and done about my influence in others' lives, will they know Your love because of me? I need You to reset my value system. Remind me that people are to be loved, not used. I want to love others to the extent that it becomes the defining characteristic of my leadership. Thank You for loving me. In Your loving Name, Amen.

_____

_____

_____

_____

_____

_____

_____

_____

_____

THE POWER OF PRESENCE

PEACE I LEAVE WITH YOU; MY PEACE I GIVE YOU. I DO NOT GIVE TO YOU AS THE WORLD GIVES. DO NOT LET YOUR HEARTS BE TROUBLED AND DO NOT BE AFRAID

JOHN 14:27

Jesus understood the power of presence in helping people make it through difficult times. He spent significant time with His disciples at the Last Supper and in Gethsemane; He told them He was going to prepare a place for them to be with Him forever; He told them to meet Him in Galilee after He had risen; before He ascended, He promised to be with them always. How does Jesus' presence in your life give you confidence as you face change? Who needs your presence to reassure them as they face change?

PRAYER

Jesus, thank You for being with me no matter what changes life brings. Your presence brings me confidence and courage. Help me to encourage others with the encouragement You give me, and to be encouraged by their presence in my life. Thank You for the gift of Your presence and the gift of brothers and sisters in Christ. In Jesus' Name, Amen.

THINK ON THESE THINGS

AND NOW, DEAR BROTHERS AND SISTERS, ONE FINAL THING. FIX YOUR THOUGHTS ON WHAT IS TRUE, AND HONORABLE, AND RIGHT, AND PURE, AND LOVELY, AND ADMIRABLE. THINK ABOUT THINGS THAT ARE EXCELLENT AND WORTHY OF PRAISE. KEEP PUTTING INTO PRACTICE ALL YOU LEARNED AND RECEIVED FROM ME—EVERYTHING YOU HEARD FROM ME AND SAW ME DOING. THEN THE GOD OF PEACE WILL BE WITH YOU.
PHILIPPIANS 4:8-9 (NLT)

What fills your mind? As leaders, others are looking to us for perspective and guidance. Are you allowing God's truth to shape your worldview and your leadership perspective? What are you reading or listening to that reinforces Christ-centered servant leadership principles?

PRAYER

Lord, thank You for Scripture, thank You for these words to think on when I am tempted toward discouragement or temptation. I know that my mind-set is greatly affected by the things I allow into it. Help me today to focus on things that strengthen my faith and commitment to You, and that shape me into a leader who looks like You. In Jesus' Name, Amen.

_____

_____

_____

_____

_____

_____

_____

_____

 WHAT DO YOU FEAR?

SO DO NOT FEAR, FOR I AM WITH YOU; DO NOT BE DISMAYED, FOR I AM YOUR GOD. I WILL STRENGTHEN YOU AND HELP YOU; I WILL UPHOLD YOU WITH MY RIGHTEOUS RIGHT HAND.
ISAIAH 41:10

What causes you to fear? Are you concerned about what the future holds? Do you wonder if you have what it takes to succeed? Are circumstances around you uncertain? Do the challenges in front of you appear overwhelming? Are people threatening you? Have you fallen into temptation recently? Remember that the fear of man is a trap. The fear of the Lord brings courage and strength in meeting present challenges and ultimately confidence in facing the future.

PRAYER
Lord, thank You for promising to be with me. Thank You for being my God. Thank You for promising to strengthen and help me and hold me up. I want these truths and promises to define my life and leadership today. In Jesus' Name, Amen.

 # WHEN RESOURCES AREN'T ENOUGH

"SACRIFICE THANK OFFERINGS TO GOD, FULFILL YOUR VOWS TO THE MOST HIGH, AND CALL UPON ME IN THE DAY OF TROUBLE; I WILL DELIVER YOU, AND YOU WILL HONOR ME."
PSALM 50:14-15

When God called Gideon to lead Israel as they faced an overwhelming enemy, God removed many of the people on whom Gideon could have relied for courage and strength. God chose to make sure that Gideon would trust in God alone as He led. At times, God does the same thing for us: He places us in seemingly impossible situations with fewer resources (people, time, or money) than we would like and calls us to lead with faith in Him. Where is God calling you to trust Him to extraordinary levels so that it will be obvious that God is at work?

PRAYER
Lord, when times come where I seem inadequate to the task and resources are lacking, help me trust You more than the resources You supply. Help me live and lead faithfully, seeking Your wisdom and way and seeing You at work. In Jesus' Name, Amen.

WHO IS THE GREATEST?

ABOUT THAT TIME THE DISCIPLES CAME TO JESUS AND ASKED, "WHO IS GREATEST IN THE KINGDOM OF HEAVEN?" JESUS CALLED A LITTLE CHILD TO HIM AND PUT THE CHILD AMONG THEM. THEN HE SAID, "I TELL YOU THE TRUTH, UNLESS YOU TURN FROM YOUR SINS AND BECOME LIKE LITTLE CHILDREN, YOU WILL NEVER GET INTO THE KINGDOM OF HEAVEN. SO ANYONE WHO BECOMES AS HUMBLE AS THIS LITTLE CHILD IS THE GREATEST IN THE KINGDOM OF HEAVEN."
MATTHEW 18:1-4 (NLT)

Greatness in the world's eyes is often characterized by confidence and accomplishment; greatness in Jesus' eyes is characterized differently. Jesus offers a child as the example of greatness in God's kingdom. Humility allows us to respond to Jesus' call to servant leadership and allows Him the freedom to place us and use us as He desires. Are you humbly depending on Jesus to use you today?

PRAYER
Jesus, even more than looking great in the world's eyes, I want to be great in Your eyes. I place myself at Your disposal. I want You to have freedom to use me as You desire today. In Jesus' Name, Amen.

A DANGEROUS HABIT

FOR THE WORD OF GOD IS LIVING AND ACTIVE. SHARPER THAN ANY DOUBLE-EDGED SWORD, IT PENETRATES EVEN TO DIVIDING SOUL AND SPIRIT, JOINTS AND MARROW; IT JUDGES THE THOUGHTS AND ATTITUDES OF THE HEART.
HEBREWS 4:12

Reading Scripture is a dangerous habit. The Bible is clear about its content and purpose. Writer after writer claims that these are the very words of God with power to change lives. Isaiah declares that God's Word will accomplish the purpose for which God gave it. Jesus claimed to be the Living Word of God who perfectly revealed the Father. Those who read Scripture risk being conformed to the image of Christ, or they risk becoming hardened to God's voice. How has God's Word shaped your life?

PRAYER
God, thank You for recording Your thoughts and preserving them through the ages. Change me today because I have spent time being exposed to Your thoughts in Scripture. As risky as it is, I want Your Word to cut away everything in me that doesn't look like Jesus. In His Name Amen.

A GOD WHO CARES

DO NOT BE ANXIOUS ABOUT ANYTHING, BUT IN EVERYTHING, BY PRAYER AND PETITION, WITH THANKSGIVING, PRESENT YOUR REQUESTS TO GOD. AND THE PEACE OF GOD, WHICH TRANSCENDS ALL UNDERSTANDING, WILL GUARD YOUR HEARTS AND YOUR MINDS IN CHRIST JESUS.
PHILIPPIANS 4:6-7

God reveals Himself to Moses as a God who listens to His people, is concerned about them, and chooses to act to make a difference. Not only is God concerned about His people as a whole, but He is concerned about His leaders and their concerns. He spends time listening to Moses' concerns and meeting Moses at his point of need. God is concerned about you today as you prepare to serve others. Where can He meet you at your point of need?

PRAYER

Lord, thank You for caring for us, and thank You for caring for me. You know the things that concern me as I prepare to serve Your people today. Thank You that I can bring these things to You. Guard my heart and mind with the awareness that You are present, You hear, You are concerned, and You will act. In Jesus' Name, Amen.

A LEADER'S BOAST

THIS IS WHAT THE LORD SAYS: "DON'T LET THE WISE BOAST IN THEIR WISDOM, OR THE POWERFUL BOAST IN THEIR POWER, OR THE RICH BOAST IN THEIR RICHES. BUT THOSE WHO WISH TO BOAST SHOULD BOAST IN THIS ALONE: THAT THEY TRULY KNOW ME AND UNDERSTAND THAT I AM THE LORD WHO DEMONSTRATES UNFAILING LOVE AND WHO BRINGS JUSTICE AND RIGHTEOUSNESS TO THE EARTH, AND THAT I DELIGHT IN THESE THINGS. I, THE LORD, HAVE SPOKEN!
JEREMIAH 9:23-24 (NLT)

Are you boastful? Most of us would not think of boastfulness as a spiritual characteristic. Scripture calls us to humility, repentance, worship, prayer, and service. We are called to seek wisdom, reconciliation with our brothers and sisters in Christ, and a right understanding of ourselves in relationship to God. At last we find that we have something to boast about: We know the Lord of all the earth! The things you boast about reveal what you value most. Where does knowing God fit on your list of values?

PRAYER
O Lord, forgive and cleanse me from my tendency to boast about myself or the ways in which You have blessed me, but let me never stop boasting about who You are! Thank You that I can tell others about Your goodness and influence them to know You. In Jesus' Name, Amen.

♥ A LEADER'S TEMPTATIONS

THEN HE SAID TO THE CROWD, "IF ANY OF YOU WANTS TO BE MY FOLLOWER, YOU MUST TURN FROM YOUR SELFISH WAYS, TAKE UP YOUR CROSS DAILY, AND FOLLOW ME. IF YOU TRY TO HANG ON TO YOUR LIFE, YOU WILL LOSE IT. BUT IF YOU GIVE UP YOUR LIFE FOR MY SAKE, YOU WILL SAVE IT. AND WHAT DO YOU BENEFIT IF YOU GAIN THE WHOLE WORLD BUT ARE YOURSELF LOST OR DESTROYED?"
LUKE 9:23-25 (NLT)

The temptation for instant gratification, recognition, power, and prestige leads to using others instead of serving them. While pride and fear tempt us to cling to self-serving methods and mind-sets, we can discover freedom in finding our fulfillment and security in Christ alone. When temptation presses in, surrender; surrender not to temptation, but to God. Where is God calling you to surrender to His plan, trusting that by doing so you will find lasting satisfaction?

PRAYER
Lord, You know the temptations I face, temptations to find satisfaction in my ways, not Yours. I hear Your call to surrender. Here I am. Free me. Save me from myself and my selfish ways. Help me find true life. In Jesus' Name, Amen.

_____
_____
_____
_____
_____
_____
_____
_____

A LEADER'S TESTIMONY

THE LORD IS MY SHEPHERD; I HAVE ALL THAT I NEED. HE LETS ME REST IN GREEN MEADOWS; HE LEADS ME BESIDE PEACEFUL STREAMS. HE RENEWS MY STRENGTH. HE GUIDES ME ALONG RIGHT PATHS, BRINGING HONOR TO HIS NAME. EVEN WHEN I WALK THROUGH THE DARKEST VALLEY, I WILL NOT BE AFRAID, FOR YOU ARE CLOSE BESIDE ME. YOUR ROD AND YOUR STAFF PROTECT AND COMFORT ME. YOU PREPARE A FEAST FOR ME IN THE PRESENCE OF MY ENEMIES. YOU HONOR ME BY ANOINTING MY HEAD WITH OIL. MY CUP OVERFLOWS WITH BLESSINGS. SURELY YOUR GOODNESS AND UNFAILING LOVE WILL PURSUE ME ALL THE DAYS OF MY LIFE, AND I WILL LIVE IN THE HOUSE OF THE LORD FOREVER.
PSALM 23 (NLT)

David's faith in God and his testimony to God's prominence in his life flow across the pages of the Old Testament. In Psalm 23, David reflected on God's sufficient and sustaining provision. His trust in God permeated his life and leadership, through good times and bad, giving him courage and confidence to face the future. How do his words strengthen you today?

PRAYER

Lord, David's words ring across the millennia, stirring my heart and soul to trust in You today. Thank You for the power of Your word. May my testimony inspire others to follow You, too. In Jesus' Name, Amen.

_____
_____
_____
_____
_____
_____
_____
_____

 A SIMPLE QUESTION

FOR TO ME, TO LIVE IS CHRIST AND TO DIE IS GAIN.
PHILIPPIANS 1:21

Why do you lead? Is it to exercise power over others? Is it to maintain a sense of control? Is it because you want to make a name for yourself? OR is it because you see the needs around you? Is it because Jesus compels you? Is it because the goal is worthy? Is it out of love for the One who loved you and calls you to follow in His footsteps? Paul, whose life was changed by encountering the risen Christ, simply said that, for him, to live was Christ. Why do you lead?

PRAYER

Jesus, examine my heart. Search my motives. Show me where my leadership motives are not pure. Cleanse me. Open my eyes to the needs surrounding me. Show me how I can make a difference. I want to lead from a servant heart, a transformed heart. In Jesus' Name, Amen.

A WORLD-CHANGING CONVERSATION

A SERVANT OF THE LORD MUST NOT QUARREL BUT MUST BE KIND TO EVERYONE, BE ABLE TO TEACH, AND BE PATIENT WITH DIFFICULT PEOPLE.
2 TIMOTHY 2:24 (NLT)

Acts 15 describes a turning point in the early church. When membership qualifications for non-Jewish believers were called into question, leaders came together to resolve the issue. What could have become a divisive shouting match resulted in a unifying decision and implementation plan. This happened because all involved were committed to discovering God's way forward. Are you committed to finding God's way when it comes to the issues that you face? Are you willing to humbly seek His will together with others in the interests of unity?

PRAYER

Father, I want to emulate the early church leaders who were able to come together in Your Spirit to solve problems. Help me to discern spiritual truth and rightly apply it to the problems I face today. Give me godly influence that leads to unity and shared vision for our work. In Jesus' Name, Amen.

ACCEPTING GOD'S CORRECTION

MY CHILD, DON'T REJECT THE LORD'S DISCIPLINE, AND DON'T BE UPSET WHEN HE CORRECTS YOU. FOR THE LORD CORRECTS THOSE HE LOVES, JUST AS A FATHER CORRECTS A CHILD IN WHOM HE DELIGHTS.
PROVERBS 3:11-12 (NLT)

When pride and fear rule us, we don't like to admit that we have done something wrong or that we are afraid of the consequences of our mistakes. Instead of these misconceptions, Scripture tells us that God corrects us because He loves us, wants to conform us to the image of Christ, and wants to be able to expand our influence in other's lives. Humbly accepting His correction brings forgiveness and freedom.

PRAYER
Lord, help me to trust You when You need to discipline me. Overcome my pride and fear with an awareness of Your love. Train me so that I can become the person You created me to be; shape me so that I reflect Jesus more clearly to others. In Jesus' Name, Amen.

BE STILL AND KNOW

"BE STILL, AND KNOW THAT I AM GOD; I WILL BE EXALTED AMONG THE NATIONS, I WILL BE EXALTED IN THE EARTH."
PSALM 46:10

In the midst of the noise and the hurry, where do you find quiet and rest? How do you slow down enough to hear God's still, small voice? When was the last time that you sat and allowed Him to sort through your priorities and commitments, your calendar and task list? What does He think about all of the thoughts that swirl through your mind? Take time even now to meditate on the above verse.

PRAYER

My Lord and my God ... Abba Father ... Jesus ... Spirit ... slow me down. Quiet my mind. Remind me that this world and all that is in it belong to You. You are accomplishing Your purposes. As I focus on You, accomplish Your purposes in me and be exalted in my life. In Jesus' Name, Amen.

BIBLICAL DECISION-MAKING

ALL SCRIPTURE IS INSPIRED BY GOD AND IS USEFUL TO TEACH US WHAT IS TRUE AND TO MAKE US REALIZE WHAT IS WRONG IN OUR LIVES. IT CORRECTS US WHEN WE ARE WRONG AND TEACHES US TO DO WHAT IS RIGHT. GOD USES IT TO PREPARE AND EQUIP HIS PEOPLE TO DO EVERY GOOD WORK.

2 TIMOTHY 3:16-17 (NLT)

Some decisions have to be weighed carefully, while others are clear cut. Jesus didn't have to second-guess what to do when Satan tempted Him in the wilderness. His thinking and decision-making were grounded in Scripture. What guides your decisions? How clearly are you able to analyze choices in light of Scripture? How strongly does a biblical perspective shape your thinking and value system?

PRAYER

Father, thank You for preserving Your thoughts in Scripture so that I can gain a biblical perspective. I want Your truth, not other's opinions or even my own opinions, to shape my value system. Teach me Your truth today; show me what is wrong in my life; correct me where I need to be corrected. Reshape my thinking and actions through Your Word. In Jesus' Name, Amen.

 BUILDING TRUST

BUT GOD DEMONSTRATES HIS OWN LOVE FOR US IN THIS: WHILE WE WERE STILL SINNERS, CHRIST DIED FOR US.
ROMANS 5:8

Trust is an essential ingredient in servant leadership. The Pharisees constantly overdrew their trust accounts with people, making unreasonable demands and claiming higher privileges. Jesus, on the other hand, built trust with people as He interceded for them, acted in their best interests, and pointed them to the Father. What are you doing to build trust with the people God has entrusted to your leadership?

PRAYER

Jesus, thank You for loving me at great cost to Yourself. I know that I can trust Your love for me and Your influence in my life. Help me not to abuse my leadership by demanding things of people. Rather, help me to serve others in love, and show me how to build trusting relationships with them. In Jesus' Name, Amen.

 CHOOSING YOUR TEAM

ONE OF THOSE DAYS JESUS WENT OUT TO A MOUNTAINSIDE TO PRAY, AND SPENT THE NIGHT PRAYING TO GOD. WHEN MORNING CAME, HE CALLED HIS DISCIPLES TO HIM AND CHOSE TWELVE OF THEM, WHOM HE ALSO DESIGNATED APOSTLES.
LUKE 6:12-13

Jesus took the task of choosing His team members very seriously. He spent extended time talking with the Father before taking the step of naming the twelve who would be his protégés. As leaders, we need to consider well those with whom we link our lives and leadership. Choosing team members is a spiritual matter. In selecting them, we take on the responsibility to invest in their development. Who has God entrusted to your care and leadership? Are they teachable? What potential exists within them? How are you praying for them?

PRAYER
Father, what a privilege it is to invest myself in the development of others on my team. Thank You that I can come to You for wisdom and insight. Help me to be a faithful leader. I pray that their lives will be enriched because we have walked together. In Jesus' Name, Amen.

 COME

LET US THEN APPROACH THE THRONE OF GRACE WITH CONFIDENCE, SO THAT WE MAY RECEIVE MERCY AND FIND GRACE TO HELP US IN OUR TIME OF NEED.
HEBREWS 4:16

God invites us to come to Him when we need help as servant leaders. Jesus opened the way into God's presence for us. The door is always open now, and we are free to enter at any time. Wanting to be in God's presence is a normal desire for His children; as His leaders, we are first His children, and then His servants. Being a servant leader doesn't mean we have all the answers; it means we know the One who has the answers and are committed to seeking His will and His wisdom for ourselves and others.

PRAYER
Thank You, Jesus, for making the way for me to freely and confidently come to the Father to receive the help I need. Thank You that mercy and grace is available for me and for the ones I am called to serve. Thank You, Father, for welcoming me into Your presence through Jesus. In His Name, Amen.

COMMENDED FOR THEIR FAITH

THESE WERE ALL COMMENDED FOR THEIR FAITH, YET NONE OF THEM RECEIVED WHAT HAD BEEN PROMISED.
HEBREWS 11:39

How do you want to be remembered? Which of your accomplishments cause others to want to emulate you? All of the people listed in the "Hall of Faith" in Hebrews 11 were commended for their faith. Their faith was revealed by their response to times of great difficulty. Men and women of faith do not live trouble-free lives; they live by faith in the midst of troubling times and circumstances. Where is God calling you to live by faith today? How will your life of faith influence others to live by faith?

PRAYER

Lord, I want my life to be different. I choose to follow You. I want to model my life after You; I want my response to difficulties to reflect my faith in You. Let my life be a testimony to Your faithfulness, an encouragement to others to trust You, and an example for others to follow. I want to be remembered as someone who lived by faith. In Jesus' Name, Amen.

 COMMON PURPOSE

THIS, THEN, IS HOW YOU SHOULD PRAY: "'OUR FATHER IN HEAVEN, HALLOWED BE YOUR NAME, YOUR KINGDOM COME, YOUR WILL BE DONE ON EARTH AS IT IS IN HEAVEN....'"
MATTHEW 6:9-10

How much does your relationship with Jesus impact your leadership? Are you looking for the same results that God is looking for in your leadership? Jesus could confidently pray that the Father's will be done because it was the only thing that mattered to Him as God's Son. He wanted to see God's purposes played out in His life and in the lives of others. Jesus knew that He and the Father shared this common purpose and passion. Does Jesus think the same thing about you?

PRAYER

Lord, I bring my definition of success and my leadership goals to You today. Show me if there is any discrepancy between Your purposes and mine. Realign my thinking so that I am in sync with Your purpose and passion. May Your will be done in my life and through my leadership. In Jesus' Name, Amen.

 CONFIDENT PRAYER

IF YOU REMAIN IN ME AND MY WORDS REMAIN IN YOU, ASK WHATEVER YOU WISH, AND IT WILL BE GIVEN YOU.
JOHN 15:7

How much does Scripture permeate your thinking and your prayer life? Prayer based upon and infused by God's truth brings God-shaped results. Jesus' confidence in prayer came from His intimate relationship with the Father. He knew that the Father always heard Him and that His prayers were in line with the Father's heart and mind. On what do you base your confidence in prayer?

PRAYER
Jesus, thank You for inviting me into the same kind of intimate relationship and communication that You share with the Father. What a privilege! As we talk together today, infuse my thinking with Your thoughts. Remind me of Your truth. Give me Your perspective and open my eyes to what You have in mind. In Jesus' Name, Amen.

↻ CONNECTING THE DOTS

THEY WERE TALKING WITH EACH OTHER ABOUT EVERYTHING THAT HAD HAPPENED. AS THEY TALKED AND DISCUSSED THESE THINGS WITH EACH OTHER, JESUS HIMSELF CAME UP AND WALKED ALONG WITH THEM...
LUKE 24:14-15

When times are tough, discouragement and confusion can find their way into our hearts and minds. The disciples on the road to Emmaus couldn't sort out the conflicting stories about the crucifixion, nor could they imagine that the reports of Jesus' resurrection were true. It was easier to simply give up and give in. As they spent time with Jesus, He gave them God's perspective on what had happened and revealed Himself to them. Where do you need a fresh perspective?

PRAYER
Lord, remind me to pull away for time with You when the pressure builds. I need Your perspective on the circumstances surrounding me. Most of all, I need to know that You are walking with me. In Jesus' Name, Amen.

_____

_____

_____

_____

_____

_____

_____

_____

_____

_____

CREATED TO RESPOND

SO GOD CREATED HUMAN BEINGS IN HIS OWN IMAGE. IN THE IMAGE OF GOD HE CREATED THEM; MALE AND FEMALE HE CREATED THEM. THEN GOD BLESSED THEM AND SAID, "BE FRUITFUL AND MULTIPLY. FILL THE EARTH AND GOVERN IT. REIGN OVER THE FISH IN THE SEA, THE BIRDS IN THE SKY, AND ALL THE ANIMALS THAT SCURRY ALONG THE GROUND."
GENESIS 1:27-28 (NLT)

God designed Adam and Eve to care for His creation; He called Moses to be responsible for leading His people out of Egypt, and He called Joshua to lead them into the Promised Land. Just like them, He calls us to be responsible to care for others. What situation has God placed you in? Who will you come into contact with today? What responsibility has God given you? How are you living in light of His call?

PRAYER
Thank You, God, for creating me in Your image, with the ability to act in life-giving ways wherever You place me. Help me to respond to situations and people today in ways that make a difference in the world around me. In Jesus' Name, Amen.

DELEGATING THE JESUS-WAY

THEN JESUS CAME TO THEM AND SAID, "ALL AUTHORITY IN HEAVEN AND ON EARTH HAS BEEN GIVEN TO ME. THEREFORE GO AND MAKE DISCIPLES OF ALL NATIONS, BAPTIZING THEM IN THE NAME OF THE FATHER AND OF THE SON AND OF THE HOLY SPIRIT, AND TEACHING THEM TO OBEY EVERYTHING I HAVE COMMANDED YOU. AND SURELY I AM WITH YOU ALWAYS, TO THE VERY END OF THE AGE."
MATTHEW 28:18-20

Delegation as a leadership style is often misunderstood and frequently misused. The Jesus-way of delegating appoints qualified people to be responsible for accomplishing the task, describes the work and the anticipated outcome, and provides ongoing personal support throughout the process. Jesus' way doesn't divide the work – it multiplies results. How can you multiply results in your work by delegating like Jesus?

PRAYER

Jesus, I can see the effectiveness of Your delegation style by the results; I'm here today because someone discipled me. Help me learn how to delegate like You do, not like the world does. And thank You for continuing to support me as I lead like You through serving others. In Jesus' Name, Amen.

 DO YOU LOVE ME?

THE THIRD TIME HE SAID TO HIM, "SIMON SON OF JOHN, DO YOU LOVE ME?" PETER WAS HURT BECAUSE JESUS ASKED HIM THE THIRD TIME, "DO YOU LOVE ME?" HE SAID, "LORD, YOU KNOW ALL THINGS; YOU KNOW THAT I LOVE YOU." JESUS SAID, "FEED MY SHEEP."
JOHN 21:17

Peter's journey toward servant leadership was filled with starts and stops. Peter loved Jesus, but he wanted to follow Jesus in his own strength, which translated into leading in his own strength. Jesus knew that Peter's failure would be the pathway to his transformation into a servant leader. Jesus needed others to know this, too, so after privately restoring Peter, He also publicly restored him to leadership. Love for Jesus is the primary qualification for servant leaders. What are you doing to serve others because you love Jesus?

PRAYER
Jesus, thank You that You look past my uninformed notions about leadership and straight into my heart. Thank You for bearing with me as I fumble my way toward a Christ-like understanding of servant leadership. I love You. Show me how to serve others. In Your Name, Jesus, I ask, Amen.

_____
_____
_____
_____
_____
_____
_____
_____

 # EVERYDAY LEADERSHIP

HE CHOSE DAVID HIS SERVANT AND TOOK HIM FROM THE SHEEP PENS; FROM TENDING THE SHEEP HE BROUGHT HIM TO BE THE SHEPHERD OF HIS PEOPLE JACOB, OF ISRAEL HIS INHERITANCE.
PSALM 78:70-71

When Samuel came to David's house, not even David's father could see the future king of Israel in his youngest son. David was not enrolled in the royal training academy for future kings. God's chosen training ground and curriculum for David was unusual, even by Israel's standards. But God used David's time as a shepherd to develop David's compassion, courage, and faith, all qualities that David would need as king. When the time was right, God revealed David as the leader He had been preparing all along. What leadership qualities is God developing in you through your everyday life?

PRAYER

Lord, I'm reminded that You have an infinite variety of ways to shape us as leaders. Help me learn the Your lessons in the experiences You place in my life today, so that I can become the leader You need tomorrow. In Jesus' Name, Amen.

_____
_____
_____
_____
_____
_____
_____
_____

 EXPECTANCY

MAY THE GOD OF HOPE FILL YOU WITH ALL JOY AND PEACE AS YOU TRUST IN HIM, SO THAT YOU MAY OVERFLOW WITH HOPE BY THE POWER OF THE HOLY SPIRIT.
ROMANS 15:13

What attitude colors your approach to life? Do you have an underlying sense that God is at work in the people and situations you will encounter today? Scripture teaches that the entire world belongs to God and that He is intimately involved in the details of life. He knows your next breath; He crafted this day as part of His plan and placed you in it. Where are you looking for God today? How will your example strengthen those around you to live with a sense of expectancy?

PRAYER

God of hope, fix my eyes on You today. Remind me of who You are. Let my trust in You overflow into my attitude as I face what this day holds, whether expected or unexpected, easy or difficult. I want to be a person who influences others to see You at work and to place their trust in You. In Jesus' Name, Amen.

# EVEN JESUS...

WHEN JESUS HEARD WHAT HAD HAPPENED, HE WITHDREW BY BOAT PRIVATELY TO A SOLITARY PLACE....
MATTHEW 14:13

Even Jesus needed to take time away in order to stay fresh for ministry: He withdrew to prepare Himself at the start of His ministry, to grieve when He heard the news of John's death, to strengthen Himself for the cross, and to simply recharge at the end of a long day. Sometimes He took friends with Him; sometimes it was just Jesus and the Father. If Jesus made rest a priority, it makes sense that we need to do the same. What do you do to recharge your soul and refresh your mind and spirit?

PRAYER
Jesus, thank You for modeling a lifestyle of rest and renewal in Your leadership. I don't want to try to lead in my own strength and set myself up for a fall. Show me how to incorporate time and activities that will nurture and strengthen me and my family. In Jesus' Name I ask, Amen.

_____

_____

_____

_____

_____

_____

_____

_____

FINDING ENCOURAGEMENT IN SCRIPTURE

FOR EVERYTHING THAT WAS WRITTEN IN THE PAST WAS WRITTEN TO TEACH US, SO THAT THROUGH ENDURANCE AND THE ENCOURAGEMENT OF THE SCRIPTURES WE MIGHT HAVE HOPE.
ROMANS 15:4

When times are tough, how do you overcome discouragement? God knew we would need spiritual encouragement to keep going. He offers us encouragement and inspiration through His Word: biographies of men and women who walked with God, journals of spiritual leaders, records of God's work through the ages, messages from prophets and teachers, not to mention the life and teachings of Jesus. If your strength is lagging, ask God to strengthen You through His Word.

PRAYER
Thank You, Lord, for preserving the Scriptures to encourage me and bring me hope. When I read how You carried Your people through difficult times and see the way You worked on their behalf, I am encouraged to keep going. Thank You for meeting me at my point of need. In Jesus' Name, Amen.

_____
_____
_____
_____
_____
_____
_____
_____

↺ FINISHING WELL

AND SO, DEAR BROTHERS AND SISTERS WHO BELONG TO GOD AND ARE PARTNERS WITH THOSE CALLED TO HEAVEN, THINK CAREFULLY ABOUT THIS JESUS WHOM WE DECLARE TO BE GOD'S MESSENGER AND HIGH PRIEST. FOR HE WAS FAITHFUL TO GOD, WHO APPOINTED HIM, JUST AS MOSES SERVED FAITHFULLY WHEN HE WAS ENTRUSTED WITH GOD'S ENTIRE HOUSE.
HEBREWS 3:1-2 (NLT)

Jesus was intent on completing the whole task the Father had given Him. He knew that the cross was not something simply to be endured, but that there was work to be done in the midst of the suffering. He still had to speak truth to Pilate, maintain His composure before Herod, forgive the thief on the cross beside Him, make provision for His mother's care, and forgive His persecutors. When all was said and done, the prophecy was fulfilled, forgiveness was purchased, and a hardened soldier had a spiritual breakthrough. How does Jesus' dedication to finishing well inspire you to faithfully serve God today?

PRAYER
Jesus, thank You for finishing well. Thank You for not settling for half-done. Don't let difficulties blind me to the work You want to accomplish in and through me. Keep me focused on You and Your example, and on the work You have called me to do. In Jesus' Name, Amen.

♥ FRUIT OF THE SPIRIT

BUT THE FRUIT OF THE SPIRIT IS LOVE, JOY, PEACE, PATIENCE, KINDNESS, GOODNESS, FAITHFULNESS, GENTLENESS AND SELF-CONTROL. AGAINST SUCH THINGS THERE IS NO LAW.
GALATIANS 5:22-23

Jesus lived a life of complete dependence upon the Holy Spirit. His attitude exhibited confidence in God's presence and power. He overflowed with qualities that Paul called "the fruit of the Spirit." We can live lives that reflect the transforming power of Christ as we depend on the Spirit like Jesus did. As our leadership is transformed by the Spirit's power, others experience His presence through our actions and attitudes. How will your leadership reflect the Spirit's presence today?

PRAYER
Jesus, thank You that I can live a life of complete dependence on the Spirit, just like You did. Help me to meditate on these qualities as I move through today. I want to live and move in sync with You, just as You did with the Father. In Jesus' Name, Amen.

 GOD'S DELIGHT

HE TAKES NO PLEASURE IN THE STRENGTH OF A HORSE OR IN HUMAN MIGHT. NO, THE LORD'S DELIGHT IS IN THOSE WHO FEAR HIM, THOSE WHO PUT THEIR HOPE IN HIS UNFAILING LOVE.
PSALM 147:10-11 (NLT)

Does God delight in you? Does that seem like a crazy question? Did you immediately start checking to see how you measure up or how long it has been since you disobeyed? Scripture offers a different perspective. What God delights in is a heart that trusts Him, a person who believes that God exists and that He rewards those who seek Him (Hebrews 11:6). Such faith brings a smile to God's heart, and it opens the door for Him to use you in other's lives. How will your faith and hope in God's unfailing give wings to your leadership today?

PRAYER
Lord, in these moments, let me rest in Your unfailing love. Let me feel Your pleasure in the gift of my faith, the only gift I have to bring to You. Renewed and refreshed by Your Spirit and time in Your presence, use me today to bless others. In Jesus' Name, Amen.

 # HARD CHOICES

"AND I WILL ASK THE FATHER, AND HE WILL GIVE YOU ANOTHER COUNSELOR TO BE WITH YOU FOREVER—THE SPIRIT OF TRUTH. THE WORLD CANNOT ACCEPT HIM, BECAUSE IT NEITHER SEES HIM NOR KNOWS HIM. BUT YOU KNOW HIM, FOR HE LIVES WITH YOU AND WILL BE IN YOU."
JOHN 14:16-17

What hard choices are you facing today? Every leader has them. Anyone can make easy choices when resources are plentiful, harmony and unity exist, and everything is going as planned. It's when difficulties erupt that Christ-like leaders and godly wisdom are needed most. Jesus promised that the Holy Spirit would help us discern right from wrong and show us the way to go. Where do you need the Spirit's guidance today?

PRAYER

Jesus, thank You for giving us the Holy Spirit to be our Counselor. I am grateful that He is always available to guide me and remind me of Your wisdom. I need wisdom that comes from beyond my understanding as I face hard choices. Be my wisdom today, I pray, in Your Name, Amen.

↻ HONORING OTHERS

BE DEVOTED TO ONE ANOTHER IN BROTHERLY LOVE. HONOR ONE ANOTHER ABOVE YOURSELVES.
ROMANS 12:10

Our treatment of people who are hard to deal with reveals where we are on the journey of becoming servant leaders. We see Jesus treating a broken woman with mercy, answering people's questions with dignity, rebuking judgmental leaders, and restoring a fallen disciple. Even when Jesus needed to be forceful or direct with people, He never resorted to using or manipulating them. How does your treatment of others compare to Jesus' interactions with people?

PRAYER

Jesus, I need Your wisdom in my interactions with people. It's easy for my world to shrink down to my personal needs or the task in front of me. When that happens, I disregard the needs of those around me. Help me to treat others with respect, even when I need to be firm. Help me reflect You in my relationships with others. In Jesus' Name, Amen.

HOW WOULD JESUS DO MY JOB DIFFERENTLY?

AND GOD IS ABLE TO MAKE ALL GRACE ABOUND TO YOU, SO THAT IN ALL THINGS AT ALL TIMES, HAVING ALL THAT YOU NEED, YOU WILL ABOUND IN EVERY GOOD WORK.
2 CORINTHIANS 9:8

How would Jesus do your job differently? Have you stopped to ask yourself this question recently? What immediately comes to mind? Would He be more single-minded about focusing on the task? Would He treat people differently? Jesus maintained a laser-like focus on accomplishing the world-changing task the Father had given Him; simultaneously, He developed His core followers so that the work continued after He was gone. He exemplified servant leadership in all that He did. How will you lead more like Jesus today?

PRAYER

Jesus, when all is said and done, I need You to focus me so that I reflect You as I do my job each day. Thank You that Your grace abounds to me, that through You I can focus on both task and people, and that I don't have to sacrifice one for the other. Help me exemplify You today, Lord. In Jesus' Name, Amen.

 INSPIRED BY VISION

THEN I HEARD THE VOICE OF THE LORD SAYING, "WHOM SHALL I SEND? AND WHO WILL GO FOR US?" AND I SAID, "HERE AM I. SEND ME!"
ISAIAH 6:8

Isaiah's ministry was inspired by his vision of who God is. He realized that he and the society in which he lived were totally out of sync with the Lord. This clear understanding broke his heart, brought him to his knees, and caused him to offer himself when God called. How well do you know the Lord? Is your knowledge of Him producing humility and a desire to serve Him? How is God calling you to serve in His name?

PRAYER

Lord Almighty, open my eyes today to see You as You are, high and exalted. Thank You for extending mercy, grace and forgiveness to me. Let me live my life today in light of Your life and holiness, and let my realization of who You are motivate me to serve others. In Jesus' Name, Amen.

↻ INTERPERSONAL RELATIONSHIPS

... OUR CONSCIENCE TESTIFIES THAT WE HAVE CONDUCTED OURSELVES IN THE WORLD, AND ESPECIALLY IN OUR RELATIONS WITH YOU, IN THE HOLINESS AND SINCERITY THAT ARE FROM GOD. WE HAVE DONE SO NOT ACCORDING TO WORLDLY WISDOM BUT ACCORDING TO GOD'S GRACE.
2 CORINTHIANS 1:12

Leadership begins at a very personal level as we turn our lives over to the care and direction of God, but it doesn't end there. As He begins to transform us into men and women who bear His image, our relationships with others begin to change. While other people may or may not be on the journey of following Jesus, it is our responsibility to treat them with love and respect. What is your interaction like with those closest to you? How does your interaction with them reflect Jesus?

PRAYER
Jesus, let my interactions with my family, friends, and colleagues reflect Your presence in my life. Use me to lay the groundwork for You to intersect their lives. Show me what this looks like in all of my relationships, not just the ones that are easy. In Jesus' Name, Amen.

_____

_____

_____

_____

_____

_____

_____

_____

 JESUS' ADVISORS

PRIDE ONLY BREEDS QUARRELS, BUT WISDOM IS FOUND IN THOSE WHO TAKE ADVICE.
PROVERBS 13:10

Who do you trust to give you feedback and advice? Jesus turned to God in prayer regularly, seeking His Father's perspective on His ministry and decisions. He also turned to His disciples to ask how His message was being received by the crowds and to evaluate how He was doing at influencing them personally. Even though He was God, He wanted their human feedback and perspective. Don't let your pride get in the way of hearing the things God wants you to hear. Whose perspective are you seeking about how you are doing as a servant leader?

PRAYER
God, it is easy to allow my pride and fear to isolate me from real relationships where I can ask honest questions and receive honest feedback. Help me to find trusted advisors who will give me good advice and then give me the courage to ask them for the feedback I need. Thank You for modeling this for me, Jesus. Thank You, Holy Spirit, for opening my eyes to how I need to become more like Jesus. In His Name, Amen.

✋ LEADERSHIP 101

... THE LORD HAS TOLD YOU WHAT IS GOOD, AND THIS IS WHAT HE REQUIRES OF YOU: TO DO WHAT IS RIGHT, TO LOVE MERCY, AND TO WALK HUMBLY WITH YOUR GOD.
MICAH 6:8 (NLT)

For some people, the thought of being a "leader" is overwhelming. What does a leader do? At the most basic level, leaders help. They see where they can make a difference and offer assistance. It might be as simple as answering a person's question or showing the way to perform a task. The behaviors of a spiritual leader are surprisingly similar: to live in right relationship with God and others. How are you practicing the basics of leadership today?

PRAYER
Lord, today I want to simply and honestly live in light of Your mercy in my life and share it with others. Let me be a help to those around me, offering what You've given me to help them. In Jesus' Name, Amen.

_____

_____

_____

_____

_____

_____

_____

_____

LEAVING CHILDISH UNDERSTANDING

YOU INTENDED TO HARM ME, BUT GOD INTENDED IT FOR GOOD TO ACCOMPLISH WHAT IS NOW BEING DONE, THE SAVING OF MANY LIVES.
GENESIS 50:20

As a child, Joseph thought leadership was about being in a place of prominence. It comes as no surprise that his older brothers reacted violently against his vision of ruling over them. God used hardships and difficulty to teach Joseph that leadership was about servanthood. When Joseph was reunited with his brothers at last, he had learned that leadership wasn't about self-promotion or ruling over people; as a result, God was able to use him powerfully. How is God using hardships and difficulties to move you from a childish understanding and shape you for His purposes?

PRAYER

God, Joseph's story is a good reminder for me that leadership isn't about speaking things into being but about serving others. Keep me from falling into the temptation to promote myself or trying to lead by power. Instead, help me to humbly submit to You in difficulties and yield to Your training so that I can be used by You to bless others, wherever You place me. In Jesus' Name, Amen.

LIVING ON PURPOSE

JESUS GAVE THEM THIS ANSWER: "I TELL YOU THE TRUTH, THE SON CAN DO NOTHING BY HIMSELF; HE CAN DO ONLY WHAT HE SEES HIS FATHER DOING, BECAUSE WHATEVER THE FATHER DOES THE SON ALSO DOES."
JOHN 5:19

There were times when Jesus walked away or moved on: when the crowd tried to stone Him, when they tried to crown Him king, when people tried to provoke a quarrel with Him. There were other times that He chose to unexpectedly engage with people or change His travel plans. Why? He lived in accordance with God's call on His life, eliminating or adding whatever it took to accomplish the Father's purpose. What would it look like for you to do the same in your life? What things would you add, and what would you take away?

PRAYER
Jesus, I want to live my life with clarity of purpose. Take away the things in my life and schedule that do not accomplish Your purposes. Show me what to add in order to align my life with Your call. In Jesus' Name, Amen.

_____

_____

_____

_____

_____

_____

_____

_____

 LIVING EXAMPLE

**AND YOU YOURSELF MUST BE AN EXAMPLE TO THEM BY DOING
GOOD WORKS OF EVERY KIND. LET EVERYTHING YOU DO REFLECT
THE INTEGRITY AND SERIOUSNESS OF YOUR TEACHING.**
TITUS 2:7 (NLT)

What do you believe about leadership? How do your beliefs drive your
attitudes and actions? How would people who know you answer these
questions about you? What do they know about servant leadership by
observing your attitudes and actions toward them? If you want to know
how you are doing in living out your beliefs, ask those around you.

PRAYER

*Jesus, these are soul-searching questions. I realize that the answers
that matter are not what I think but what You think and what others
think. How am I doing from Your perspective, Lord? And who can I ask
for feedback? What do I need to start, stop, or continue doing to lead
more like You? Show me, I pray. In Jesus' Name, Amen.*

_____

_____

_____

_____

_____

_____

_____

_____

♥ LOVING YOUR ENEMIES

"BUT I TELL YOU WHO HEAR ME: LOVE YOUR ENEMIES, DO GOOD TO THOSE WHO HATE YOU, BLESS THOSE WHO CURSE YOU, PRAY FOR THOSE WHO MISTREAT YOU."
LUKE 6:27-28

It's easier to lead people whom we genuinely like and who genuinely like us. Loving and leading our enemies, the people who wish us harm and don't respect us, is harder. Yet Jesus made it clear that this is part of our call. Ananias heard this call very specifically. He resisted at first, but eventually he was used by God in transforming Saul the persecutor into Paul the apostle. Like Ananias, your willingness to respond sets the stage for God to work through you.

PRAYER
Jesus, when I pray for You to use me, I naturally think of the people I love and care about. Break through my resistance to letting You use me in the lives of people I don't like or people I fear. Help me to love and lead with courage, compassion, and obedience. In Jesus' Name, Amen.

MY PART OF OUR JOB

THE ONE WHO PLANTS AND THE ONE WHO WATERS WORK TOGETHER WITH THE SAME PURPOSE. AND BOTH WILL BE REWARDED FOR THEIR OWN HARD WORK.
1 CORINTHIANS 3:8

God has assigned each one of us a role to play in serving others. Our roles are specifically suited to how He has gifted us. His vision for the world is too big to be captured by just one person's heart or accomplished by a single individual's strength and energy. His strategy is to plant one piece of His vision within each of us as His followers and to use His Spirit to harness us into a team that works together for His purpose. Which part of God's vision drives you as a servant leader?

PRAYER

God, I continue to be amazed and humbled that You give me a way to serve Your purposes in the world. Help me to humbly offer what You have given me to be used to reach others with the message of Jesus through following His model of servant leadership. In His Name, Amen.

_____
_____
_____
_____
_____
_____
_____
_____

♥ NO OTHER GODS

YOU SHALL HAVE NO OTHER GODS BEFORE ME.
EXODUS 20:3

When God first called Moses, Moses could only look at his own inadequacy and insecurity. Fear overwhelmed him to the point that he couldn't go forward without Aaron at his side. As Moses walked with God through the exodus experience, He eventually came to the place where his loyalty and security were grounded in God's presence alone. He realized that no human being could take God's place in his life. What do you place your trust in when it comes to leadership: your own strengths, the people around you, or God's presence and His power to fulfill His call on your life?

PRAYER
Lord, I know that my confidence needs to rest in You alone. Thank You for the strength You provide and the people You have given me to work with. Don't let me idolize them by looking to them instead of You. You are the only One worthy of worship and the only One who deserves first place in my life. In Jesus' Name, Amen.

_____

_____

_____

_____

_____

_____

_____

_____

 PLACED BY GOD

THE LORD GOD TOOK THE MAN AND PUT HIM IN THE GARDEN OF EDEN TO WORK IT AND TAKE CARE OF IT.

GENESIS 2:15

Human beings are the crowning achievement of God's creation. Think of it, God placed Adam and Eve in the midst of the glory of the universe—the sun, moon, and stars and the intricacies, power, and beauty of creation—so they could care for the world on His behalf. He continues to place His people where He needs them, to care for others and cultivate a setting where God's purposes are accomplished. Where has God placed you?

PRAYER

Lord, it changes my perspective on daily life to consider that You have placed me where I am for Your purposes. Help me to align myself with You today, to see others as You see them, to treat them with respect, and to be part accomplishing Your purposes. In Jesus' Name, Amen.

 # PRIDEFUL PRAYER

"FOR WHO HAS KNOWN THE MIND OF THE LORD THAT HE MAY INSTRUCT HIM?" BUT WE HAVE THE MIND OF CHRIST.

1 CORINTHIANS 2:16

When you pray, what drives you? Is it a desire to tell God what to do, how to think, how to feel? Or is it a time of heartfelt connection and communication with Him? Do you come prepared to listen, honor, love, and connect with Him? Pride reveals itself in our prayer lives when we think that telling God what is on our minds is more important than asking Him to talk to us about the things on His mind. What does God want to talk with you about today?

PRAYER

Lord Jesus, You know how easily my thoughts become consumed with my own perspective. I confess that I need to stop clinging to my own ideas, thinking that I know better than You how to run the world. Cleanse me from self-centered, misdirected thinking. Fill my mind with the things You think about; help me see people and situations from Your perspective. In Jesus' Name, Amen.

# REMAINING NIMBLE

YOU WILL KEEP IN PERFECT PEACE ALL WHO TRUST IN YOU, ALL WHOSE THOUGHTS ARE FIXED ON YOU!
ISAIAH 26:3 (NLT)

Life moves quickly, circumstances change, and needs arise. As leaders, whether at home or in the marketplace, it is up to us to respond to changing times and circumstances. A steadfast trust in God and His unchanging truth and faithfulness gives us the ability to respond in the present with wisdom from above. Confidence in God frees us to think clearly and make decisions in the moment. How will your response to changing circumstances reflect your trust in God?

PRAYER

God, thank You for this time to get an eternal perspective in the midst of my day. I know that the changing circumstances of my life never catch You by surprise. Keep me focused on Your purposes and aligned with Your Spirit. Help me to lead well today, and may my responses reflect my faith in You. In Jesus' Name, Amen.

ROLE MODELS NEEDED

ONE DAY JESUS WAS PRAYING IN A CERTAIN PLACE. WHEN HE FINISHED, ONE OF HIS DISCIPLES SAID TO HIM, "LORD, TEACH US TO PRAY, JUST AS JOHN TAUGHT HIS DISCIPLES."
LUKE 11:1

People are watching you. Children, teens, and adults are looking for role models. Even people who don't know you notice what you do or don't do, what you say or don't say, as your life intersects with theirs. Who are you modeling your life after? Whose leadership example have you taken as your own? What will people be able to learn about leading like Jesus from your example today?

PRAYER
Lord, it is humbling to think that other people are watching me the way Your disciples watched You. Do they see a life of faith? Do they see a person who depends on You through prayer? Do they see a person who leads with focus and compassion? Do they see a leader who serves them as You served Your disciples? Make me that leader, Lord, I pray, in Jesus' Name, Amen.

_____

_____

_____

_____

_____

_____

_____

_____

 # SHAPED BY GOD

FOR YOU CREATED MY INMOST BEING; YOU KNIT ME TOGETHER IN MY MOTHER'S WOMB. I PRAISE YOU BECAUSE I AM FEARFULLY AND WONDERFULLY MADE; YOUR WORKS ARE WONDERFUL, I KNOW THAT FULL WELL.
PSALM 139:13-14

Where do you live? What do you like to do? What experiences have you had in life? David came to see clearly that God's design and workmanship were woven throughout his life. God knows just what He is doing as He works in you. He placed the framework in place before you were born, and He continues to shape you through His Spirit. How has God shaped you? How is He using you to influence others?

PRAYER

Creator God, thank You for thinking of me. Thank You for reminding me that You are the One who has been at work in my life from before I was born. Thank You for continuing Your work in me through the years. As I live today, I want to remain pliable, sensitive to the ongoing work of Your Spirit. Use the challenges of this day to continue to shape me to be like Jesus. In His Name, Amen.

THE JOURNEY OF A LIFETIME

"... I HAVE COME THAT THEY MAY HAVE LIFE, AND HAVE IT TO THE FULL."
JOHN 10:10

Do you like to travel, discover new places, and experience a sense of adventure? The journey of servant leadership is big enough to fill a lifetime and consuming enough to bring significance to each moment. Each day offers new opportunities, challenges and experiences. Jesus is a guaranteed traveling companion and guide. You will meet people who long to know the freedom and adventure of traveling with Jesus. What will today hold for you on the Lead like Jesus journey?

PRAYER
Jesus, I hear Your invitation to join You on the journey, to discover life as You designed it to be lived. Sometimes fear holds me back, and sometimes I pridefully opt out of the day's itinerary. Today, I want to join you in serving others. In Jesus' Name, Amen.

_____
_____
_____
_____
_____
_____
_____
_____
_____

THE LORD WILL FULFILL HIS PURPOSE

THE LORD WILL FULFILL [HIS PURPOSE] FOR ME; YOUR LOVE, O LORD, ENDURES FOREVER—DO NOT ABANDON THE WORKS OF YOUR HANDS.
PSALM 138:8

How do you respond to feelings of inadequacy or moments of personal failure? Feelings of disappointment in ourselves, discouragement from constant opposition, sorrow, and fear of failing God and being cast aside can overwhelm us. Our inadequacies and failures do not surprise God. His forgiveness and power to redeem are ever-present to meet us, even at our lowest moments. He longs to pick you up and re-orient your life and leadership. Where do You need the Lord's restoration so you can serve Him with renewed faithfulness?

PRAYER

Lord, I am so grateful that my life and leadership doesn't depend on me. Thank You for being the One who calls, equips, protects, preserves, and empowers me. I trust in Your enduring love and power to accomplish all that You desire. I commit myself to You. Be exalted in my life. In Jesus' Name, Amen.

THE RIGHT WORD AT THE RIGHT TIME

LISTEN TO ADVICE AND ACCEPT INSTRUCTION, AND IN THE END YOU WILL BE WISE.

PROVERBS 19:20

When Moses had his hands full leading God's people, God brought his father-in-law Jethro to offer him advice. Jethro exemplifies a servant leader's approach to supporting an established leader. He observed a problem, he had the relational basis to be able to offer a different perspective, and he allowed Moses to determine whether he wanted to take action on the advice. When Moses discerned the wisdom behind Jethro's words, he implemented the plan and saw God use it to multiply ministry. Who does God use to offer you good advice? Where do you need godly advice today?

PRAYER

Thank you, God, for sending people with different perspectives into my life. Help me to listen and discern whether their advice is from you. Show me how I can better serve the needs of Your people. In Jesus' Name, Amen.

 # THE WAY FORWARD

TRUST IN THE LORD WITH ALL YOUR HEART AND LEAN NOT ON YOUR OWN UNDERSTANDING; IN ALL YOUR WAYS ACKNOWLEDGE HIM, AND HE WILL MAKE YOUR PATHS STRAIGHT.
PROVERBS 3:5-6

Trusting God to show us the way brings courage and confidence to take the next step, whatever it may be. He will be sure to lead us along the pathway He has designed. Especially in uncertain times, trusting unreservedly in Him is the best choice. When you don't know which way to go, He knows the way forward. Trust Him ... and take the next step. Where do you need the Lord to make your path straight today?

PRAYER
Lord, You know how I can move forward with what is in front of me. I don't want to waste time or effort, or mislead others by wandering around aimlessly. I know I can trust You to take me in the right direction. I will follow You today. Please lead me along Your path. In Jesus' Name, Amen.

 THROUGH, NOT AROUND

YOUR PATH LED THROUGH THE SEA, YOUR WAY THROUGH THE MIGHTY WATERS, THOUGH YOUR FOOTPRINTS WERE NOT SEEN.
PSALM 77:19

What insurmountable obstacles are you facing? Our human tendency is to want God to remove the obstacles in our paths, yet Scripture reveals that God's way is often through, not around. God led Moses and the Israelites to the Red Sea so that He could once again show them His power as they moved forward in faith. How does God want to reveal Himself to you today as you step out in faith?

PRAYER

Lord, You know the impossibilities facing me right now, and You know the path that led me here. Sometimes I feel overwhelmed when I look at the situation from my perspective. Give me your perspective today, and courage to take the steps of faith You reveal. I want to look forward, not backward, and see Your power revealed as I follow You into the future. In Jesus' Name, Amen.

_____

_____

_____

_____

_____

_____

_____

_____

_____

VIRAL ATTITUDES

BE JOYFUL IN HOPE, PATIENT IN AFFLICTION, FAITHFUL IN PRAYER.
ROMANS 12:12

For better or for worse, a leader's attitudes are contagious. When we are joyful, patient, and faithful, others notice and tend to emulate us. When we are discouraged, impatient, and faithless, they notice that, too. If poor attitudes continue over an extended period of time, morale begins to deteriorate. Our attitudes are indicators of our spiritual health. Spiritual habits like meditating on God's Word, prayer, and spending time with other believers strengthen us spiritually. As our spiritual health and vitality increases, so does our ability to influence the thinking, behavior, and development of others.

PRAYER

Jesus, it strikes me that joy, patience, and faithfulness are all fruit of the Spirit. Thank You that as I focus on the hope You offer in spite of circumstances, consistently seek You during hard times, and spend time communicating with You, You will develop these attitudes in me. Please make me a virus for good during hard times. In Jesus' Name, Amen.

WEEDING OUT BITTERNESS

SEE TO IT THAT NO ONE MISSES THE GRACE OF GOD AND THAT NO BITTER ROOT GROWS UP TO CAUSE TROUBLE AND DEFILE MANY.
HEBREWS 12:15

Jonah heard God's call clearly, so clearly that he decided to run from it. When God told him to go to the enemies who were oppressing God's people, Jonah said, "No!" The second time God told him, Jonah obediently went and saw God use him to transform hearts and lives. The only life not transformed was Jonah's. Don't cling to bitterness and unforgiveness and miss the blessing of being transformed by God. Where do you need to ask God to change your heart?

PRAYER
Lord, weed out any bitterness in my heart. Don't let me be a stumbling block to others. And please don't let me miss Your grace and mercy in the midst of offering it to other people. I don't want to just talk like someone who leads like Jesus; I want to live a transformed life as I serve in His name. In Jesus' Name, Amen.

WHEN JESUS ASKS

REMAIN IN ME, AND I WILL REMAIN IN YOU. FOR A BRANCH CANNOT PRODUCE FRUIT IF IT IS SEVERED FROM THE VINE, AND YOU CANNOT BE FRUITFUL UNLESS YOU REMAIN IN ME. YES, I AM THE VINE; YOU ARE THE BRANCHES. THOSE WHO REMAIN IN ME, AND I IN THEM, WILL PRODUCE MUCH FRUIT. FOR APART FROM ME YOU CAN DO NOTHING.
JOHN 15:4-5 (NLT)

What questions does Jesus ask you on a regular basis? Does He want to talk about your heart attitudes and motivations? Does He challenge your thinking and beliefs? Does He focus on how you are interacting with others? Does He call you to deeper intimacy in your relationship with Him? Jesus wants you to find your home in Him, to be so connected with Him that your life is simply and naturally an extension of His life.

PRAYER

Jesus, thank You for probing me, for challenging me to examine my life, my leadership, and my connection to You. I don't want to wither away; I want my life to flow from You and Your life through me to others. In Jesus' Name, Amen.

 WHEN THE ODDS ARE OVERWHELMING

THEN HE SAID TO ME, "THIS IS WHAT THE LORD SAYS TO ZERUBBABEL: IT IS NOT BY FORCE NOR BY STRENGTH, BUT BY MY SPIRIT, SAYS THE LORD OF HEAVEN'S ARMIES."
ZECHARIAH 4:6 (NLT)

How do you respond when the task in front of you seems overwhelming? Perhaps it is so large that you don't know if you can accomplish it. Perhaps others have tried and failed. Perhaps you doubt your own abilities. Perhaps you have failed at this in the past. Perhaps all the odds are against you. God delights in using people who know their only hope of success is in Him. What is God calling you to do that can only be accomplished through dependence on Him?

PRAYER

Lord, You know where I am feeling overwhelmed. Do I have my eyes on the right things? What does success look like to You when it comes to this situation? Correct my thinking and give me Your perspective. Show me where I am trying to force results or achieve them in my own strength. Lead me, Spirit, and help me depend on You. In Jesus' Name, Amen.

WHO DO YOU LEARN FROM?

THE FEAR OF THE LORD IS THE BEGINNING OF KNOWLEDGE, BUT FOOLS DESPISE WISDOM AND DISCIPLINE.
PROVERBS 1:7

Even Jesus was a learner while He was here on earth. Though He was God, He learned obedience, and He learned to suffer and to fight temptation. Who or what has God used to teach you in your life? Good friends, authors, parents, children, colleagues, pastors? Suffering, success, failure, obedience, disobedience? How open are you to learning from others? For the person who is open to hearing God speak, the teachers are endless. What does God want to teach you today?

PRAYER

Lord, thank You for being willing to teach me. Open my eyes to the teachers and lessons You send me today. If Jesus needed to learn obedience and how to suffer and fight temptation, I know I need to learn these lessons, also. Let me learn from Your hand, Jesus' example, and Your Word, and from all those You send into my life. In Jesus' Name, Amen.

_____

_____

_____

_____

_____

_____

_____

_____

_____

 A DUAL FOCUS

FOR WE ARE GOD'S HANDIWORK, CREATED IN CHRIST JESUS TO DO GOOD WORKS, WHICH GOD PREPARED IN ADVANCE FOR US TO DO.
EPHESIANS 2:10

Are you task-oriented or relationship-oriented? Relationships offer opportunities for reflecting the kindness, compassion, and wisdom of Jesus. Tasks to be done provide opportunities to serve others at their point of need and reflect character qualities of integrity and perseverance. Jesus modeled a life that blended a dual focus on accomplishing tasks with highly valuing relationships with God and people. How can you emulate Him today?

PRAYER

God, You made me according to Your design. You planned how You would use me to serve others and what You want me to accomplish in life. Help me to not lose sight of You in the midst of my daily tasks. Show me how You want me to focus my life today so I accomplish Your purpose. I ask in Jesus' name, Amen.

 A GOOD RECEIVER

YET TO ALL WHO DID RECEIVE HIM, TO THOSE WHO BELIEVED IN HIS NAME, HE GAVE THE RIGHT TO BECOME CHILDREN OF GOD—CHILDREN BORN NOT OF NATURAL DESCENT, NOR OF HUMAN DECISION OR A HUSBAND'S WILL, BUT BORN OF GOD.
JOHN 1:12-13

Have you ever known anyone who had a hard time receiving gifts? Whether an expression of gratitude or the offer of help, some people have a hard time receiving. They prefer to be on the giving side of things, perhaps so they won't be indebted to anyone, even God. Through Jesus, God offers a new heart, real life, and the freedom to be more than we ever imagined we could be. Have you received His gift?

PRAYER

God, I am by nature self-centered, and I cannot be the person or the leader I want to be unless I receive a new heart from You. Thank You that Jesus came to serve me at my point of need, and that He made the way for me to become Your child. Help me to live as Your child today, as Jesus did. In His Name, Amen.

A TIME OF PREPARATION

"EVERY BRANCH THAT DOES BEAR FRUIT HE PRUNES SO THAT IT WILL BE EVEN MORE FRUITFUL."
JOHN 15:2

God uses our life experiences to prepare us to serve others. As we seek Him through the seasons of our lives, we develop wisdom, confidence, and courage. These qualities not only prepare us for the future, they provide the platform from which we can influence those around us. Many times the very circumstances that we would choose to avoid become the catalyst for God to use us in other people's lives. How is God preparing you today to serve others?

PRAYER
Lord, what would it look like today to pray, not for escape from difficulties but for more faith to trust You, open eyes to see You at work, and a spirit and will yielded to Your purposes and pruning process in my life? I want to be fruitful in my service. Please mold me and make me someone You can use to serve other people. In the name of Your servant Jesus, Amen.

AN IMPOSSIBLE TASK

"I AM THE LORD'S SERVANT," MARY ANSWERED. "MAY YOUR WORD TO ME BE FULFILLED."
LUKE 1:38 (NLT)

Has God ever called you to an impossible task? Something that you knew you could not (or cannot) accomplish in your own strength, something that you know will require you to depend wholly on Him. Something that will serve to draw you closer to His side, to seek His wisdom, to cling to Him for strength, and to follow Him more closely. What impossible task is God calling you to today?

PRAYER

Lord, thank You for Mary's example of hearing Your call to a seemingly impossible task and yielding all that she was to You. You continue to call us today to carry Your name and message to others. May Your word to us be fulfilled. May we today hear Your voice and follow Mary's example of humility and confidence. May we serve in Jesus' Name, Amen.

_____

_____

_____

_____

_____

_____

_____

_____

 ARE YOU EAGER?

FOR I KNOW YOUR EAGERNESS TO HELP, AND I HAVE BEEN BOASTING ABOUT IT TO THE MACEDONIANS, TELLING THEM THAT SINCE LAST YEAR YOU IN ACHAIA WERE READY TO GIVE; AND YOUR ENTHUSIASM HAS STIRRED MOST OF THEM TO ACTION.
2 CORINTHIANS 9:2

What gets you up and going each day? What inspires you to give your all? What causes you to say yes to sacrifice and surrender? How does your vision of God, your understanding of who He is and how He works, influence your life? Today, ask Him to permeate your thinking with an awareness of who He is and what He is doing around you.

PRAYER

Lord, stir up my eagerness to be used by You. Remind me of the greatness of Your salvation and of who You are. I want to be ready to give my all, whatever You need or ask. Revive my spirit, reshape my thinking, help me to re-engage in the transformational journey of leading like Jesus, in whose Name I pray, Amen.

_____

_____

_____

_____

_____

_____

_____

_____

_____

↻ ARE YOU USEFUL?

THOSE WHO CLEANSE THEMSELVES FROM THE LATTER WILL BE INSTRUMENTS FOR SPECIAL PURPOSES, MADE HOLY, USEFUL TO THE MASTER AND PREPARED TO DO ANY GOOD WORK.
2 TIMOTHY 2:21

Jesus prepared Himself for being used by God. He became part of the world He came to save, filled His mind with Scripture, affirmed His desire to fulfill God's call in His life, resisted temptation, spent time re-connecting with the Father, and surrounded Himself with a spiritual support community. What are you doing to prepare yourself to be used by God?

PRAYER
God, if Jesus needed and lived by these spiritual habits in order to be an instrument for Your purposes, then I know that I need to practice them, too. How can I prepare myself to be of greater use for You? What do I need to add? What do I need to take away? Show me and make me useful to You, I pray, in Jesus' Name, Amen.

❤ BACK TO THE BEGINNING

AS FOR YOU, SEE THAT WHAT YOU HAVE HEARD FROM THE BEGINNING REMAINS IN YOU. IF IT DOES, YOU ALSO WILL REMAIN IN THE SON AND IN THE FATHER. AND THIS IS WHAT HE PROMISED US—ETERNAL LIFE.
1 JOHN 2:24-25

Leading like Jesus does not guarantee that the journey will be easy or that the outcomes will always be the ones for which we hope. On days when the struggles seem to outweigh the benefits, it's a good idea to go back to the beginning. Remember Jesus' journey as a servant leader; remember how He called you; remember His presence with you today. How do these things strengthen you to continue leading in His name?

PRAYER

Jesus, thank You for reminding me that You are the beginning from which my whole life flows. Thank You for calling me back to relationship with You as the basis for facing this day. Help me lead from the core of my relationship with You. It is in Your Name that I ask, Amen.

DAILY OPPORTUNITIES

YOU DID NOT CHOOSE ME, BUT I CHOSE YOU AND APPOINTED YOU SO THAT YOU MIGHT GO AND BEAR FRUIT—FRUIT THAT WILL LAST—AND SO THAT WHATEVER YOU ASK IN MY NAME THE FATHER WILL GIVE YOU.
JOHN 15:16

Each day provides new opportunities to serve God and others. Your opportunities will be unique to your life and situation. Don't miss them. God has placed you where He needs you in order to serve others in Jesus' name. What opportunities will God bring you today?

PRAYER
Lord, I want my life to bear fruit for You. I don't want to miss the opportunities that You bring my way. Help me to see the opportunities You place in front of me and respond by serving others. Use me, I ask, in Jesus' Name, Amen.

FAITHFUL IN GOD'S HOUSE

THEREFORE, HOLY BROTHERS AND SISTERS, WHO SHARE IN THE HEAVENLY CALLING, FIX YOUR THOUGHTS ON JESUS, WHOM WE ACKNOWLEDGE AS OUR APOSTLE AND HIGH PRIEST. HE WAS FAITHFUL TO THE ONE WHO APPOINTED HIM, JUST AS MOSES WAS FAITHFUL IN ALL GOD'S HOUSE.
HEBREWS 3:1-2

God's call asks for a response. Abraham, Moses, Joshua, Deborah, Esther, Samuel, David, John the Baptist, Jesus, Simon Peter, Andrew, the rest of the disciples: Each person heard and responded to the call of God. Scripture tells us that each one was found faithful in doing their part. What is God's call on your life? Will you be found faithful?

PRAYER
God, I know You have called me to love You and to love others. The natural outflow of my love for You is to serve others and carry the message of Jesus to others as I live my life. I want to be found faithful in Your house, like Jesus, in whose Name I pray, Amen.

_____
_____
_____
_____
_____
_____
_____
_____
_____

 # FOCUS

...AND LET US RUN WITH PERSEVERANCE THE RACE MARKED OUT FOR US, FIXING OUR EYES ON JESUS, THE PIONEER AND PERFECTER OF FAITH.
HEBREWS 12:1-2

What is your focus in life? Jesus expressed His goal as simply doing whatever the Father was doing; Paul spoke about pressing on toward the goal of knowing Christ and being found in Him. God has called you into relationship with Himself through Jesus Christ in order for you to be caught up in His purposes in the world. How will your leadership influence others for Him today?

PRAYER

Jesus, some days the little things in life eat away at my sense of being caught up in pursuing You and Your purposes. Thank You for being faithful to fulfilling God's purposes, not only on the cross but also every single day that You lived. Help me to run with perseverance today as I fix my eyes on You. It is in Your Name that I pray, Amen.

 FOOD FOR THOUGHT

THE SPIRIT GIVES LIFE; THE FLESH COUNTS FOR NOTHING. THE WORDS I HAVE SPOKEN TO YOU—THEY ARE FULL OF THE SPIRIT AND LIFE.
JOHN 6:63

A balanced diet is as important to maintaining good spiritual health as it is for physical health. What feeds your heart and mind spiritually? Are you taking in enough spiritual nourishment to strengthen you to serve sacrificially? Scripture is food for the soul. Spend time in God's Word today. Savor it slowly, allowing the Holy Spirit to apply it to your heart and mind. Allow it to infuse your leadership with power from above.

PRAYER
Jesus, today I want Your words to nourish my heart, my mind, my interactions with others. As I meditate on Scripture, refresh my weary soul, reshape my perspective, and replenish my spiritual strength so that I can serve others as You did. I pray in Jesus' Name, Amen.

 # FORGIVENESS

BEAR WITH EACH OTHER AND FORGIVE ONE ANOTHER IF ANY OF YOU HAS A GRIEVANCE AGAINST SOMEONE. FORGIVE AS THE LORD FORGAVE YOU.
COLOSSIANS 3:13

When was the last time you forgave someone who offended you or hurt you? Most of us have the opportunity to offer and receive forgiveness on a regular basis. Forgiveness is a gift that God gives us in order for us to pass it on to others. Forgiveness that is hoarded without being shared freely is not being used for God's intended purpose. How does your willingness to forgive reflect the forgiveness of Jesus? Who do you need to forgive today?

PRAYER
Jesus, I confess that at times I have hoarded Your forgiveness to myself, and I have not always forgiven others as You forgive me. Thank You for the freedom and hope that Your forgiveness has brought me. Help me to offer forgiveness today so that others find the freedom and courage to move forward in life. In Jesus' Name I pray, Amen.

_____

_____

_____

_____

_____

_____

_____

_____

HE UNDERSTANDS

FOR WE DO NOT HAVE A HIGH PRIEST WHO IS UNABLE TO EMPATHIZE WITH OUR WEAKNESSES, BUT WE HAVE ONE WHO HAS BEEN TEMPTED IN EVERY WAY, JUST AS WE ARE—YET HE DID NOT SIN.
HEBREWS 4:15

Jesus understands the challenges you face. He knows how hard it is to stand against temptation as you try to live as a servant leader. He has experienced what it's like to be misunderstood and used. He has made the right decisions in quiet moments, cared deeply for others in His private life, and stood courageously against opposition in public settings. He can help you as you face any situation. Where do you need Him to strengthen you today?

PRAYER

Jesus, thank You for being able to empathize with me, especially with my weakness. Thank You for facing temptation, for knowing what it takes to stand up under pressure, so that You can help me when I am tempted to give up and give in. Help me today to do what is right both privately and publicly. I ask in Jesus' Name, Amen.

 IN JESUS' NAME

WITH THIS IN MIND, WE CONSTANTLY PRAY FOR YOU, THAT OUR GOD MAY MAKE YOU WORTHY OF HIS CALLING, AND THAT BY HIS POWER HE MAY BRING TO FRUITION YOUR EVERY DESIRE FOR GOODNESS AND YOUR EVERY DEED PROMPTED BY FAITH. WE PRAY THIS SO THAT THE NAME OF OUR LORD JESUS MAY BE GLORIFIED IN YOU, AND YOU IN HIM, ACCORDING TO THE GRACE OF OUR GOD AND THE LORD JESUS CHRIST.
2 THESSALONIANS 1:11-12

To many people today, the words "in Jesus' Name" are tacked on at the end of a prayer before saying "Amen." Yet the book of Acts tells a different story. The early disciples boldly stepped out to serve in Jesus' name. In Jesus' Name, people were forgiven, healed, restored, baptized, and commissioned. What about you? Is Jesus' Name just a catch phrase for you? Or does His Name compel you to serve others as He did and carry His message to others?

PRAYER
Jesus, I don't want to speak Your Name in vain, nor do I want to live in vain. I want Your Name to be the impulse for every desire and every deed in my life. Fan this longing into flame, and let my life bring glory to You. I ask this in Jesus' Name, Amen.

JESUS IS PRAYING FOR YOU

... BECAUSE JESUS LIVES FOREVER, HE HAS A PERMANENT PRIESTHOOD. THEREFORE HE IS ABLE TO SAVE COMPLETELY THOSE WHO COME TO GOD THROUGH HIM, BECAUSE HE ALWAYS LIVES TO INTERCEDE FOR THEM.
HEBREWS 7:24-25

Jesus' ministry on our behalf continues in heaven. He has now rested from the work of providing salvation, yet He continues to care for and strengthen His own. He is praying for you today, asking the Father to help you live and lead like Him. How do you want Him to pray for you today?

PRAYER

Jesus, what an overwhelming thought, that even now in heaven You are continuing to serve me. If I could ask for one thing today, it would be _____. Thank You for hearing my prayer and for interceding with the Father on my behalf. I need You to strengthen me to serve You and those You place in my life. Please continue to use me, I humbly ask in Jesus' Name, Amen.

_____

_____

_____

_____

_____

_____

_____

_____

IMITATE YOUR LEADERS

REMEMBER YOUR LEADERS, WHO SPOKE THE WORD OF GOD TO YOU. CONSIDER THE OUTCOME OF THEIR WAY OF LIFE AND IMITATE THEIR FAITH. JESUS CHRIST IS THE SAME YESTERDAY AND TODAY AND FOREVER.
HEBREWS 13:7-8

Who is your role model of a Christ-like servant leader? Who embodies the heart, head, hands, and habits of Jesus? What can you thank God for in their example? What do you want to imitate in their faith and lifestyle? While our eyes are first to be on Jesus, men and women through the ages have followed Him, providing examples of faith and servant leadership. Circumstances and situations may change, but Jesus' example of servant leadership is timeless.

PRAYER
Jesus, thank You for providing a role model for all time, and thank You for the people whose faithfulness have impacted my life. I want to be used by You in the same way that You used them in my life. Help me to rise to new levels of faithfulness and service in Jesus' Name, Amen.

 IMPOSSIBLE SITUATIONS

DEAR FRIEND, DO NOT IMITATE WHAT IS EVIL BUT WHAT IS GOOD. ANYONE WHO DOES WHAT IS GOOD IS FROM GOD. ANYONE WHO DOES WHAT IS EVIL HAS NOT SEEN GOD.
3 JOHN 1:11

Some days it can seem impossible to see how God can possibly transform the situations around us. Yet situations are shaped by the choices and responses of the people involved in them. When we focus on being Christ-like servant leaders, God can use us to influence people, and consequently situations. What difference does God want to make, not in your situation or those around you, but in you today?

PRAYER
Lord, You know the things that cause me to despair that things will ever change. Yet You are continually at work, transforming me so that I can be a change agent in my seemingly impossible situations. Thank You for never giving up on me; help me to keep on imitating You as a servant leader so that others might see You. I ask in Jesus' Name, Amen.

 # LIKE YOU

I HAVE SET YOU AN EXAMPLE THAT YOU SHOULD DO AS I HAVE DONE FOR YOU.

JOHN 13:15

What would the world look like today if every person followed your example? What if the words they spoke carried the same tone and message as yours? What if their responses echoed your responses? What if their actions mimicked your actions? Would people look more like Jesus? Would relationships reflect His forgiveness and compassion? Would the world be any different?

PRAYER

Jesus, You offer Yourself as an example for me to follow. You call me to love others, serving them, honoring them above myself, and sacrificially caring for them. Some days I don't really believe it matters how I live—at least that's what my actions seem to indicate. Yet I know that it matters to You how I live, and it matters to those who look to me as a living example of You. Help me today to live as You lived. I ask in Jesus' Name, Amen.

_____
_____
_____
_____
_____
_____
_____
_____
_____

 LISTEN!

"WHOEVER HAS EARS, LET THEM HEAR."
MATTHEW 13:9

How often do you find yourself listening during the day? Not just hearing words or noise, but actually listening. Listening to what people are saying and listening to God. Jesus frequently included a call to hear in His parables. What He was saying was, "Stop, pay attention, listen, understand, and respond!" When you take time to listen, you take a giant step toward becoming a servant leader.

PRAYER

Jesus, You have given me ears. Open my ears, Lord, to hear Your word to me and to hear the heart cries of people around me. Forgive me for being so busy listening to myself that I miss what You want to say and how You want me to respond. May I listen well today, through God-tuned ears. I ask in Jesus' Name, Amen.

 # LIVING AS IF

HE HAS SAVED US AND CALLED US TO A HOLY LIFE—NOT BECAUSE OF ANYTHING WE HAVE DONE BUT BECAUSE OF HIS OWN PURPOSE AND GRACE.
2 TIMOTHY 1:9

The early disciples lived life with an awareness of being caught up in God's purpose for the world. What does it mean for you to live today in light of God's purpose? As if every person you encounter is valuable to God. As if your interaction with people holds the potential to demonstrate the reality of a living, personal God who cares about them. As if God were orchestrating events to bring about His purposes in this time and place. What difference would this make?

PRAYER
Lord, lift my eyes from the daily tasks that fill my day so that I re-focus on Your purpose and grace. Let me look at the people with whom I interact through Your eyes and help me to accomplish Your purposes in what I do and say. May my life reveal Your life to them as I serve them in Jesus' Name, I pray, Amen.

♥ NOT SO WITH YOU

JESUS CALLED THEM TOGETHER AND SAID, "YOU KNOW THAT THE RULERS OF THE GENTILES LORD IT OVER THEM, AND THEIR HIGH OFFICIALS EXERCISE AUTHORITY OVER THEM. NOT SO WITH YOU. INSTEAD, WHOEVER WANTS TO BECOME GREAT AMONG YOU MUST BE YOUR SERVANT, AND WHOEVER WANTS TO BE FIRST MUST BE YOUR SLAVE—JUST AS THE SON OF MAN DID NOT COME TO BE SERVED, BUT TO SERVE, AND TO GIVE HIS LIFE AS A RANSOM FOR MANY."
MATTHEW 20:25-28

Jesus' words regarding how His followers are to lead are clear and unequivocal. We are not to copy the world's leadership pattern of exercising power and authority for our own benefit. There is to be a clear-cut difference between how servant leaders and self-serving leaders approach influencing others. How will this difference be evident in your leadership today?

PRAYER
Lord Jesus, may it be evident today that there is only one Lord in my life – You. As I interact with others today, may they sense that I have been in Your presence. I ask in Jesus' Name, Amen.

 PRAYER

BUT WHEN YOU PRAY, GO INTO YOUR ROOM, CLOSE THE DOOR AND PRAY TO YOUR FATHER, WHO IS UNSEEN. THEN YOUR FATHER, WHO SEES WHAT IS DONE IN SECRET, WILL REWARD YOU.
MATTHEW 6:6

What does your prayer life reveal about your leadership? Are you spending time talking with God about your heart, head, hands, and habits? Do you trust your own ability to influence others, or are you seeking to align yourself with what God wants for them? Are you bringing people and their challenges before God, asking for Him to move in their lives and situations? Take time to pray today.

PRAYER

Lord, as I talk with You today, I want to move beyond the formalities of prayer into a real conversation about how You want to shape me and use me. Open my ears so that I can hear from You; when I walk out into the world, I want to be attuned to Your servant heart. In the Name of Jesus, who taught me to come to You, Amen.

♥ READY OR NOT, HERE I COME

THEN I HEARD THE VOICE OF THE LORD SAYING, "WHOM SHALL I SEND? AND WHO WILL GO FOR US?" AND I SAID, "HERE AM I. SEND ME!"
ISAIAH 6:8

There are times when opportunities to serve are suddenly thrust upon us. We may not feel ready for them, yet God isn't obligated to ask our permission or opinion about who or how He wants us to serve. He reserves the right to change our situations any time He wants to in order to accomplish His purposes. What unexpected opportunities is God placing in front of you? How will you respond? Are you ready to say "yes"?

PRAYER

Lord, I want to think that I would quickly and easily say "yes" to You whenever or however You call me to serve. In this quiet moment, I confess that sometimes I place conditions on serving You. Forgive me for the times and places where I resist Your call to serve. Today, I want to say "yes" to Your call. In the Name of Jesus, whose response to You was always "yes," Amen.

SHOW ME YOUR WAY

CONSIDER HIM WHO ENDURED SUCH OPPOSITION FROM SINNERS, SO THAT YOU WILL NOT GROW WEARY AND LOSE HEART.
HEBREWS 12:3

How did Jesus do it, dealing with fallen people every day, training slow-learning disciples (like you and me), combatting leaders who were set in their ways, and wrestling against spiritual opposition? How did He manage to reflect the truth, grace, love, and compassion of God through His life in spite of the obstacles in front of Him? When we get discouraged, we can always look to Him and His example. What can you emulate from His approach to life that will strengthen you in the midst of challenges?

PRAYER

Jesus, thank You for living with Your disciples in such a way that they knew Your endurance came from a vibrant relationship with the Father. Thank You for speaking about Scripture and spiritual matters with them. Please speak with me today and show me how You want to strengthen me to live and lead like You. In Jesus' Name, Amen.

 SPIRITUAL POWER AND AUTHORITY

FINALLY, BE STRONG IN THE LORD AND IN HIS MIGHTY POWER. PUT ON THE FULL ARMOR OF GOD, SO THAT YOU CAN TAKE YOUR STAND AGAINST THE DEVIL'S SCHEMES. FOR OUR STRUGGLE IS NOT AGAINST FLESH AND BLOOD, BUT AGAINST THE RULERS, AGAINST THE AUTHORITIES, AGAINST THE POWERS OF THIS DARK WORLD AND AGAINST THE SPIRITUAL FORCES OF EVIL IN THE HEAVENLY REALMS.
EPHESIANS 6:10-12

Trying to lead in your own power and authority will never achieve God's results. God's purposes are birthed through prayer and listening to His voice and lived out in humble dependence and obedience. His work is accomplished through Spirit-led servant leaders who live in daily awareness of Jesus' presence and commands. Whose power and authority guides your life today?

PRAYER
Lord, forgive me for edging You out of my life, for the times when I try to do things in my own interests and power. I lay these down today. Clothe me instead in Your name and power so that I can be used by You. I want my life to exalt You only. Accomplish Your purposes through me, I ask in Jesus' Name, Amen.

TAKING THINGS IN STRIDE

PREACH THE WORD; BE PREPARED IN SEASON AND OUT OF SEASON; CORRECT, REBUKE AND ENCOURAGE—WITH GREAT PATIENCE AND CAREFUL INSTRUCTION.
TIMOTHY 4:2

Our world is filled with ups and downs, highs and lows. Just as Jesus came into the world because we needed a Savior, God sends us into situations because people still need to see Jesus' example and hear His wisdom. He calls us to leadership roles because He needs someone to represent Jesus, especially when the challenges come. When difficulties arise, how will you reflect Jesus' example of servant leadership to those around you?

PRAYER
Jesus, I am humbled to realize that You call me to represent You to the people I come into contact with today. Prepare me now with the patience and wisdom I will need. Remind me that I represent You when challenges and blessings come. Make me one who patiently reflects Your wisdom in the midst of dealing with difficulties. In Your Name, Amen.

 UNLIKELY CHOICE

AND WE ALL, WHO WITH UNVEILED FACES CONTEMPLATE THE LORD'S GLORY, ARE BEING TRANSFORMED INTO HIS IMAGE WITH EVER-INCREASING GLORY, WHICH COMES FROM THE LORD, WHO IS THE SPIRIT.
2 CORINTHIANS 3:18

Knowing yourself as you do, what makes you an unlikely choice as a person whom God wants to use? Is it pride, fear, lack of training, questions and doubts, lack of consistency in your spiritual life? Jesus has a knack for picking people that the rest of the world overlooks and undervalues. He looks for a heart that responds to His call, a person who wants to be transformed and used for His purposes. How will your life reflect the transformational power of God to those around you?

PRAYER
Lord, I want to see You as You are in all Your glory, and be transformed into Your image. Overwhelm me with who You are; overshadow my inadequacies and forgive my sin; let Your presence shine through me. In the transformational Name of Jesus, I pray, Amen.

UNMET EXPECTATIONS

DO NOT REPAY ANYONE EVIL FOR EVIL. BE CAREFUL TO DO WHAT IS RIGHT IN THE EYES OF EVERYONE. IF IT IS POSSIBLE, AS FAR AS IT DEPENDS ON YOU, LIVE AT PEACE WITH EVERYONE.
ROMANS 12:17-18

How do you respond when you fall short of meeting people's expectations, or when their responses fall short of meeting your expectations? Do you automatically assume a defensive posture, or do you tend to take a solution-oriented approach? When you stop and think it about it, it becomes obvious that one response flows from pride and fear, while the other flows from humility and confidence. How do you need God to refocus and reshape your responses?

PRAYER

Jesus, thank You that my self-worth is found in You, not in perfection. Thank You that You are remaking me by refocusing my priorities and expectations, for myself and for others, too. Remake me today, so that when difficulties arise, I will do what is right in the eyes of everyone. In Jesus' Name I ask, Amen.

WHAT ARE YOU LEARNING?

BUT WHEN HE, THE SPIRIT OF TRUTH, COMES, HE WILL GUIDE YOU INTO ALL THE TRUTH. HE WILL NOT SPEAK ON HIS OWN; HE WILL SPEAK ONLY WHAT HE HEARS, AND HE WILL TELL YOU WHAT IS YET TO COME. HE WILL GLORIFY ME BECAUSE IT IS FROM ME THAT HE WILL RECEIVE WHAT HE WILL MAKE KNOWN TO YOU.
JOHN 16:13-14

What are you learning? Each day holds multiple opportunities for us to learn how to live as servant leaders. Servant leaders are lifelong learners, as the pages of Scripture and the changing nature of relationships remind us. The good news is that Jesus is on the journey with you, and He gives you His Spirit to be your teacher and guide. What does He want to teach you today?

PRAYER

Jesus, thank You for sending the Holy Spirit to be my guide on this journey. Just when I think I have it all figured out, I find that You have something new for me. What do You want me to learn today? In Jesus' Name I pray, Amen.

 WHAT DO YOU SEE?

ONCE MORE JESUS PUT HIS HANDS ON THE MAN'S EYES. THEN HIS EYES WERE OPENED, HIS SIGHT WAS RESTORED, AND HE SAW EVERYTHING CLEARLY.
MARK 8:25

What do you see when you look at the people around you? Do you see people whom God loves and desires to save? Sometimes it can be hard to see God's design in fallen people or to realize how far God has brought another person on the journey. As you allow God to transform your vision, you will be able to see the world through God's eyes.

PRAYER

God, when I stop and think about it, I realize that You are at work around me in ways that I cannot see unless I see through Your eyes. I want to see, I want to perceive Your purposes and ways, I want to catch a glimpse of You at work. Restore my sight so that I see both people and the world through Jesus' eyes, in whose Name I pray, Amen.

# A PRAYER FOR THE DISCOURAGED

TURN TO ME AND BE GRACIOUS TO ME, FOR I AM LONELY AND AFFLICTED. RELIEVE THE TROUBLES OF MY HEART AND FREE ME FROM MY ANGUISH.
PSALM 25:16-17

Every leader faces times when things don't go the way they planned, times when troubles come fast and furious, when no choice seems like a good choice. In times such as these, we have the example of men and women of faith who turned to God for help. God never intended for us to face difficulties in our own strength. He wants us to depend on Him. The Psalms help us give voice to our need.

PRAYER

Lord, I cry out to You in David's words, asking You to turn to me and be gracious to me. Ease my heart; release me from the burden of trying to carry my stresses alone. I look for You, I hunger for Your voice, I long for Your touch, I need You to intervene. I give You the praise for what You are going to do, in Jesus' Name, Amen.

A TRUSTWORTHY TEACHER

"YOU CALL ME 'TEACHER' AND 'LORD,' AND RIGHTLY SO, FOR THAT IS WHAT I AM. NOW THAT I, YOUR LORD AND TEACHER, HAVE WASHED YOUR FEET, YOU ALSO SHOULD WASH ONE ANOTHER'S FEET."
JOHN 13:13-14

Jesus was clear with His disciples. He told them that they could trust Him to tell the truth about God and the way to life. He told them to focus on building the kingdom of God and loving others. He told them that they were to follow His example of servant leadership, regardless of how others responded to them. He told them that the Spirit would empower them and teach them day by day. How are these truths shaping Your life today?

PRAYER

Lord Jesus, thank You for telling us the truth about God, our purpose in life, and what to expect as we live for You. Thank You for sending Your Spirit to empower us and teach us. Show me how I need to embrace and live out what You taught. Empower me to live and lead in Jesus' Name today, Amen.

_____
_____
_____
_____
_____
_____
_____
_____
_____

ACTIONS SPEAK LOUDER THAN WORDS

DEAR CHILDREN, LET US NOT LOVE WITH WORDS OR SPEECH BUT WITH ACTIONS AND IN TRUTH.
1 JOHN 3:18

How do you demonstrate a servant lifestyle? Serving others may involve words, but you earn the right to be heard by the way you treat people. Sometimes the most important leadership tools are a listening ear and willing hands. Faithfully demonstrating a Christ-like attitude toward others may result in openings for conversations about leading like Jesus. How will you demonstrate servant leadership through your attitude and actions today?

PRAYER

God, words are so much easier to say than they are to live. Yet I realize that all my talk about servant leadership will fall on deaf ears if I don't put it into practice in daily life. Who can I serve today in Jesus' name? Let me be His hands and feet today. I pray in His name, Amen.

_____

_____

_____

_____

_____

_____

_____

_____

_____

BACKGROUND NOISE

I MEDITATE ON YOUR PRECEPTS AND CONSIDER YOUR WAYS. I DELIGHT IN YOUR DECREES; I WILL NOT NEGLECT YOUR WORD.
PSALM 119:15-16

What thoughts hover in the background of your mind? Your thoughts and beliefs form the basis for decisions and actions. Worry, anxiety, and fear can act like static that keeps you from clearly hearing God's voice. Instead of letting these things cloud your thinking, choose to replace debilitating thoughts with the truth found in Scripture. Inviting God's Spirit to invade your thinking will strengthen you to lead like Jesus. Where do you need to focus on God's truth in order to bring clarity to your thinking?

PRAYER

God, You know the background noise that plays in my mind, keeping me from hearing and believing You. Today, I choose to meditate on You and Your truth. Speak to me through Your word. Fill my mind with Your thoughts, not my own, and strengthen me with courage and confidence in You. I ask in Jesus' Name, Amen.

♥ BE THE PERSON GOD DESIGNED YOU TO BE

FOR WE ARE GOD'S HANDIWORK, CREATED IN CHRIST JESUS TO DO GOOD WORKS, WHICH GOD PREPARED IN ADVANCE FOR US TO DO.
EPHESIANS 2:10

The temptation to compare ourselves to other leaders is always present. In the process of learning from others, we can find ourselves copying them instead of imitating Christ. But God uniquely created each of us to fulfill the role that He has planned for us. He knows who He designed you to reach and how He wants to use you. Your life, yielded to Him, will accomplish His purposes in the world. How does God want to use you today?

PRAYER

God, I want to be the person You created me to be so that You can use me like You used Jesus. Help me keep my eyes on Him so that I become who You created me to be and accomplish what You want to accomplish through me. In Jesus' name I pray, Amen.

GOD'S PLANS AND PURPOSES

BUT THE PLANS OF THE LORD STAND FIRM FOREVER, THE PURPOSES OF HIS HEART THROUGH ALL GENERATIONS.

PSALM 33:11

How do you respond to unexpected change? While change is a constant factor in life, some people have a greater capacity for change than others. Are you more adventurous, or do you tend to desire familiarity and security? Trusting that God is in control and is working out His plan can bring stability when circumstances are unpredictable. What helps you handle unwelcome or unexpected change? How can you use these insights to help others deal with change?

PRAYER

Lord, thank You for the reminder that You are always working out Your purposes even when I am caught off guard by change. Help me focus on Your plans and purposes in my life, no matter what changing circumstances I face today. In Jesus' Name, Amen.

 CHANGE

THEREFORE, AS WE HAVE OPPORTUNITY, LET US DO GOOD TO ALL PEOPLE, ESPECIALLY TO THOSE WHO BELONG TO THE FAMILY OF BELIEVERS.
GALATIANS 6:10

What change do you want to see in your family? At work? At church? In your community? What opportunity do you have to live the change that God desires to bring to pass? What would it look like today to live so that others can see the difference God makes in one person's life? God's vision for your circumstances begins to come to light as you yield yourself to Him and live as His servant. As you trust Him, He will equip you to live the change He wants to bring about in and through your life.

PRAYER

Lord Jesus, thank You that each day holds new opportunities to be part of changing the world through following Jesus' model of servant leadership. Prepare me to take advantage of the opportunities You offer me today to reveal Jesus to other people through my actions and attitudes. Strengthen me to lead like You today. I ask this in Your Name, Amen.

_____

_____

_____

_____

_____

_____

_____

_____

↻ CONFIDENCE IN PRAYER

THIS IS THE CONFIDENCE WE HAVE IN APPROACHING GOD: THAT IF WE ASK ANYTHING ACCORDING TO HIS WILL, HE HEARS US. AND IF WE KNOW THAT HE HEARS US—WHATEVER WE ASK—WE KNOW THAT WE HAVE WHAT WE ASKED OF HIM.
1 JOHN 5:14-15

How often does God hear your voice? Is talking to Him as natural to you as talking to others? Scripture tells us that we can confidently approach God, tell Him what is on our hearts, and ask Him to get involved in the details of our lives. Scripture also teaches that we need to come to Him worshipfully, humbly, and thankfully, trusting that He will do what is best. What are you talking with the Father about today?

PRAYER
God my Father, thank You for never being too busy or too distracted to listen to me when I pray. Thank You for tuning Your ear to my voice as a parent listens for his or her child. Here is my life. Do what is best, I pray in Jesus' Name, Amen.

EXPECT THE UNEXPECTED

SEE, I AM DOING A NEW THING! NOW IT SPRINGS UP; DO YOU NOT PERCEIVE IT? I AM MAKING A WAY IN THE WILDERNESS AND STREAMS IN THE WASTELAND.

ISAIAH 43:19

You can plan for opportunities to serve others, but sometimes situations change unexpectedly. Your plans fall apart, and you begin to look for God's plan in the midst of changing circumstances. That is when it gets exciting. All of a sudden you realize it isn't about you and your plans, but about God and what He is up to. Life takes on a fresh expectancy as God begins to reveal His plan. Where is God stirring in your circumstances? What is He up to in your life?

PRAYER

God, You have a way of changing things up just when I am getting used to the old way of doing things. A desire for security and stability tugs at my soul, but You are the untamable God who beckons me into the future You envision. You are my security and my guide, and I will follow where You lead. In Jesus' Name, Amen.

_____

_____

_____

_____

_____

_____

_____

_____

_____

 # FORWARD

BUT YOU WILL RECEIVE POWER WHEN THE HOLY SPIRIT COMES ON YOU; AND YOU WILL BE MY WITNESSES IN JERUSALEM, AND IN ALL JUDEA AND SAMARIA, AND TO THE ENDS OF THE EARTH."
ACTS 1:8

The earliest disciples frequently prayed together and met together. Their desire to speed, not hinder, the spread of the gospel, compelled them to work through the challenges facing them. Always, their focus was on Jesus' commission to make disciples and be His witnesses, and they found ways to keep moving forward in spite of opposition. What focus in your life propels you forward?

PRAYER

Jesus, I need You to sharpen my focus on Your call to make disciples and be Your witness. I want to move forward in Your Spirit's power. I want this day to count for Your kingdom. How do You want to use me today? How do I need to equip myself to be more useful to You? Propel me forward, I ask in Jesus' Name, Amen.

FROM GENERATION TO GENERATION

HE DECREED STATUTES FOR JACOB AND ESTABLISHED THE LAW IN ISRAEL, WHICH HE COMMANDED OUR ANCESTORS TO TEACH THEIR CHILDREN, SO THE NEXT GENERATION WOULD KNOW THEM, EVEN THE CHILDREN YET TO BE BORN, AND THEY IN TURN WOULD TELL THEIR CHILDREN. THEN THEY WOULD PUT THEIR TRUST IN GOD AND WOULD NOT FORGET HIS DEEDS BUT WOULD KEEP HIS COMMANDS.
PSALM 78:5-7

It is easy to think of leadership as something that is practiced outside of the home. Yet Scripture is clear that it is within a family that spiritual truths are to be lived out, taught, and passed on. Whether or not you are a parent, you are part of the family of God, and you are part of passing on faith in Jesus. Who are you influencing? How are you modeling servant leadership for those who look up to you?

PRAYER

Lord, as others interact with me today, I want to be a living, breathing example of faith. Help me to serve others well, so that when they think of being a servant leader, they can follow my example. I want the next generation to know You and serve You. In Jesus' Name I pray, Amen.

FUELED BY THE SPIRIT

ARE YOU SO FOOLISH? AFTER BEGINNING BY MEANS OF THE SPIRIT, ARE YOU NOW TRYING TO FINISH BY MEANS OF THE FLESH?
GALATIANS 3:3

Don't be fooled into thinking that leading like Jesus is about a book, a Leadership Encounter, or reading these devotions. Servant leadership is a one-time change of direction that gives rise to ongoing choices to lead like Jesus. Actions that flow from the Spirit's work in a servant leader's heart have great power, releasing the life-changing grace of God into the lives of those around us. How is God's Spirit reshaping Your leadership point of view?

PRAYER

Lord, I know that Your work can only be accomplished in Your way by Your power. Thank You for giving me the Spirit to transform me into the image of Jesus from the inside out. I want to increasingly yield myself to Him instead of trying to lead like Jesus in my own strength. I pray in His Name, Amen.

 GOD KNOWS BEST

COME, LET US BOW DOWN IN WORSHIP, LET US KNEEL BEFORE THE LORD OUR MAKER; FOR HE IS OUR GOD AND WE ARE THE PEOPLE OF HIS PASTURE, THE FLOCK UNDER HIS CARE.

PSALM 95:6-7

Time with God, worshiping Him and allowing Him to care for us, is essential for the servant leader. He designed us to worship, then gave us the choice as to who or what we would worship. He created us and knows best how to nurture us, but He gave us the choice to receive His love and care. How is time in His presence reshaping you?

PRAYER

Lord, I come to worship You, the Lord of heaven and earth, my God. I bow my heart and my head as I kneel before You. Search me, cleanse me, nurture me with Your word and Your Spirit. Let me rest for these moments in Your love and care. As I go, let me pour out to others what I have received from You. In Jesus' name I pray, Amen.

_____

_____

_____

_____

_____

_____

_____

_____

_____

↺ GOD SPEAKS

IN THE PAST GOD SPOKE TO OUR FOREFATHERS THROUGH THE PROPHETS AT MANY TIMES AND IN VARIOUS WAYS, BUT IN THESE LAST DAYS HE HAS SPOKEN TO US BY HIS SON, WHOM HE APPOINTED HEIR OF ALL THINGS, AND THROUGH WHOM HE MADE THE UNIVERSE.
HEBREWS 1:1-2

The wonder of God is that He speaks to us. Scripture records the life-giving words of God. In Genesis, He breathes and speaks creation into existence. In Exodus, He speaks to call a deliverer for His oppressed people. Through the prophets, He speaks to correct, guide, and protect His people. In Jesus, He speaks the ultimate words of life, revealing His heart, His salvation, and hope for the future. What does He want to say to you today? Are you listening?

PRAYER
God, I worship You as the living God who speaks to people through all time and in every place. Thank You for Your words, recorded for our benefit. Thank You for Your Son, Your greatest Word, and for Your Spirit, who helps me to hear what You are saying. Speak to me today, I ask in the Name of Jesus, Amen.

 HEARTS REVEALED

BUT GOD DEMONSTRATES HIS OWN LOVE FOR US IN THIS: WHILE WE WERE STILL SINNERS, CHRIST DIED FOR US.
ROMANS 5:8

The interaction between Jesus and a Gentile woman in Matthew 15:21-28 provides a glimpse into the hearts of those involved. The woman's request reveals her faith. The disciples' response reveals how much they still had to learn. Jesus revealed His heart by honoring her request, not that of His disciples. What does your response to the needs around you reveal about your heart? Does your response reveal the heart of Jesus?

PRAYER
Lord, I am forever grateful that You were not content to love simply with words or speech, but that You demonstrated Your love for us in serving us at our point of need. Change my heart. Give me Your servant heart to replace my self-serving heart, Your compassion to replace my self-absorption. Change me, I pray in Jesus' Name, Amen.

_____

_____

_____

_____

_____

_____

_____

_____

_____

 # I WILL IF HE WILL

FOR IT IS BY GRACE YOU HAVE BEEN SAVED, THROUGH FAITH—AND THIS IS NOT FROM YOURSELVES, IT IS THE GIFT OF GOD—NOT BY WORKS, SO THAT NO ONE CAN BOAST.
EPHESIANS 2:8-9

Where would we be if Jesus' attitude had been, "I will if they will"? What if His mercy and grace were predicated upon us deserving His grace? It is actually just the opposite, according to Scripture. Jesus came to serve and save those who not only did not deserve His love and intervention, but those who desperately needed it all the same. Who do you know who needs to be shown mercy? How can you serve them in Jesus' Name?

PRAYER

Jesus, You came to serve and save me when I could not save myself. I am so grateful that You came to me at my point of need and drew me to Yourself. Your love has transformed my life, teaching me what true love is and how to love others. Help me to love those who are unlovable. Help me to serve them in Jesus' Name, Amen.

 IN A MOMENT

THE NEXT DAY JOHN WAS THERE AGAIN WITH TWO OF HIS DISCIPLES. WHEN HE SAW JESUS PASSING BY, HE SAID, "LOOK, THE LAMB OF GOD!" WHEN THE TWO DISCIPLES HEARD HIM SAY THIS, THEY FOLLOWED JESUS.
JOHN 1:35-37

Some moments in life are life-changing. From that time forward, everything is different. God opens our eyes, and suddenly we hear, we see, we understand that life needs to change. Perhaps we realize that we need to change direction. Or perhaps it becomes clear that we need to continue in the same direction, only now with eyes of faith. Where do you need to see Jesus so that you can follow Him?

PRAYER
God, I am grateful for the times You have spoken into my life through other people, through Scripture, through the Spirit. I want to follow You into the future, living a life of faith and walking in the light of Your truth and understanding. Show me Jesus passing by today, so that I can follow Him, in whose Name I pray, Amen.

 IT'S THE SMALL THINGS

"'WELL DONE, MY GOOD SERVANT!' HIS MASTER REPLIED. 'BECAUSE YOU HAVE BEEN TRUSTWORTHY IN A VERY SMALL MATTER, TAKE CHARGE OF TEN CITIES.'"
LUKE 19:17

The character of leadership is built one moment, one truth, one action at a time. It isn't about the big public displays, but the private character that inevitably shines through in those public moments. It's about thinking of others as more important than ourselves, faithfulness in our relationship with God and those closest to us, integrity, kindness, and honor. What small things do you need to pay attention to in your life?

PRAYER
Lord, the public displays of leadership may draw people's attention, but I want to live for You in the details of my life. Keep me focused on Your still, small voice, and shape my heart, mind, and soul to look like Jesus, who obeyed You with His whole life. I want to faithfully obey You in the small things, and hear Your "well done, my good servant." I ask this in Jesus' Name, Amen.

_____

_____

_____

_____

_____

_____

_____

_____

♥ LEARNING FROM FAILURE

DO NOT GLOAT OVER ME, MY ENEMY! THOUGH I HAVE FALLEN, I WILL RISE. THOUGH I SIT IN DARKNESS, THE LORD WILL BE MY LIGHT.
MICAH 7:8

One of the amazing things about the Bible is that it shows us not only the good side of the people God used, it also shows us their faults and mistakes. Take Peter, who put his foot in his mouth on a regular basis, and even denied knowing Christ. Or David, known as the man after God's heart, who used his power for his own advantage at times. A wise person learns from their own mistakes, as well as from the mistakes of others. What lessons have you learned from failure?

PRAYER
Lord, how I thank You that in Your economy, failure is not final for the humble person. Like Israel of old, I trust in You to forgive, purify, teach, and restore me as I humbly turn to You. I pray in the name of Jesus, whose sacrifice covers all my sin, and whose Spirit leads me in the way of life. Amen.

_____

_____

_____

_____

_____

_____

_____

_____

OBEYING GOD'S DIRECTION

**I WILL INSTRUCT YOU AND TEACH YOU IN THE WAY YOU SHOULD
GO; I WILL COUNSEL YOU WITH MY LOVING EYE ON YOU.**
PSALM 32:8

The crowds constantly came looking for Jesus, trying to get Him to do
what they wanted Him to do. They wanted more bread to eat, more
people healed, more stories told. Scripture shows us that at times Jesus
responded to the ever-present demands, while at other times He walked
away. Knowing when to stay and serve and when to walk away requires
sensitivity and obedience to God's direction. How do you tune your
heart to His so that You know what He wants you to do?

PRAYER

*Lord, I need You to guide me as a servant leader today. Show me the
opportunities for me to make a difference in someone else's life. Show
me, too, the situations I need to pass by, leaving the person and the
outcome in Your hands. I want to be Your obedient servant, like Jesus,
in whose Name I pray, Amen.*

_____
_____
_____
_____
_____
_____
_____
_____

 ONCE UPON A TIME

YET THIS I CALL TO MIND AND THEREFORE I HAVE HOPE: BECAUSE OF THE LORD'S GREAT LOVE WE ARE NOT CONSUMED, FOR HIS COMPASSIONS NEVER FAIL. THEY ARE NEW EVERY MORNING; GREAT IS YOUR FAITHFULNESS.
LAMENTATIONS 3:21-23

When you were a child, what were your dreams for your life? When did God enter into those dreams? Even more importantly, when did you begin to realign your life with God's dream for the world? God's vision for the world includes your personal transformation into a Christ-like servant leader who is captured by God's dream to touch and change the world with Christ's love. It is never too late to begin living God's dream. You can start today.

PRAYER
Lord, thank You that no matter how recently I have failed, I am free to re-engage in being part of Your dream to change the world. All I have to do is turn to You and let You do Your forgiving, healing, and transforming work in me. Thank You for Your forgiveness, Your power to remake me in Jesus' image. Help me to dream Your dreams for my life and the lives of others. In Jesus' name, Amen.

READY TO STAY, READY TO GO

WHETHER THE CLOUD STAYED OVER THE TABERNACLE FOR TWO DAYS OR A MONTH OR A YEAR, THE ISRAELITES WOULD REMAIN IN CAMP AND NOT SET OUT; BUT WHEN IT LIFTED, THEY WOULD SET OUT. AT THE LORD'S COMMAND THEY ENCAMPED, AND AT THE LORD'S COMMAND THEY SET OUT. THEY OBEYED THE LORD'S ORDER, IN ACCORDANCE WITH HIS COMMAND THROUGH MOSES.

NUMBERS 9:22-23

The Israelites had a visible sign of God's presence and direction in the cloud that hovered above the tabernacle. The timing and direction of their coming and going was totally up to God. To lead like Jesus, we must stay attuned to God's presence and leading. How quickly do you respond to God's direction? Are you ready to stay or go at His command?

PRAYER

Sovereign Lord, You know the way I should go and when the time is right for me to move in a new direction. You know, too, where I need to hear this in my life. In all my comings and goings, may I bring glory to You. In Jesus' Name I pray, Amen.

RECOGNIZING GOD'S VOICE

"MY SHEEP LISTEN TO MY VOICE; I KNOW THEM, AND THEY FOLLOW ME."
JOHN 10:27

How do you know when God is talking to you? How do you tune your ear to His voice? Elijah had to pour out his discouragement to God and listen intently before he heard Him. Habakkuk poured out his questions to God and waited patiently for an answer. Saul had to be forcibly stopped by Jesus Himself while he was in the middle of pursuing his own agenda before he could hear God's direction for his life. What about you?

PRAYER
Jesus, I have heard Your voice call me to follow You and find life. Many things compete with the sound of Your voice in the midst of my daily responsibilities, yet I know You still call me to follow You. Help me to hear Your voice and Your message as I listen to You right now. In Your Name, Amen.

_____

_____

_____

_____

_____

_____

_____

_____

_____

RESPONDING TO GOD'S CALL

I BECAME A SERVANT OF THIS GOSPEL BY THE GIFT OF GOD'S GRACE GIVEN ME THROUGH THE WORKING OF HIS POWER.
EPHESIANS 3:7

From being driven by pride, Paul became a man who lived with humility and confidence born of an encounter with Jesus Christ. In response to God's call, Paul lived his life with a new focus of taking the message of Christ to both Jews and Gentiles. God's call and God's grace reshaped Paul's perspective and approach to life. How are God's call and grace reshaping your perspective and approach?

PRAYER

Who would I be without You, Jesus? I would still be left in the self-centered mind-set of pride and fear. Thank You for freeing me from these traps and giving me a new perspective on life. I want to live today in light of Your call and Your grace. It is in Jesus' Name that I ask, Amen.

 SATISFACTION

I KNOW THAT THERE IS NOTHING BETTER FOR PEOPLE THAN TO BE HAPPY AND TO DO GOOD WHILE THEY LIVE. THAT EACH OF THEM MAY EAT AND DRINK, AND FIND SATISFACTION IN ALL THEIR TOIL— THIS IS THE GIFT OF GOD.
ECCLESIASTES 3:12-13

Have you ever watched someone doing what God gifted them to do? A mom in action, a teacher teaching, a craftsperson at work all have one thing in common: They are caught up in doing what God created them to do. At the end of the day, each person's ability to feel satisfaction and joy in the work flows from being able to function out of his giftedness. How many moments like that do you have in your day? What about those around you?

PRAYER
Lord, thank You for the gifts You give each of us, and thank You for the gift of work. How will I be able to bless others today by using the gifts You have given me? Please give me opportunities to bless others today by doing what You created me to do. In Jesus' Name, Amen.

 # THE EYES SAY IT ALL

YOU SAVE THE HUMBLE BUT BRING LOW THOSE WHOSE EYES ARE HAUGHTY.
PSALM 18:27

Eyes are windows into a person's inner being. They communicate compassion, anger, questions, and sadness. Eyes can narrow in contempt or open wide in surprise and joy. A glance can demean or encourage others. Eyes also allow us to receive information and insight about life. Humble eyes look at life from God's perspective, not from a human perspective. They see what He sees. What will your eyes reveal about you today?

PRAYER

Lord, too often I look at You and others with haughty eyes, thinking I know best. In this moment, I cast my eyes down in humility before You, and I look up for Your forgiveness. Let me see the world through Your eyes, I pray. I offer my eyes to you today, to be used to encourage and strengthen others. In Jesus' Name I pray, Amen.

 THE GREAT EXCHANGE

YOU, O LORD, KEEP MY LAMP BURNING; MY GOD TURNS MY DARKNESS INTO LIGHT. WITH YOUR HELP I CAN ADVANCE AGAINST A TROOP; WITH MY GOD I CAN SCALE A WALL.
PSALM 18:28-29

How tightly do you cling to your accomplishments and possessions? Pride in self-accomplishment frequently pushes God out of the picture as the giver of all good things. God calls us to exchange pride in self for humble thanksgiving and reliance on Him. As we daily acknowledge His presence as Creator and Sustainer, we come to trust Him as the source of all our confidence and power. Who are you trusting in today, yourself or God?

PRAYER
God, today I want to exchange my self-confidence for God-confidence. You are the One who sustains me and brings light to my life. With you, I can overcome any challenge facing me. Thank You for the opportunity to live courageously and confidently, as Jesus did, in whose Name I pray, Amen.

 THE POWER OF LOVE

DEAR FRIENDS, LET US LOVE ONE ANOTHER, FOR LOVE COMES FROM GOD. EVERYONE WHO LOVES HAS BEEN BORN OF GOD AND KNOWS GOD.
JOHN 4:7

What impact has the love of God made in your life? God's love changes the human heart. It creates new life, transforming hardened hearts and creating new patterns of living. Just as Jesus' love for His Father was revealed in His sacrificial love for others, those transformed by Jesus' unconditional love cannot remain the same. Where is God's transforming love at work in you? How is it changing your relationships with others?

PRAYER

Jesus, Your love for the Father shaped Your life and relationships, and Your love for me has created a new future and a new hope for me. I want to live in the awareness of Your love today so that my love for You pours into the relationships I have with others. Transform me with Your love, Lord, so that I look like You. I pray in Jesus' Name, Amen.

THE PRIORITY OF PRAYER

YET THE NEWS ABOUT HIM SPREAD ALL THE MORE, SO THAT CROWDS OF PEOPLE CAME TO HEAR HIM AND TO BE HEALED OF THEIR SICKNESSES. BUT JESUS OFTEN WITHDREW TO LONELY PLACES AND PRAYED.
LUKE 5:15-16

When new opportunities appear, decisions must be made, relationships are strained, and goals must be met, is it your practice to turn to God? Jesus modeled a life of prayer as a daily spiritual practice, especially as the demands on Him increased. The larger the crowds and the greater His success, the more determined He was to guard His relationship with His Father. This allowed Him to stand for God even when the world turned against Him. What about you?

PRAYER

Heavenly Father, I confess that at times I try to lead in my own strength. Jesus' life reminds me that I need to guard my relationship with You, both in times of success and times of stress. Meet with me today, I pray, and align me with Your purposes. I ask in Jesus' Name, Amen.

⟲ TIME TO PRAY

DEVOTE YOURSELVES TO PRAYER, BEING WATCHFUL AND THANKFUL.
COLOSSIANS 4:2

Looking at the world around us, it is easy to assume that the only way to lead is to look out for ourselves. Jesus offers a different perspective. We hear His words, "Not so with you." We see Him wash His disciples' feet. His words and actions model a new way of leadership. Whose model of leadership are you following?

PRAYER

God, I come desiring time with You. I am humbled and grateful that You invite me into Your presence. As I quiet myself before You now, I worship You. I seek Your face. As I spend time in Your presence, tune my ears to hear You speak. Shape my heart and my thoughts. Give me the wisdom I need for what is in front of me. Help me to lead like Jesus, in whose Name I pray, Amen.

_____

_____

_____

_____

_____

_____

_____

_____

_____

 TREMBLE

TREMBLE, EARTH, AT THE PRESENCE OF THE LORD, AT THE PRESENCE OF THE GOD OF JACOB, WHO TURNED THE ROCK INTO A POOL, THE HARD ROCK INTO SPRINGS OF WATER.

PSALM 114:7-8

What circumstances unsettle you? Fear, trembling at what is currently happening or might happen in the future, interferes with our ability to sense the very real presence of the Lord. We underestimate His power to act on behalf of His children. Fear should drive us to the Lord, to remembering His greatness and His provision in the past. Then we tremble at the right thing: the presence and power of our God.

PRAYER

Lord, thank You for the way You showed Yourself strong on behalf of the Israelites, generation after generation. When I am tempted to fear, remind me of who You are and cause me to tremble at Your greatness. I honor You today, and ask that You would accomplish Your purposes through my life. I pray in Jesus' Name, Amen.

VALUES-BASED PARTNERSHIPS

AS FOR TITUS, HE IS MY PARTNER AND CO-WORKER AMONG YOU; AS FOR OUR BROTHERS, THEY ARE REPRESENTATIVES OF THE CHURCHES AND AN HONOR TO CHRIST.

CORINTHIANS 8:23

The leaders of the early church faced a rapidly changing situation. In the midst of phenomenal growth, tremendous opposition, and limited communication, they demonstrated a focused commitment to Christ. Partnerships between the disciples and newly emerging leaders grew from shared values that provided guidance for goal-setting and decision-making. What values guide your life decisions?

PRAYER

Lord Jesus, I want to be described as an honor to You by my friends and co-workers. I want to pass on Your values to my family and friends. I want to be a faithful partner to people who serve You. I want my decisions to reflect Your presence in my life. I want to be more like You today than I was yesterday. In Jesus' Name I pray, Amen.

WHAT ARE YOU KNOWN FOR?

"NOW THEN, MY CHILDREN, LISTEN TO ME; BLESSED ARE THOSE WHO KEEP MY WAYS. LISTEN TO MY INSTRUCTION AND BE WISE; DO NOT DISREGARD IT. BLESSED ARE THOSE WHO LISTEN TO ME, WATCHING DAILY AT MY DOORS, WAITING AT MY DOORWAY."
PROVERBS 8:32-34

"Even a child is known by his actions..." What about your life reveals that you are God's child? How is He training you to handle yourself as His son or daughter? Would those around you be surprised to learn that you are God's child? Spend some time today talking with your Heavenly Father about how He would answer these questions and how He wants you to respond to His guidance.

PRAYER

Lord, I need Your wisdom and discipline. I need Your guidance. I want to You to be pleased with me. I want my life and leadership to reflect You. Speak to me today about my life, my leadership. Give me ears to hear Your voice and a spirit yielded to Your discipline. I ask these things in the name of Your Son, Jesus Christ, Amen.

_____

_____

_____

_____

_____

_____

_____

_____

_____

 # WHAT DRIVES YOU?

SOME TRUST IN CHARIOTS AND SOME IN HORSES, BUT WE TRUST IN THE NAME OF THE LORD OUR GOD.
PSALM 20:7

Peter was driven by pride when he boasted that he would never deny Jesus, only to find himself driven by fear when he denied Jesus a few hours later. When pride or fear drive us, we find ourselves attempting to overcome circumstances in our own strength or furiously trusting in our own efforts to protect ourselves. What circumstances tempt you to place your trust in yourself instead of God? Where do you need to exchange trusting yourself for trust in God?

PRAYER
Lord, forgive me for putting my trust in things and people (including myself) and letting pride and fear drive me instead of humility and confidence in You. Sometimes I find myself unexpectedly relying on Your gifts instead of on Your presence and power. Like Jesus, I want my life to be a demonstration of a person who humbly and confidently trusts in You. In Jesus' Name I pray, Amen.

♥ WHAT DO YOU DESIRE

BUT IF SERVING THE LORD SEEMS UNDESIRABLE TO YOU, THEN CHOOSE FOR YOURSELVES THIS DAY WHOM YOU WILL SERVE, WHETHER THE GODS YOUR ANCESTORS SERVED BEYOND THE EUPHRATES, OR THE GODS OF THE AMORITES, IN WHOSE LAND YOU ARE LIVING. BUT AS FOR ME AND MY HOUSEHOLD, WE WILL SERVE THE LORD.
JOSHUA 24:15

What do you desire? Your desires, devotion, or lack of devotion to the Lord have enormous impact for you and for those around you. Your life choices matter. They matter to the Lord, and they matter in terms of your influence on your family, friends, and co-workers. Where have you been tempted to serve someone other than the Lord with your life? How can you fan the flame of desire for serving Him today?

PRAYER

Lord, Joshua's words to the Israelites prompt me to search my heart. You have done so much for me. You have rescued me, redeemed me, and brought me into Your kingdom. Rekindle my desire to serve You today, and let my example inspire others to serve You as well. In Jesus' Name, Amen.

_____

_____

_____

_____

_____

_____

_____

_____

# WHERE DO YOU PLACE YOUR HOPE?

WHY, MY SOUL, ARE YOU DOWNCAST? WHY SO DISTURBED WITHIN ME? PUT YOUR HOPE IN GOD, FOR I WILL YET PRAISE HIM, MY SAVIOR AND MY GOD.
PSALM 42:11

What keeps you going when life gets difficult? Where do you look to renew your hope when things seem hopeless? God is our only secure hope. He doesn't change like the circumstances; He remains faithful and sure. Confidence grounded in anything other than Him is misplaced. When challenging days come, when the future is cloudy, look to God. He alone is worthy of your confidence and hope. He will faithfully lead you and renew your vision and hope as you look to Him.

PRAYER

My Savior and my God, I fix my eyes on You. You hold the future securely in Your hand, and You invite me to follow You into the future You are creating. I praise You today, in Jesus' Name, Amen.

_____

_____

_____

_____

_____

_____

_____

_____

✋ WHEREVER YOU GO

"THEREFORE GO AND MAKE DISCIPLES OF ALL NATIONS, BAPTIZING THEM IN THE NAME OF THE FATHER AND OF THE SON AND OF THE HOLY SPIRIT, AND TEACHING THEM TO OBEY EVERYTHING I HAVE COMMANDED YOU. AND SURELY I AM WITH YOU ALWAYS, TO THE VERY END OF THE AGE."
MATTHEW 28:19-20

Jesus' call to make disciples and be servant leaders is all-inclusive. He calls every Christian in every time and place to take the message of new life in Christ into every sphere of their lives. Servant leadership opportunities have no boundaries; the possibilities are endless. Where is God calling you to lead like Jesus today?

PRAYER

Jesus, thank You for a call that transcends every other call in life and is simultaneously applicable to every situation in which I find myself. No matter what I am doing today, help me see my role in light of Your call to be a servant and make disciples. May I be found faithful, Lord. In Jesus' Name I ask, Amen.

 WHICH COMES FIRST?

SO I TELL YOU THIS, AND INSIST ON IT IN THE LORD, THAT YOU MUST NO LONGER LIVE AS THE GENTILES DO, IN THE FUTILITY OF THEIR THINKING. THEY ARE DARKENED IN THEIR UNDERSTANDING AND SEPARATED FROM THE LIFE OF GOD BECAUSE OF THE IGNORANCE THAT IS IN THEM DUE TO THE HARDENING OF THEIR HEARTS.
EPHESIANS 4:17-18

Which comes first, the heart or the head? Paul tells us that, spiritually speaking, the condition of the heart influences the working of the mind. A humble heart, transformed by God and yielded to Him, transforms our thinking so that we can consciously join God in what He is doing in the world around us. What condition is your heart in? How is God transforming your thinking?

PRAYER
Lord, search out the hard places in my heart. Soften them with Your Spirit and Your grace. Let me hear Your voice. I yield myself to You. In Jesus' Name I pray, Amen.

 # WHO'S IN CHARGE?

"WHOEVER SERVES ME MUST FOLLOW ME; AND WHERE I AM, MY SERVANT ALSO WILL BE. MY FATHER WILL HONOR THE ONE WHO SERVES ME."
JOHN 12:26

It is only human to want to know who is in charge in any given setting. Some of us are naturally wired for leadership; others just want to know who is in charge so they can get their marching orders. God is in the business of recalibrating our leadership compass so that it always points to Jesus. He is the leader whose directions we listen for and with whose agenda we choose to align. In which direction is Jesus pointing you today?

PRAYER
God, thank You for recalibrating my heart and mind so that I am attuned to Your Spirit. I hear Jesus say that to serve Him I must follow Him, and Lord, I want to be a better follower. I realize that means laying down my tendency to take charge so that He can lead the way. Help me today to align with Jesus, in whose Name I pray, Amen.

WISDOM THAT OVERFLOWS

GIVE ME WISDOM AND KNOWLEDGE, THAT I MAY LEAD THIS PEOPLE, FOR WHO IS ABLE TO GOVERN THIS GREAT PEOPLE OF YOURS?
2 CHRONICLES 1:10

Solomon's wisdom wasn't limited to settling a dispute between two women quarreling over a lost child, although that was not a small matter. Solomon's wisdom extended to forming alliances, building the temple, writing proverbs and composing songs, negotiating trade deals, worker compensation and scheduling, and knowledge about plants and animals. In short, God gave Solomon the wisdom he needed for everything He had called him to do in his life. What kind of wisdom do you need from God?

PRAYER

Lord, today I need Your wisdom in order to lead well, and so I pray Solomon's prayer: "Give me wisdom and knowledge that I may lead those around me." As this day unfolds before me, remind me to consciously and expectantly seek Your perspective above all others. In Jesus' Name I pray, Amen.

_____

_____

_____

_____

_____

_____

_____

_____

 A LEADER'S CONFIDENCE

THOSE WHO KNOW YOUR NAME TRUST IN YOU, FOR YOU, LORD, HAVE NEVER FORSAKEN THOSE WHO SEEK YOU.

PSALM 9:10

Where does your confidence come from? A servant leader's confidence does not rest in himself or herself; a servant leader's confidence is in the One who created and sustains the universe. The living God who directs all things according to His purposes can be trusted to guide you today, no matter what situation you find yourself in. He will provide wisdom, strength, and discernment. He delights to answer those who seek Him.

PRAYER

Lord, how grateful I am to know You. I place my trust in You as I face this day, a day that You have given me to live for You. As I encounter people and face different situations, remind me that You remain the same, a God who is eternally present and eternally trustworthy. Steady me so that I can confidently represent You. In Jesus' Name I pray, Amen.

_____

_____

_____

_____

_____

_____

_____

_____

♥ A LEADER'S EMOTIONS

FOR THIS REASON HE HAD TO BE MADE LIKE THEM, FULLY HUMAN IN EVERY WAY, IN ORDER THAT HE MIGHT BECOME A MERCIFUL AND FAITHFUL HIGH PRIEST IN SERVICE TO GOD, AND THAT HE MIGHT MAKE ATONEMENT FOR THE SINS OF THE PEOPLE.

HEBREWS 2:17

"Jesus wept" (John 11:35). Two words, packed with significance. Jesus, the Son of God, was about to raise Lazarus from the dead, and He was overcome with emotion. Servant leadership wasn't an intellectual pursuit for Jesus; it engaged His whole being. Jesus poured out His emotions in prayer, shared them with His close friends, and expressed them in the midst of serving others. How can you emulate Him?

PRAYER

Jesus, thank You for being the perfect embodiment of a servant leader. Thank You for embracing humanity in every way, including experiencing emotions. Help me to engage emotionally with people, to enter into their lives, and to empathize with their emotions, just as You do with me. Help me to serve from a heart like Yours. I pray in Jesus' Name, Amen.

♥ A LEADER'S HOPE

BUT YOU, LORD, ARE A SHIELD AROUND ME, MY GLORY, THE ONE WHO LIFTS MY HEAD HIGH. I CALL OUT TO THE LORD, AND HE ANSWERS ME FROM HIS HOLY MOUNTAIN. I LIE DOWN AND SLEEP; I WAKE AGAIN, BECAUSE THE LORD SUSTAINS ME. I WILL NOT FEAR THOUGH TENS OF THOUSANDS ASSAIL ME ON EVERY SIDE.
PSALM 3:3-6

Where does a leader find hope when hopelessness overwhelms him or her? Where do you find hope? The psalmist found hope in the Lord. When people oppose you, when circumstances seem insurmountable, when you feel alone and nothing is going right, turn your eyes to the Lord. Humble yourself before Him. Find in Him the hope you need to keep going.

PRAYER
Lord, I am never alone because You are always with me, and in this, I find hope. You are everything Scripture reveals You to be - my shield and my glory, the One who answers my cry, gives me rest, and sustains me. You are the antidote to fear and hopelessness. Let my leadership reflect my confidence and hope in You. In Jesus' name, Amen.

A LEADER'S REST

IN PEACE I WILL LIE DOWN AND SLEEP, FOR YOU ALONE, LORD, MAKE ME DWELL IN SAFETY.

PSALM 4:8

The demands of leadership are many and varied. The changing needs of people around us can drain us and lessen our effectiveness. Even when the rewards match the demands and leading is exhilarating, leadership can drain our physical, emotional, and mental energy. The Christ-like servant leader finds rest in God Himself: His sovereignty, His presence, and His watchful care and protection.

PRAYER

Lord, let me find my place of safety and rest in You. When rest is hard to come by and sleep is elusive, let Your Spirit turn my thoughts to You. Flood my mind with Your peace and an awareness of Your presence. Let me rest in You and allow the sleep You give to rejuvenate me so that I can awake to serve with renewed energy, a clear mind, and a willing spirit. In Jesus' Name I pray, Amen.

 ALL OF YOU

TRUST IN THE LORD AND DO GOOD; DWELL IN THE LAND AND ENJOY SAFE PASTURE. TAKE DELIGHT IN THE LORD, AND HE WILL GIVE YOU THE DESIRES OF YOUR HEART.COMMIT YOUR WAY TO THE LORD; TRUST IN HIM AND HE WILL DO THIS: HE WILL MAKE YOUR RIGHTEOUS REWARD SHINE LIKE THE DAWN, YOUR VINDICATION LIKE THE NOONDAY SUN.
PSALM 37:3-6

God wants all of you – your whole heart, mind, and soul. He wants your whole life, every relationship, every setting in which you find yourself. Likewise, His call to lead like Jesus embraces every facet of your life. He wants to transform every part of you, every thought, impulse, dream, desire, and delight, so that You look, live, and lead like Jesus. Trust Him. Delight in Him. Commit your way to Him. Let Him have all of you.

PRAYER

Lord God, my Creator and Redeemer, I long to know Your transforming power and the fulfillment of Your promises. Let Your words, "Trust, take delight, commit!" ring in my mind as I live this day. I pray this in Jesus' name, Amen.

BE STILL AND WAIT

BE STILL BEFORE THE LORD AND WAIT PATIENTLY FOR HIM; DO NOT FRET WHEN PEOPLE SUCCEED IN THEIR WAYS, WHEN THEY CARRY OUT THEIR WICKED SCHEMES.
PSALM 37:7

Scripture is full of stories of people who had to wait on the Lord to see His plans and promises come to fulfillment. Abraham waited twenty-five years for Isaac's birth, David waited twenty years to ascend the throne, and today we are waiting for Christ's return. Waiting is a faith-building process, causing us to seek God and allowing Him to mold us for His purposes. How is God shaping you as you wait on Him?

PRAYER

God, it is easy to see how You shaped Abraham and David as they waited on You. I wait on You now, patiently, trustingly, with a quiet heart, confident in You. Shape my heart, my head, and hands, and my habits. Make me a servant leader, like Jesus, in whose Name I pray, Amen.

 BLESSING OTHERS AS GOD HAS BLESSED YOU

WHOEVER WELCOMES ONE OF THESE LITTLE CHILDREN IN MY NAME WELCOMES ME; AND WHOEVER WELCOMES ME DOES NOT WELCOME ME BUT THE ONE WHO SENT ME.
MARK 9:37

How has God blessed you? What difference has Jesus made in your life? Has He met you at a point of need? Has He forgiven you much? Has He redeemed your mistakes? How are you passing on to others the blessing God has given you? Who are you devoting yourself to in Christ's name? Who are you meeting at their point of need? Who will you serve today in His name?

PRAYER
Jesus, thank You for stopping to bless the children alongside the road! Thank You for blessing me with forgiveness, eternal life, unconditional love, and unending grace. As Your child and Your servant, make me a blessing to those I meet today, at home, along the way, at work, and especially those in the family of God. I ask in Jesus' name, Amen.

_____

_____

_____

_____

_____

_____

_____

_____

DOING GOD'S WORK IN GOD'S WAY

THEN MANOAH PRAYED TO THE LORD: "PARDON YOUR SERVANT, LORD. I BEG YOU TO LET THE MAN OF GOD YOU SENT TO US COME AGAIN TO TEACH US HOW TO BRING UP THE BOY WHO IS TO BE BORN."
JUDGES 13:8

When Samson's parents learned that they were going to have a son, they first asked God to show them how to raise their son. They didn't try to do God's work in their own strength or understanding. They knew they would need His wisdom and direction to know how to do what He had called them to do. What has God called you to do? How does He want you to do it?

PRAYER
Lord, thank You for calling me to be part of extending Your kingdom. Show me today how to do what You have called me to do. Step-by-step, day by day, I know I need to depend on You. I ask for wisdom, courage, strength, and discernment, in Jesus' Name, Amen.

_____
_____
_____
_____
_____
_____
_____
_____
_____

♥ FIRST YOU RECEIVE

IN HIM WE HAVE REDEMPTION THROUGH HIS BLOOD, THE FORGIVENESS OF SINS, IN ACCORDANCE WITH THE RICHES OF GOD'S GRACE THAT HE LAVISHED ON US.
EPHESIANS 1:7-8

As a servant leader, you cannot give what you have not first received. To extend unconditional love to others, you must first accept it from God. To extend forgiveness, you must receive God's forgiveness. To extend grace, you must experience God's grace restoring and freeing you. Only then can you find yourself moving in the currents of God's grace, love, and forgiveness. Take time to receive today, then freely give.

PRAYER
Lord, let the reality of Your redemption and forgiveness flood my soul. Let the riches of Your grace overwhelm me. Let Your passion for all people come alive within me, and give me opportunities to pass on the hope I have found in You. Let my words and life reflect the depth of the work You are doing within me. In Jesus' Name I pray, Amen.

GO IN THE STRENGTH YOU HAVE

THE LORD TURNED TO HIM AND SAID, "GO IN THE STRENGTH YOU HAVE AND SAVE ISRAEL OUT OF MIDIAN'S HAND. AM I NOT SENDING YOU?"
JUDGES 6:14

Do you ever feel unequal to the task to which God has called you? If so, you can probably relate to Gideon. Gideon rightly assessed the situation in front of him; he knew that the Midianites were a formidable enemy. When Gideon talked with God about the seeming hopelessness of his people's situation, he discovered that God had a role for him to play. What overwhelming situation are you facing? What is God telling you to do to face this challenge?

PRAYER

Lord God, I draw hope from Gideon's story. Even when Your people's distress came from disobedience, You were willing to save them. You called Gideon to move from hopeless resignation to faith-based action. Let Gideon be my example as I move forward in the strength I have, as You send me in Jesus' Name, Amen.

🤍 GOD'S INVITING LOVE

BUT I, BY YOUR GREAT LOVE, CAN COME INTO YOUR HOUSE; IN REVERENCE I BOW DOWN TOWARD YOUR HOLY TEMPLE.
PSALM 5:7

God's love opens the way into His presence. His love draws people to Jesus, just as it drew you. God's love invites you to know Him better and makes the way for you to worship Him with your life. He invites you to come into His presence, to meet with Him, to worship Him, to let your life be transformed by time spent in His presence. Will you accept His invitation today?

PRAYER

Lord, I am humbled that You would invite me into Your presence. I am humbled at Your great love, love that came looking for me and spoke to my heart. Yes, Lord, I want to come into Your house. I bow before You in reverence and worship. As I stay here in Your presence, transform me, and send me out to share Your love and invitation with others. In Jesus' name I pray, Amen.

GOD'S WORK ON DISPLAY

"NEITHER THIS MAN NOR HIS PARENTS SINNED," SAID JESUS, "BUT THIS HAPPENED SO THAT THE WORKS OF GOD MIGHT BE DISPLAYED IN HIM."
JOHN 9:3

When Jesus' early disciples saw a blind man, they wanted to know whose fault it was that he was born blind. Do you ever fall into the trap of judging others instead of seeing their need for God's touch? Jesus knew that this man's blindness could be powerfully used by God, and He reached out to heal him. As a result of Jesus' touch, the man's eyesight was restored, and he became a living example to Jesus' transformational power.

PRAYER

Jesus, give me new eyes, eyes that see the world and people around me as You do. Remove the blindness in me that tempts me to judge others. Make me a living example of Your grace. Transform me into a person who helps others focus on the difference You can make in their lives. I ask in Jesus' Name, Amen.

 HE TOUCHED ME

SIMON'S MOTHER-IN-LAW WAS IN BED WITH A FEVER, AND THEY IMMEDIATELY TOLD JESUS ABOUT HER. SO HE WENT TO HER, TOOK HER HAND AND HELPED HER UP. THE FEVER LEFT HER AND SHE BEGAN TO WAIT ON THEM.

MARK 1:30-31

Can you imagine Simon Peter's mother-in-law telling others about how Jesus healed her? All she knew was that one moment she was incapacitated, caught up in her own suffering, unable to make herself well, and then came the touch of a hand on hers. Relief, health, wholeness, clarity, strength, and energy flowed into and through her being. Other people came into focus. Purpose and grace transformed her existence. Where do you need His touch today?

PRAYER

Oh, Lord, I need Your touch. Free me from what binds me. Infuse my life with Your life-giving power. Bring the world around me into focus. Fill me with Your grace and power to serve others. In Jesus' Name I pray, Amen.

_____

_____

_____

_____

_____

_____

_____

_____

_____

♥ HEART CHECK: FORGIVENESS

THEN PETER CAME TO JESUS AND ASKED, "LORD, HOW MANY TIMES SHALL I FORGIVE MY BROTHER OR SISTER WHO SINS AGAINST ME? UP TO SEVEN TIMES?" JESUS ANSWERED, "I TELL YOU, NOT SEVEN TIMES, BUT SEVENTY-SEVEN TIMES."
MATTHEW 18:21-22

Do you remember when Peter asked Jesus how many times he needed to forgive? It's a question that anyone who has been hurt can relate to. Jesus' answer made it clear that forgiveness is not an option for His followers, especially for those who want to follow in His footsteps as Christ-like servant leaders. Forgiving others keeps our hearts humble and allows God to use us.

PRAYER

Jesus, thank You for forgiving me time and time again. Help me to extend that same forgiveness and grace to those around me. Help me to make forgiveness a way of life so that I can remain pliable and useful in Your kingdom. Thank You for not giving up on me; help me to not give up on others. I pray in Jesus' Name, Amen.

♥ HEART CHECK: LOVING OTHERS

THIS IS MY COMMAND: LOVE EACH OTHER
JOHN 15:17

Jesus gave us a living example of love throughout His life, patiently teaching His slow-to-learn disciples, mercifully serving the hungry, healing the sick, and bestowing honor on the outcasts. His death on the cross was the ultimate act of love, giving Himself for those who didn't understand how He was loving and saving them. Love for God naturally overflows into love for others, love that takes shape in our words and actions, our attitudes and relationships. Who are you loving like Jesus loves them?

PRAYER
Jesus, thank You for living a life of love. The examples of how You treated others with unconditional love in the Bible convince me that You can love me, and they help me understand how you expect me to love others. May others know I am Your disciple by my love. In Jesus' Name I pray, Amen.

HEART CHECK: MISUNDERSTANDING

HEAR ME, LORD, MY PLEA IS JUST; LISTEN TO MY CRY. HEAR MY PRAYER—IT DOES NOT RISE FROM DECEITFUL LIPS. LET MY VINDICATION COME FROM YOU; MAY YOUR EYES SEE WHAT IS RIGHT. THOUGH YOU PROBE MY HEART, THOUGH YOU EXAMINE ME AT NIGHT AND TEST ME, YOU WILL FIND THAT I HAVE PLANNED NO EVIL; MY MOUTH HAS NOT TRANSGRESSED.
PSALM 17:1-3

Your response to being misunderstood reveals the condition of your heart. Humbly opening yourself up to the scrutiny of the Holy Spirit and accountability to trusted friends can provide needed correction or valuable insight, leading to honest communication and possible reconciliation. Prideful defense of yourself in ways that malign others reveals a need to humbly seek forgiveness and make amends. What do your responses reveal about your heart?

PRAYER
Lord, probe my heart. Where I need to ask for forgiveness, show me. Where I need to seek reconciliation, give me courage. Where I need to trust You to defend my reputation, let me hide myself in You. In Jesus' Name I pray, Amen.

_____
_____
_____
_____
_____
_____
_____
_____
_____
_____

HOW ARE YOU PRAYING?

FOR THIS REASON, SINCE THE DAY WE HEARD ABOUT YOU, WE HAVE NOT STOPPED PRAYING FOR YOU...
COLOSSIANS 1:9

How are you praying for others? Jesus prayed for His disciples, the crowds who came to hear Him and see His miracles, and those who would be impacted by the disciples' ministry—that's us! He told His disciples to pray in His name, asking the Father for whatever we need in order to extend the Kingdom. For whom are you praying and what are you asking God to do? Don't stop!

PRAYER
God, I come to You in Jesus' name today, realizing that people don't need more of me; they need more of You. I lift up the people in my life, those You have called me to serve. Meet them where they are, make Yourself real to them, and work in ways that reveal Your power. Heal, forgive, restore, challenge, strengthen, soften, motivate, and encourage them. Use me as Your instrument, I ask in Jesus' Name, Amen.

INSIDE-OUT AND UPSIDE-DOWN

JESUS CALLED THEM TOGETHER AND SAID, "YOU KNOW THAT THOSE
WHO ARE REGARDED AS RULERS OF THE GENTILES LORD IT OVER THEM,
AND THEIR HIGH OFFICIALS EXERCISE AUTHORITY OVER THEM. NOT SO
WITH YOU. INSTEAD, WHOEVER WANTS TO BECOME GREAT AMONG YOU
MUST BE YOUR SERVANT, AND WHOEVER WANTS TO BE FIRST MUST BE
SLAVE OF ALL."

MARK 10:42-44

Listen to Jesus telling His disciples that they were not to follow the
world's leadership values or methods. Jesus knew He was teaching them
a countercultural concept, one that required intentional realignment of
thoughts, values, and interpersonal relationships. He knew His followers
would need to be transformed from the inside out in order to turn the
world upside down. How is He transforming your thinking
and relationships?

PRAYER

*Jesus, You turned my world upside down by coming from heaven to serve
me in love. God became man, master became servant, and ruler became
friend. Turn my heart inside out, Lord, and transform my thinking. Help
me to hear those four important words, "Not so with you...instead..."
Remake me in Your image, I ask in Jesus' Name, Amen.*

LEADING IN THE WILDERNESS

REMEMBER HOW THE LORD YOUR GOD LED YOU ALL THE WAY IN THE WILDERNESS THESE FORTY YEARS, TO HUMBLE AND TEST YOU IN ORDER TO KNOW WHAT WAS IN YOUR HEART, WHETHER OR NOT YOU WOULD KEEP HIS COMMANDS.
DEUTERONOMY 8:2

Sometimes the servant leader's journey goes through the wilderness. In the wilderness, Moses heard God's call and learned lessons that he would need later to lead God's people through the same wilderness. Jesus voluntarily went into the wilderness to prepare Himself for public ministry, resisting temptation, and being ministered to by angels. What lessons has God taught you through wilderness experiences?

PRAYER

Lord, thank You for faithfully traveling with Your people, making Your home with them, even though they found themselves in the wilderness through disobedience. Thank You for using the wilderness to shape leaders like Moses, Joshua, and Jesus. Shape me, please, and make me a blessing to others who are journeying through the wilderness. In Jesus' Name I pray, Amen.

 # LIVING A NEW WAY

THAT, HOWEVER, IS NOT THE WAY OF LIFE YOU LEARNED WHEN YOU HEARD ABOUT CHRIST AND WERE TAUGHT IN HIM IN ACCORDANCE WITH THE TRUTH THAT IS IN JESUS.
EPHESIANS 4:20-21

How is your leadership different because you follow Jesus' servant model? Have you replaced pride with humility, and confidence with fear? Are people aware that you value them? How are you influencing the thinking, behavior, and development of others? What habits are you cultivating in order to keep your focus on Christ? Jesus doesn't want you to admire His teaching and model of servanthood; He wants you to become a servant. How are you doing?

PRAYER

Jesus, it's easy to admire Your example and Your teaching about servanthood. It is harder to actually move Your teaching from my heart to my head, hands, and habits. But I know You didn't come to amaze me; You came to transform my thinking and my life. May my life reflect You; change me from the inside out, I ask in Jesus' Name, Amen.

_____

_____

_____

_____

_____

_____

_____

_____

_____

_____

✋ LIVING THE TRUTH

... ANYONE WHO HAS SEEN ME HAS SEEN THE FATHER. HOW CAN YOU SAY, 'SHOW US THE FATHER'? DON'T YOU BELIEVE THAT I AM IN THE FATHER AND THAT THE FATHER IS IN ME? THE WORDS I SAY TO YOU I DO NOT SPEAK ON MY OWN AUTHORITY. RATHER, IT IS THE FATHER, LIVING IN ME, WHO IS DOING HIS WORK.
JOHN 14:9-10

When people look at you, do they see Jesus? Jesus' life accurately represents the reality of who God is and what He feels and thinks about every facet of life, including leadership. Empowered by God, the servant leader reflects God by meeting people at their point of need, extending God's forgiveness, and freeing people from Satan's lies by proclaiming God's truth.

PRAYER
Jesus, I want to live a life that accurately reflects You to others, just as Your life truthfully reflected the Father. I need You to live in me and work through me. I want people to know the Father better because they have experienced His touch through their interaction with me. I humbly ask this in Jesus' Name, Amen.

MEDITATING ON GOD'S WORD

**FOR THE LORD WATCHES OVER THE WAY OF THE RIGHTEOUS,
BUT THE WAY OF THE WICKED LEADS TO DESTRUCTION.**
PSALM 1:6

What keeps you going when the road of servant leadership is hard? What fills your thoughts when you are discouraged? The psalmist tells us that those who delight in God's law, in God's truth, and meditate on it will find refreshment and nourishment for the long haul. Those who turn their thoughts toward Him, God blesses. Those who look to Him will find life and strength to keep going. What will fill your thoughts today?

PRAYER
Lord, shield my thoughts from discouragement and the temptation to abandon Your path of servant leadership and turn to worldly leadership methods of power and control. You have called me to serve others, following Jesus' example, even when it is hard. I want to be found walking in Your ways. Strengthen my mind with Your Word so that today I can lead like Jesus, in whose Name I pray, Amen.

♥ NO ONE IS EXEMPT

SO, IF YOU THINK YOU ARE STANDING FIRM, BE CAREFUL THAT YOU DON'T FALL! NO TEMPTATION HAS OVERTAKEN YOU EXCEPT WHAT IS COMMON TO MANKIND. AND GOD IS FAITHFUL; HE WILL NOT LET YOU BE TEMPTED BEYOND WHAT YOU CAN BEAR. BUT WHEN YOU ARE TEMPTED, HE WILL ALSO PROVIDE A WAY OUT SO THAT YOU CAN ENDURE IT.
1 CORINTHIANS 10:12-13

No believer is exempt from temptation, not even servant leaders. Pride can lure us into thinking that we are above temptation, or even into excusing our particular vices as not being as "bad" as sins that others practice. Paul warned against "setting our hearts on evil things": idolatry, sexual immorality, testing Christ, and grumbling. What is your heart set on?

PRAYER
God, thank You for being faithful to me and for providing Jesus as the forgiver, cleanser, transformer, and strength of my life. Keep me attentive to the condition of my heart, so that pride does not gain a foothold and I do not fall to temptation. In Jesus' Name I pray, Amen.

_____

_____

_____

_____

_____

_____

_____

_____

_____

 PARADOXES

THEN HE SAID TO THEM ALL: "WHOEVER WANTS TO BE MY DISCIPLE MUST DENY THEMSELVES AND TAKE UP THEIR CROSS DAILY AND FOLLOW ME. FOR WHOEVER WANTS TO SAVE THEIR LIFE WILL LOSE IT, BUT WHOEVER LOSES THEIR LIFE FOR ME WILL SAVE IT."
LUKE 9:23-24

Life is full of paradoxes for Christ-followers: serve to lead, the last are first, the least is the greatest, die to live, and lose to save. What do you stand to lose today by denying yourself and following Jesus? What do you stand to lose by serving others and exalting God instead of yourself? What do you stand to gain?

PRAYER

Lord Jesus, today, help me to keep my eyes on You, my heart tuned to Your Spirit, and to walk in simple obedience. Let me filter all of life through the command to love God and love others. Today I want to lose my life so that I can truly live. In Jesus' Name I pray, Amen.

 # POSSIBILITIES

AND WHATEVER YOU DO, WHETHER IN WORD OR DEED, DO IT ALL IN THE NAME OF THE LORD JESUS, GIVING THANKS TO GOD THE FATHER THROUGH HIM.

COLOSSIANS 3:17

The different settings in which we find ourselves – home, work, and church – allow God's presence to spread into the life and fabric of our communities. Jesus took advantage of every opportunity to point people to His Father. We also have the opportunity to share Jesus' message through our words, actions, and attitudes. Who will your servant lifestyle influence today?

PRAYER

Lord Jesus, whatever I do today, wherever I go, whoever I meet, I want to make the most of every opportunity to reflect You. What if I am the only servant leader that comes across their path today? Will they have seen You and been touched by Your hand? May it be so, Lord Jesus, I ask in Jesus' Name, Amen.

_____

_____

_____

_____

_____

_____

_____

_____

READY, SET, GO

IN THE MORNING, LORD, YOU HEAR MY VOICE; IN THE MORNING I LAY MY REQUESTS BEFORE YOU AND WAIT EXPECTANTLY.
PSALM 5:3

Where are you waiting on God's direction? Perhaps a better question is, how are you waiting on God's direction? Is your heart anxious, or are you confident in God? Is your mind filled with thoughts of performing well, or is focused on exalting God? Once your heart is ready and your mind is set upon the things of God, all that is left is to go at His command. Are you ready? Are you set? Listen now for His voice.

PRAYER

Lord, clear my mind of distractions; focus me on You alone. Creator and Sovereign of the universe, You deserve all praise; You are unfolding Your plan even as I bow before You now. My heart is confident in You; ready me for Your purposes; set my mind on exalting You today. I ask in Jesus' Name, Amen.

 TEACH US TO PRAY

ONE DAY JESUS WAS PRAYING IN A CERTAIN PLACE. WHEN HE FINISHED, ONE OF HIS DISCIPLES SAID TO HIM, "LORD, TEACH US TO PRAY, JUST AS JOHN TAUGHT HIS DISCIPLES."
LUKE 11:1

Jesus knew the power of prayer. It was prayer that kept Him connected with His Father. It was prayer that undergirded each decision. It was prayer that prepared Him to face the challenge of the cross. He prayed for Himself, for His disciples, for those who needed healing, and for those who cursed Him. His disciples asked Him to teach them to pray. Where do you need Jesus to teach you to pray?

PRAYER

Lord, teach us to pray. Teach us to pray for ourselves, that we might become leaders who lead with spiritual power. Teach us to pray for those whom we influence, and let our lives of prayer inspire them to pray. Teach us to pray for those who are hurting, and for the difficult people we have to deal with. Teach us to pray, we ask in Jesus' Name, Amen.

_____

_____

_____

_____

_____

_____

_____

_____

 # TO EXALT JESUS

I EAGERLY EXPECT AND HOPE THAT I WILL IN NO WAY BE ASHAMED, BUT WILL HAVE SUFFICIENT COURAGE SO THAT NOW AS ALWAYS CHRIST WILL BE EXALTED IN MY BODY, WHETHER BY LIFE OR BY DEATH.
PHILIPPIANS 1:20

Paul's desire was that others would see Christ through his life, whether living or dying. What about you? Is exalting God your goal and motivation? How would you live today if it were? Would your relationship with God change? Would you treat people differently? Would you spend more time with family, or do your job differently? Who will you exalt today, yourself or God?

PRAYER

Lord Jesus, thank You for transforming my heart, head, hands, and habits so that, like Paul, I can exalt You through my life. Infuse me with humility, confidence, and courage that are born out of a vibrant relationship with You. Let others see Your work in me and take hope that You can do the same for them. In Jesus' Name I pray, Amen.

❤ UNEXPECTED MOMENTS

AS YOU COME TO HIM, THE LIVING STONE—REJECTED BY HUMANS BUT CHOSEN BY GOD AND PRECIOUS TO HIM—YOU ALSO, LIKE LIVING STONES, ARE BEING BUILT INTO A SPIRITUAL HOUSE TO BE A HOLY PRIESTHOOD, OFFERING SPIRITUAL SACRIFICES ACCEPTABLE TO GOD THROUGH JESUS CHRIST.
1 PETER 2:4-5

What unexpected moments will come your way today? People to respond to, problems to solve, places to serve: Each one is an opportunity to display the servant heart of Jesus through your attitude, behavior, and words. Each one is an opportunity to catch a glimpse of how God is transforming your heart, and each one gives you an opportunity to be transformed by responding to the prompting of God's Spirit. What will unexpected moments reveal in you today?

PRAYER
Lord Jesus, please continue to transform me—my heart, my beliefs and thinking, my actions and attitudes, my words and behavior—so that I respond like You in the unexpected moments that come my way today. I ask in Your powerful Name, Jesus, Amen.

WORDS OF BLESSINGS

"THE LORD BLESS YOU AND KEEP YOU; THE LORD MAKE HIS FACE SHINE ON YOU AND BE GRACIOUS TO YOU; THE LORD TURN HIS FACE TOWARD YOU AND GIVE YOU PEACE."
NUMBERS 6:24-26

Words are powerful. God spoke, and the universe was created. Jesus, the Living Word, spoke through His life, teaching, death, and resurrection, bringing life to all who trust in Him. Scripture, the Word of God, continues to speak today, revealing the way to eternal life. God gave Moses the words of blessing for the priests to speak over the Israelites. As His priests and servants, what words will you use to bless others today?

PRAYER

Jesus, Your words spoke forgiveness to those who crucified You, blessing to children, healing and strength to the hurting, and correction and encouragement to Your disciples. May my words today bless, strengthen, and encourage those whom I meet, and most of all, point them to You. I ask in Jesus' Name, Amen.

♥ FORGIVE AND BE FORGIVEN

"AND WHEN YOU STAND PRAYING, IF YOU HOLD ANYTHING AGAINST ANYONE, FORGIVE THEM, SO THAT YOUR FATHER IN HEAVEN MAY FORGIVE YOU YOUR SINS."
MARK 11:25

Who do you need to forgive? Whose is the first name that comes to mind? Unforgiveness, resentment, and bitterness find their foothold quietly, secretly, sometimes even imperceptibly, in hearts. Pride and fear, two familiar enemies, flourish, and your relationship with God suffers, along with your relationships with others. Who do you need to forgive today so that God can forgive you?

PRAYER
Father, I confess that I need Your forgiveness. Search my heart for strongholds of unforgiveness, fear, and pride. Show me where, and how, I need to forgive. Fill me with an awareness of Your forgiveness, cleansing, and transformation, and help me pass that on to others. In Jesus' Name, who brought me forgiveness, I pray, Amen.

 # GOOD BEGINNINGS

THE FEAR OF THE LORD IS THE BEGINNING OF WISDOM; ALL WHO FOLLOW HIS PRECEPTS HAVE GOOD UNDERSTANDING. TO HIM BELONGS ETERNAL PRAISE.
PSALM 111:10

How did your day start? It is easy for the demands of life to insert themselves: family members who need attention, a phone call that awakens you from sleep, pressing deadlines, unresolved problems. Yet each day is God's new beginning; each breath invites you to turn afresh to Him. Find in Him eternal wisdom to guide you today.

PRAYER
Lord, thank You for the new beginning You have given me in this new day. Thank You for teaching me to fear You, so that I might find wisdom to live life as You designed it. I want to grow in understanding. Give me fresh insight for this new day, and lead me along the path of wisdom, I pray. In Jesus' Name, I commit this day to You, Amen.

 GREAT THINGS

AND MARY SAID: "MY SOUL GLORIFIES THE LORD AND MY SPIRIT REJOICES IN GOD MY SAVIOR, FOR HE HAS BEEN MINDFUL OF THE HUMBLE STATE OF HIS SERVANT. FROM NOW ON ALL GENERATIONS WILL CALL ME BLESSED, FOR THE MIGHTY ONE HAS DONE GREAT THINGS FOR ME—HOLY IS HIS NAME."
LUKE 1:46-49

"The Mighty One has done great things for me," proclaimed Mary. Was she perhaps echoing Psalm 126, "The Lord has done great things for us, and we are filled with joy"? Mary's psalm of praise, like Hannah's (1 Samuel 1) before her, and that of men and women throughout the ages, overflowed from her personal gratefulness for God's presence and power. What great things has He done in your life?

PRAYER
Mighty One, Lord, God my Savior, You have done great things in my life and in the lives of Your people throughout time. Thank You for revealing Yourself to us. I praise You today with a grateful heart, especially for sending Jesus, in whose Name I pray, Amen.

THE PATH OF LIFE

YOU MAKE KNOWN TO ME THE PATH OF LIFE; YOU WILL FILL ME WITH JOY IN YOUR PRESENCE, WITH ETERNAL PLEASURES AT YOUR RIGHT HAND.
PSALM 16:11

Each step along a path provides an increasingly clearer perspective on your surroundings. The past is put into perspective – things that seem blurry from a distance come into sharper focus as you move toward them. Joy comes from walking the path in the presence of One who loves you and promises always to be with you, and who is Himself "the way, and the truth, and the life" (John 14:6). Where is Jesus taking you on the path of life?

PRAYER

Jesus, how good it is to be Your companion as I journey through life. Show me the path of life today, fill me with joy in Your presence, and lead me into the future You have planned. Help me to live, love, and lead like You as we walk together today. I pray in Jesus' Name, Amen.

♥ TRUSTING RELATIONSHIPS

DO EVERYTHING IN LOVE.
1 CORINTHIANS 16:14

Paul and Peter could disagree and still endorse one another in ministry because they both knew the unconditional love of Jesus. An awareness of being fully accepted by Him allowed them to speak the truth in love and challenge one another to faithfulness. A secure foundation in God's unconditional love and acceptance allows us to trust God and one another. Treating others with unconditional love helps to build trusting relationships with family members, friends, co-workers, and community members. How will your words and actions reflect Christ's unconditional love to others today?

PRAYER

Jesus, thank You for loving me unconditionally and forgiving me fully and freely! Thank You that I am secure in my relationship with You. May this realization help me to love others the way You love me. May love be the motivation for my words and actions today. In Jesus' Name I pray, Amen.

 # A TIMELY WORD

THE HEARTS OF THE WISE MAKE THEIR MOUTHS PRUDENT, AND THEIR LIPS PROMOTE INSTRUCTION.

PROVERBS 16:23

Have you ever noticed how Jesus always had the right words at the right time? He never seemed to be flustered, whether He was interacting with His disciples or with those who opposed Him. When a comforting word was needed, it was on His lips. When a rebuke was required, He gave it firmly and concisely, but without malice. When truth was needed, it poured readily from within Him. What situations will you face today? Are you ready and willing to speak with humble confidence as God directs you?

PRAYER

Lord, fill my heart with wisdom from Your lips so that my lips will speak Your truth today. All of my thoughts pale in comparison to the life-giving nature of Your wisdom and words. May my words point people to You. I ask in Jesus' name, in whose Name I live and lead, Amen.

KEEP ON LOVING ONE ANOTHER

KEEP ON LOVING ONE ANOTHER AS BROTHERS AND SISTERS.
HEBREWS 13:1

Jesus loved His disciples to the end of His life, and He commanded His disciples to love one another just as He had loved them. John referred to himself as "the one Jesus loved," and urged his hearers to love others with action and in truth. Actively loving others is an undeniable indication that we have experienced the transformational, unconditional love of God. How has the love of God changed you? Who will you meet today who needs to experience the love of God?

PRAYER

Lord, thank You for loving me. Like John, help me to find my identity in being loved by You. Thank You for loving me "to the end" forgiving, cleansing, and transforming me. May the reality of being loved by You overflow into my relationships with others today. I pray in the Name of Jesus, whose love has changed my life, Amen.

 LEVEL GROUND

TEACH ME TO DO YOUR WILL, FOR YOU ARE MY GOD; MAY YOUR GOOD SPIRIT LEAD ME ON LEVEL GROUND.
PSALM 143:10

Rocky ground makes the journey harder; even small pebbles can make your feet slip and slide. What a difference a smooth, well-designed path makes, especially when traveling into unknown areas. Level ground allows you to walk more confidently and focus on the people and setting around you. Fear and pride can lead us to straying from God's path instead of humbly and confidently following where He leads. Where are you seeking God's will so that He can lead you on level ground?

PRAYER

God, I am grateful that You make a way even in the midst of challenges. Lead me today on level ground, I pray. Teach me to do Your will and follow Your way. Where there are rocks, give me eyes to see Your footsteps and the path You have prepared. Let me glorify You as I humbly and confidently follow You. I pray in Jesus' Name, Amen.

THE PROMISE OF GUIDANCE

I RUN IN THE PATH OF YOUR COMMANDS, FOR YOU HAVE BROADENED MY UNDERSTANDING.
PSALM 119:32

To whom do you look for wise counsel? Do you believe that God wants to speak to you about the challenges you face today? How do you put yourself in a position to hear His guidance? Jesus evidently knew Scripture well. On a moment's notice, under severe strain, He was able to meet temptation with wisdom from God's Word. His thinking was saturated with Scriptural principles and truths. When the time came, Scripture provided the guidance He needed. What about you?

PRAYER
Lord, thank You for preserving Your Word so that I can read and meditate on it today. Thank You that in Scripture I find wisdom for life, and I can move forward with confidence when I live in the light of Your truth. Broaden my understanding as I meditate on Your Word, I pray in Jesus' Name, Amen.

THE PROMISE OF PRESENCE

"...AND SURELY I AM WITH YOU ALWAYS, TO THE VERY END OF THE AGE."
MATTHEW 28:20

What could you do if you knew God was with you? Jesus did not abandon His disciples to do the work He called them to do. He promised to be with them (and us) always. Can you trust Jesus to keep His promise? His promise means that you will never face any situation alone. He is always with you, in you, to strengthen, guide, and encourage you as you make disciples. What is He calling you to do today?

PRAYER

Jesus, I know I can trust Your promises. As I face this day, remind me that I am walking with You into whatever awaits me. May I reflect spirit-infused humility and confidence in each situation. Make Your presence more real to me than anything or anyone else. Today, help me to lead like You, for it is in Jesus' Name that I pray and serve, Amen.

_____
_____
_____
_____
_____
_____
_____
_____

♥ A TRUSTWORTHY FORMULA

"VERY TRULY I TELL YOU, THE ONE WHO BELIEVES HAS ETERNAL LIFE."
JOHN 6:47

What is your formula for self-worth? Are you grounded in the unconditional love of Christ? Do you take Him at His Word when He says that He has forgiven you and now calls you His son, daughter, servant, friend, disciple? No one can take this identify from you. You are forever His. His love for you does not diminish. From this basis, you are free to lead like Jesus, loving and serving others. Live and lead as who you are in Christ today.

PRAYER

Lord Jesus, believing in You, I have been reborn to live like You lived, in intimate relationship with the Father and empowered by the Spirit. Thank You for freeing me from the trap of constantly trying to prove my worth. Let me selflessly live and lead like You today. In Jesus' Name I pray, Amen.

_____
_____
_____
_____
_____
_____
_____
_____
_____

ADVICE TO THE WISE

AS IRON SHARPENS IRON, SO ONE PERSON SHARPENS ANOTHER.
PROVERBS 27:17

What is your reaction when others offer you advice? To ask for advice reveals wisdom. To receive advice reveals humility. Paul and Barnabas asked for advice from the apostles and elders. Paul gave Peter advice when he was in the wrong. Peter later affirmed Paul's ministry. Who do you trust to give you godly advice? Are you open to what God might want to say to you through others?

PRAYER
Lord, thank You for providing godly wisdom and insight through my brothers and sisters in Christ. Open my ears to humbly listen to what You want to say to me through them so that I might grow in Christlikeness. I want to be a wise and discerning servant. In Jesus' Name I pray, Amen.

_____
_____
_____
_____
_____
_____
_____
_____

💜 AS ONE WHO SERVES

"THE KINGS OF THE GENTILES LORD IT OVER THEM; AND THOSE WHO EXERCISE AUTHORITY OVER THEM CALL THEMSELVES BENEFACTORS. BUT YOU ARE NOT TO BE LIKE THAT. INSTEAD, THE GREATEST AMONG YOU SHOULD BE LIKE THE YOUNGEST, AND THE ONE WHO RULES LIKE THE ONE WHO SERVES. ... I AM AMONG YOU AS ONE WHO SERVES."
LUKE 22:25-27

Are you serving people around you, or are you using them to meet your own needs? It's a question that those of us who aspire to lead like Jesus must face each and every day. Is it your intention to serve God or yourself? To love God and others, or to love yourself? What motivates you?

PRAYER
Jesus, today, I want to see others through Your eyes and reflect You in my interactions with them. Transform my heart, my mind, and my leadership methods. This day, may people know me as one who serves. In Jesus' Name I pray, Amen.

 # INFLUENCE

JESUS GAVE THEM THIS ANSWER: "VERY TRULY I TELL YOU, THE SON CAN DO NOTHING BY HIMSELF; HE CAN DO ONLY WHAT HE SEES HIS FATHER DOING, BECAUSE WHATEVER THE FATHER DOES THE SON ALSO DOES."
JOHN 5:19

Who or what influences your life's agenda? Jesus' life reflected the Father's influence, an influence strengthened and sustained through solitude, Scripture, and prayer. He resisted the influence of those who did not understand His call from God. How much opportunity to influence your life does the Father have? In the midst of changing circumstances and daily pressures, what are you doing to keep your focus on God and His purposes?

PRAYER

Lord Jesus, I long for these words to be true of my life, also. I know that this doesn't happen by chance. Today, I turn my thoughts toward You, and I humbly come to hear what You have to say to me. In Jesus' Name, I ask, Amen.

_____

_____

_____

_____

_____

_____

_____

_____

SERVE WHERE GOD PLACES YOU

LOOK TO THE LORD AND HIS STRENGTH; SEEK HIS FACE ALWAYS.
1 CHRONICLES 16:11

Where has God placed you? Like Naaman's servant girl in 2 Kings 5, you may find yourself taken captive by circumstances not of your making. Wherever you are, God is able to use you in the lives of others, just as He did this young woman. Through her influence, Naaman received physical healing and confessed the Lord as God. How does the Lord want to use you today?

PRAYER

Lord, these are good words, good advice. Regardless of where I find myself today, it is always the right time to look to You and Your strength. As I seek Your face, show me the opportunities I have to point people to You. May others come to know You as I praise and serve where You place me. In Jesus' Name I pray, Amen.

 # STRENGTH FOR TODAY

WHO THEN IS THE ONE WHO CONDEMNS? NO ONE. CHRIST JESUS WHO DIED—MORE THAN THAT, WHO WAS RAISED TO LIFE—IS AT THE RIGHT HAND OF GOD AND IS ALSO INTERCEDING FOR US.
ROMANS 8:34

What do you need today in order to lead like Jesus? Do you need His strength? His wisdom? His compassion? His courage? His humility? Whatever you need, Jesus is able to meet your need. Even if you can't put it into words, He knows, and He is asking the Father to supply your need so that you can serve Him today. What do you need?

PRAYER

Jesus, how grateful I am that You are alive and interceding for me today. You know my every need, including what I need to be able to live today with a focus on serving others. Thank You for freeing me from condemnation and providing what I need every day so that I may serve fully and freely in Jesus' Name, Amen.

TRUST STARTS WITH THE LEADER

BELIEVE ME WHEN I SAY THAT I AM IN THE FATHER AND THE FATHER IS IN ME; OR AT LEAST BELIEVE ON THE EVIDENCE OF THE WORKS THEMSELVES.
JOHN 14:11

Who do you trust? Who trusts you? Jesus showed Himself trustworthy with God and with people. He could be trusted to honor and obey God and speak God's truth in every situation. Jesus demonstrated godly character, commitment, competence, and concern throughout His life. Because of how He lived and how He interacts with us even now, we know we can trust Him. How will you build trust with others today?

PRAYER

Jesus, You have poured out Your grace toward me. I know that You have come from the Father, and I can trust You to lead me in in His ways. I want to honor and obey the Father. Help me to follow in Your footsteps today, building trust with those around me. I ask in Jesus' Name, Amen.

_____

_____

_____

_____

_____

_____

_____

_____

WHEN PRESSURE BUILDS

THEY WENT TO A PLACE CALLED GETHSEMANE, AND JESUS SAID TO HIS DISCIPLES, "SIT HERE WHILE I PRAY." HE TOOK PETER, JAMES AND JOHN ALONG WITH HIM, AND HE BEGAN TO BE DEEPLY DISTRESSED AND TROUBLED. "MY SOUL IS OVERWHELMED WITH SORROW TO THE POINT OF DEATH," HE SAID TO THEM. "STAY HERE AND KEEP WATCH."
MARK 14:32-34

When Jesus went to pray at Gethsemane, He knew the struggle that was ahead of Him. He needed time with His Father, and He needed the spiritual companionship of His closest disciples. Where do you turn when pressure builds?

PRAYER

Lord Jesus, thank You for showing me how to live in every season of life, including times of great pressure. Your example reminds me that when struggle comes, I can turn to the Father for help. Remind me to share my burdens with others, and help me point them to the Father in times of stress. In Jesus' Name I pray, Amen.

_____

_____

_____

_____

_____

_____

_____

_____

_____

WHEN SERVING REQUIRES COURAGE

SO WE SAY WITH CONFIDENCE, "THE LORD IS MY HELPER; I WILL NOT BE AFRAID. WHAT CAN MERE MORTALS DO TO ME?"
HEBREWS 13:6

What characteristics come to mind when you think of a servant? Do you think of courage? When Jesus faced Pilate, He displayed great presence of mind and steadfast courage, as did Stephen when facing the religious leaders, along with many faithful witnesses throughout the centuries. Christ-like courage springs from confidence that we have been called by God and are empowered by His Spirit. Where is He calling you to serve with confidence and courage?

PRAYER

Lord, You are my helper. What an amazing thought! You come to my aid, infusing me with confidence and courage to serve Your purposes in every circumstance. When fear rears its head, when my faith falters, encourage my heart and strengthen me to serve You courageously. I ask in the Name of Jesus, Amen.

WHO GETS THE GLORY?

NOT TO US, LORD, NOT TO US BUT TO YOUR NAME BE THE GLORY, BECAUSE OF YOUR LOVE AND FAITHFULNESS.
PSALM 115:1

What is your ultimate goal in life: self-glorification or God-glorification? Self-glorification is closely linked to instant gratification. Pride, power, and fear lead to ways of leading that exalt self, trample others, and force results without God's involvement. Humility and confidence exalt God, honor others, invite God's perspective, and follow His leading. Who will get glory through your life and leadership?

PRAYER

Lord, Your love and faithfulness is beyond anything I could ever deserve or imagine. May my life reflect my gratitude and the power of Your transforming love. May You receive glory through my attitude, thoughts, choices, and behavior today. I choose to exalt You rather than myself today. In Jesus' Name I pray, Amen.

 # ARE YOU WILLING?

A MAN WITH LEPROSY CAME TO HIM AND BEGGED HIM ON HIS KNEES, "IF YOU ARE WILLING, YOU CAN MAKE ME CLEAN." JESUS WAS INDIGNANT. HE REACHED OUT HIS HAND AND TOUCHED THE MAN. "I AM WILLING," HE SAID. "BE CLEAN!" IMMEDIATELY THE LEPROSY LEFT HIM AND HE WAS CLEANSED.
MARK 1:40-42

Jesus' starting point for ministry typically seems to be the needs of people. Consider His compassion in feeding the 4,000 and 5,000, healing the blind and lame, and answering the questions of ordinary people. Has He not called you, His follower, to do likewise? Who will you minister to at their point of need today?

PRAYER
Jesus, thank You for being willing to meet me in my need just as You met the leper in his need. Your willingness to heal, to forgive, to cleanse, and to restore reveals the Father's heart. Give me a willing heart so that I, too, can serve people at their point of need. I ask in Jesus' Name, Amen.

BLESSINGS FROM HEAVEN

THEREFORE ENCOURAGE ONE ANOTHER AND BUILD EACH OTHER UP, JUST AS IN FACT YOU ARE DOING.
THESSALONIANS 5:11

Who does God use to bless you? God wants to bless us through everyday interactions with people in our communities: work and ministry colleagues, friends and family members, and brothers and sisters in Christ. Jesus modeled mutually supportive human relationships with disciples and friends who blessed Him by their very presence. How are you being blessed by being in relationship with others? Who are you blessing through your interactions with them?

PRAYER
Lord, thank You for brothers and sisters in Christ who bless me by their faith and mutual encouragement. Thank You for family members and friends with whom I share loving and lasting relationships. Thank You for colleagues and neighbors who make a difference in my life. Help me to be a blessing to them today, I pray in Jesus' Name, Amen.

 INSPIRATION

WE REMEMBER BEFORE OUR GOD AND FATHER YOUR WORK PRODUCED BY FAITH, YOUR LABOR PROMPTED BY LOVE, AND YOUR ENDURANCE INSPIRED BY HOPE IN OUR LORD JESUS CHRIST.
1 THESSALONIANS 1:3

Who or what inspires you? Jesus found inspiration in His relationship with His Father, and He found fulfillment in living in light of His identity as God's Son. God's Word nourished and strengthened Him, and God's Spirit empowered Him. His life, lived in intimacy with the Father, inspired others to ask Him spiritual questions and to want to be like Him. What about you?

PRAYER
Lord Jesus, You are my inspiration. You inspire me to be more than I know myself to be. The hope You give inspires me to keep going and to trust in Your Spirit's ability to transform me. Be my life and breath today so that I inspire others to look to You. I pray in Jesus' Name, Amen.

JESUS' READING LIST

ESUS ANSWERED, "IT IS WRITTEN: 'MAN SHALL NOT LIVE ON BREAD LONE, BUT ON EVERY WORD THAT COMES FROM THE MOUTH OF GOD.'"
ATTHEW 4:4

Vhat's on your reading list? In a day and age when copies of cripture were rare and difficult to come by, Jesus, even as a young han, made a point of knowing the Scripture. His life mission was rounded in God's Word, what we today call the Old Testament. his knowledge strengthened Him for opposition and prepared Him o resist temptation. How familiar are you with the Bible that Jesus new, loved, and memorized?

RAYER

ord, give me a love for Scripture, including a longing for and insight into he Bible that Jesus knew. Reveal Your character to me as I read the Old estament. Give me deeper insight into Jesus as I study the Scripture hat He read and studied. Prepare and strengthen me for ministry hrough Your word. I pray in Jesus' Name, Amen.

LIVING IN THE LIGHT

BLESSED ARE THOSE WHO HAVE LEARNED TO ACCLAIM YOU, WHO WALK IN THE LIGHT OF YOUR PRESENCE, LORD.

PSALM 89:15

What is your vision of life? For whom do you live? Overarching vision provides direction, undergirds decision-making, and gives meaning to otherwise ordinary or difficult tasks. Jesus' vision undergirded His intimate relationship with His Father and resulted in unflagging obedience as He lived in the light of the kingdom of God. What difference will your vision of life make in how you live today?

PRAYER

Lord, I praise You, the Creator, Giver, and Sustainer of life, the One who gives light to my eyes. Give me Your vision for the world and for my life so that I may walk in the light of Your presence. Let me perceive You at work around me so that I can partner with You in establishing Your kingdom today. I pray in Jesus' Name, Amen.

_____

_____

_____

_____

_____

_____

_____

_____

OPPORTUNITY KNOCKS

EVERYONE WAS AMAZED AND GAVE PRAISE TO GOD. THEY WERE FILLED WITH AWE AND SAID, "WE HAVE SEEN REMARKABLE THINGS TODAY."
LUKE 5:26

The Gospel writers record the lives of men, women, and children who recognized and seized the opportunity to interact with Jesus: a father who begged for his daughter's life, a woman who risked what little was left of her reputation to reach out for healing, disciples who responded to His call, children who were irresistibly drawn to Jesus. Others missed out, turning away from the opportunity to know Him. What opportunities will you seize today?

PRAYER
Lord Jesus, this day is a day filled with opportunities to see You at work, to be amazed, to connect with You, to reach out for You, and to respond to Your call. Don't let me miss out. I don't want to be left behind. I want to live this day with You and for You. I pray in Jesus' Name, Amen.

TO BE FOUND FAITHFUL

THIS, THEN, IS HOW YOU OUGHT TO REGARD US: AS SERVANTS OF CHRIST AND AS THOSE ENTRUSTED WITH THE MYSTERIES GOD HAS REVEALED. NOW IT IS REQUIRED THAT THOSE WHO HAVE BEEN GIVEN A TRUST MUST PROVE FAITHFUL.
1 CORINTHIANS 4:1-2

What does faithfulness look like in your life situation today? The Lord has given you another day to live and placed you in circumstances where you can influence those around you. He invites you to draw deeply of His Spirit as you make your way through each minute. Who or what has He entrusted you with? Will you determine even now to be faithful?

PRAYER

Lord, I want to be found faithful. Wherever this day takes me, I want to go as the servant of Christ, with an awareness of my opportunity and responsibility to faithfully represent and serve You. In the Name of the One who was found faithful to the end I pray, Amen.

_____

_____

_____

_____

_____

_____

_____

_____

TO TELL THE TRUTH

ALL YOUR WORDS ARE TRUE; ALL YOUR RIGHTEOUS LAWS ARE ETERNAL."
SALM 119:160

Who do you trust to tell you the truth? Hopefully, several faces just passed in front of your mind's eye, people whom you trust to give you an honest answer and to point you in the right direction. They are typically people that you trust not only to tell you the truth, but to do so with your best interests in mind. You know that they, like God, speak the truth in order to help you and strengthen you, not to tear you down or belittle you.

PRAYER

God, I worship You as the God of truth, the One who is all-knowing and all-wise. Thank You for preserving Scripture as a source of Your truth and wisdom. Thank You for the truth-tellers that You have placed in my life. Thank You for Your Spirit who speaks truth to me in my spirit. I praise You in Jesus' Name, Amen.

 WHEN ENOUGH IS ENOUGH

THE LORD SAID, "GO OUT AND STAND ON THE MOUNTAIN IN THE PRESENCE OF THE LORD, FOR THE LORD IS ABOUT TO PASS BY."
1 KINGS 19:11

Everyone gets there at some point: the moment when energy runs out and enough is, well, enough. Serving has left the servant depleted. Ministry has drained all of the energy from body and soul. In times like these, the Lord sent His angel to care for Elijah's physical needs, and then He called Elijah to come away to meet with Him so that He personally could restore Elijah spiritually.

PRAYER
Lord, Great "I AM," You are my life-source, who restores me physically, emotionally, and spiritually. Thank You for caring about my well-being. Remind me to come away with You to hear Your whisper and be replenished for ministry. Remind me that You are still (and always) at work; remind me to listen for Your Word, which is more than enough to lead me into the future. In Jesus' Name I pray, Amen.

WISDOM FOR THE TAKING

FOR WISDOM WILL ENTER YOUR HEART, AND KNOWLEDGE WILL BE PLEASANT TO YOUR SOUL.
PROVERBS 2:10

Aren't you glad that you don't have to figure life out in your own strength? God desires to pour out His wisdom when you seek Him, His will, and His purposes. Rather than being left to your own momentary flashes of brilliance, you know the One who created, orchestrates, and sustains the universe. He lives in you and longs to share His thoughts and perspective with you.

PRAYER

O Lord, how wise You are, and how full of understanding! From before time, You have possessed knowledge and wisdom, and You freely answer me when I call to You for insight. I open my heart and mind to You. Show me how to walk in Your way today, thinking like You think, pursuing Your purposes, and speaking words that reflect Your wisdom. In Jesus' Name I pray, Amen.

 # BEING PRESENT

LET NO DEBT REMAIN OUTSTANDING, EXCEPT THE CONTINUING DEBT TO LOVE ONE ANOTHER, FOR WHOEVER LOVES OTHERS HAS FULFILLED THE LAW.
ROMANS 13:8

Where does God have you today? Who will you see? Who will you talk to? What places will you go? What will you be doing? Wherever you are, be aware of the Lord's purpose in bringing you into each situation. Like Jesus, invite the Father's presence into every task and conversation. Be present with those whom God brings your way, recognize that they are created in His image, and meet them at their point of need.

PRAYER

Father, how I thank You for Your love for me, evidenced in your gracious patience, guidance, and presence in my life. Help me to extend this same grace to those I meet today, seeing them as You see them, focusing on them as people who matter to You, as Jesus did. I pray in His Name, Amen.

EXCEEDING EXPECTATIONS

HE TOOK HIM OUTSIDE AND SAID, "LOOK UP AT THE SKY AND COUNT THE STARS—IF INDEED YOU CAN COUNT THEM." THEN HE SAID TO HIM, "SO SHALL YOUR OFFSPRING BE." ABRAM BELIEVED THE LORD, AND HE CREDITED IT TO HIM AS RIGHTEOUSNESS.
GENESIS 15:5-6

God called Abram to trust Him and follow Him into the unknown, promising that He would far exceed Abram's hope for the future. As Abram trusted and followed God, God changed him into Abraham, a person whose life and legacy were transformed by God's power. Do you want God to do the same for you?

PRAYER

Lord, how amazing that I am part of the fulfillment of Your promise to Abram. You have called me into the great family of faith, those who believe in Christ Jesus and are counted righteous by faith. Transform my life, leadership, and legacy as I trust and follow Jesus, in whose Name I pray, Amen.

FAITHFUL TO THE END

THE LORD IS MY SHEPHERD, I LACK NOTHING. HE MAKES ME LIE DOWN IN GREEN PASTURES, HE LEADS ME BESIDE QUIET WATERS, HE REFRESHES MY SOUL. HE GUIDES ME ALONG THE RIGHT PATHS FOR HIS NAME'S SAKE.
PSALM 23:1-3

When times are tough, leaders can be tempted to turn from Jesus' example of servant leadership. Yet Jesus did not call us to be servant leaders only when it feels good. He Himself washed the feet of His disciples, including Judas, on the night when He was betrayed. Where do you, like Jesus, need to draw strength from Your relationship with the Father, strength to continue serving to the end?

PRAYER

Lord, I look to You today for spiritual strength so that I can be faithful in what You've called me to do. I know my leadership needs to be more than words. Give me Jesus' courage and commitment to follow You faithfully to the end. Refresh and guide me, I pray in Jesus' Name, Amen.

FINDING THE WAY FORWARD

I TRUST IN YOU; DO NOT LET ME BE PUT TO SHAME, NOR LET MY ENEMIES TRIUMPH OVER ME. NO ONE WHO HOPES IN YOU
WILL EVER BE PUT TO SHAME, BUT SHAME WILL COME ON THOSE WHO ARE TREACHEROUS WITHOUT CAUSE.
PSALM 25:2-3

When disappointment in yourself as a person and as a leader overwhelms you, turn your focus to God, to the One whom you long to please. Find hope in His forgiveness and grace to enable you to move forward in His power. Where do you need to surrender anew to God, trusting Him to show you the way forward?

PRAYER

O Lord, I cry out to You today, seeking to see myself as You see me. My hope is in You. Where I have disappointed myself and You, forgive me. Where I have disappointed others, give me the humility and honesty to apologize and seek forgiveness from them. I place my hope in Your grace and transforming power. In Jesus' Name I pray, Amen.

_____

_____

_____

_____

_____

_____

_____

_____

 FIRST OF MANY

FOR THOSE GOD FOREKNEW HE ALSO PREDESTINED TO BE CONFORMED TO THE IMAGE OF HIS SON, THAT HE MIGHT BE THE FIRSTBORN AMONG MANY BROTHERS AND SISTERS.
ROMANS 8:29

Jesus is the perfect older brother, the firstborn of many brothers and sisters. Jesus — who called the world into being, redeemed the world, and whose name will be forever praised — is at work transforming you into His image. When the days are hard, challenges mount, and you're wondering if you'll ever be able to be a servant leader like Jesus, remember that He is for you. How will you follow His example today?

PRAYER
Father, today I want to be like Jesus. Thank You for making it possible for me to be conformed to His image through Your Spirit's transforming power. May others notice our family resemblance today as Jesus lives in and through me. I pray in Jesus' Name, Amen.

_____
_____
_____
_____
_____
_____
_____
_____

FOLLOW THE LEADER

WHETHER YOU TURN TO THE RIGHT OR TO THE LEFT, YOUR EARS WILL HEAR A VOICE BEHIND YOU, SAYING, "THIS IS THE WAY; WALK IN IT."
ISAIAH 30:21

Fluid circumstances require leaders who are both discerning and responsive to the changes and people around them. We can follow Jesus, Who knew when to continue with His stated goals and when to turn aside to respond to new developments. This discernment is a gift from God, one that is developed by listening to and obeying His Spirit's prompting. Where do you need Jesus' discernment and the Spirit's guidance today?

PRAYER

Jesus, I want to follow You today. I need Your discernment. I want Your Spirit to be my guide. Remind me to depend on the Spirit's presence in the midst of changing circumstances. Open my ears to His voice so that I respond with spiritual wisdom. I ask in Jesus' Name, Amen.

 JOY AND DELIGHT

THE LAW OF THE LORD IS PERFECT, REFRESHING THE SOUL. THE STATUTES OF THE LORD ARE TRUSTWORTHY, MAKING WISE THE SIMPLE. THE PRECEPTS OF THE LORD ARE RIGHT, GIVING JOY TO THE HEART. THE COMMANDS OF THE LORD ARE RADIANT, GIVING LIGHT TO THE EYES.
PSALM 19:7-8

Is God's Word your joy and delight? Do you long to hear Him speak to you? Do you search the Scriptures daily to hear His Word to you? How would your world be different if you no longer had access to the Bible? God has preserved His Word through the ages so that you can hear His voice and live in His ways. Will you, like Jesus, treasure His Word and make it part of your life?

PRAYER
Lord, I praise You for the refreshing, life-giving power of Scripture to those who believe. Give me a hunger to know Your Word, so that I can live by Your truth, finding joy and direction in life. I pray in Jesus' Name, Amen.

KEEPING GOD IN THE EQUATION

MANY ARE THE PLANS IN A PERSON'S HEART, BUT IT IS THE LORD'S PURPOSE THAT PREVAILS.
PROVERBS 19:21

Success, like familiarity, can breed contempt. As God hones our skills, giving us success, and vision becomes reality, we may be tempted to forget that God is the giver of our strength, skills, dreams, and vision. Prolonged prayer may dwindle to momentary pleas for help as we begin to rely more on ourselves and less on God. Whose dream and strength are you relying on, your own or God's?

PRAYER

Lord, You created me. You shape my dreams, and You continually craft the circumstances of my life so that You can use me to spread Your Kingdom vision and values throughout the earth. I am grateful to belong to You and honored to be part of what You are doing. All that I am and achieve are because of You. Use me today, I pray in Jesus' Name, Amen.

 REFLECTION

AS WATER REFLECTS THE FACE, SO ONE'S LIFE REFLECTS THE HEART.
PROVERBS 27:19

What is God doing in your life? Reflecting on God's activity in and through your life results in praise going to the One to Whom it is due rather than to yourself. Reflection provides an opportunity for you as a leader to evaluate your heart, to "altar" your ego, and to humbly and confidently realign yourself with God's perspective and purpose. What is the condition of your heart today?

PRAYER
Lord, thank You for helping me slow down and reflect on the condition of my heart. In the midst of leading others, it can be easy to start to think that it all depends on me, to forget that You are the One at work in and through me. May You receive the glory today as I refocus on You. In the Name of Jesus, who reflected You in all He said and did, I pray, Amen.

TO BE REMEMBERED

THEN THOSE WHO FEARED THE LORD TALKED WITH EACH OTHER, AND THE LORD LISTENED AND HEARD. A SCROLL OF REMEMBRANCE WAS WRITTEN IN HIS PRESENCE CONCERNING THOSE WHO FEARED THE LORD AND HONORED HIS NAME.

MALACHI 3:16

For what do you want to be remembered? Who do you want to remember you? Do you strive to be remembered for human accomplishments? Or is it your desire to lift up the name of Jesus so that He is remembered? The Lord knows those who are His, and He delights in every sacrifice made on His behalf. He Himself will be your reward. Trust Him to be true to His word.

PRAYER

Lord, I give You this day. I give You my life. I give You my desire to be remembered. If anyone is going to remember me, I want it to be You, first of all. As I live for You, my heart's desire is for Jesus to be lifted up. In Jesus' Name I pray, Amen.

🗣 A DANGEROUS PRAYER

THEN I HEARD THE VOICE OF THE LORD SAYING, "WHOM SHALL I SEND? AND WHO WILL GO FOR US?" AND I SAID, "HERE AM I. SEND ME!"
ISAIAH 6:8

Caught up in the wonder of God's forgiveness, God's majesty, and God's call for someone to take His message, Isaiah volunteered to serve. Was he expecting the next part of God's call? "Take my message to people who won't hear and won't respond." Servant leadership can be hard. Ask Isaiah, Nathan, Esther, Moses, Mary, or any of the prophets or disciples. Praying Isaiah's prayer puts you in good company. Have you heard God's call? Are you willing to volunteer?

PRAYER
Lord, I've heard Jesus' call to servant leadership. I'm willing to follow Jesus and let Him transform me. I don't know what the future holds, but I trust that You do and that You will be sufficient for me. Here am I. Send me in Jesus' Name, I pray, Amen.

A FAITHFUL WITNESS

BUT DANIEL RESOLVED NOT TO DEFILE HIMSELF WITH THE ROYAL FOOD AND WINE, AND HE ASKED THE CHIEF OFFICIAL FOR PERMISSION NOT TO DEFILE HIMSELF THIS WAY.

DANIEL 1:8

How well do you treat those in authority over you? How well do you treat those over whom you have authority? Daniel found himself in circumstances beyond his control, first taken prisoner, and then singled out for special attention. His humility and confidence are reflected in his interactions with those over him. What does your treatment of others reveal about your leadership point of view?

PRAYER

I am impressed, Lord, by Daniel's commitment to live for you in whatever circumstances he found himself. Knowing that You orchestrated his life, he moved forward in faith, respectfully seeking ways to honor You. His life of faith became a witness to those over him. He reminds me of Jesus. May I reflect Daniel's faith today, I pray in Jesus' Name, Amen.

♥ A LIFE THAT IS CHANGED

WHEN JESUS SAW HIM LYING THERE AND LEARNED THAT HE HAD BEEN IN THIS CONDITION FOR A LONG TIME, HE ASKED HIM, "DO YOU WANT TO GET WELL?"
JOHN 5:6

Person after person in Scripture was changed by an encounter with the living God. Sadly, some refused His offer of forgiveness, some hardened their hearts, and some rejected the offer of a future and a hope. What about you? Have you heard His call? He offers hope to you today. Will you accept His offer to infuse your life and circumstances with His transforming presence? Will yours be a life that is changed?

PRAYER

Jesus, today I hear Your question; I hear Your call. It is time for me to choose life, health, and hope. Yes, I want to get well. Yes, I want to experience Your transformation and infusion of purpose in my life. Yes, I accept Your offer. I pray in Jesus' Name, Amen.

_____

_____

_____

_____

_____

_____

_____

_____

A LIFE THAT WAS WASTED: JUDAS

FOR EVERYTHING IN THE WORLD—THE LUST OF THE FLESH, THE LUST OF THE EYES, AND THE PRIDE OF LIFE—COMES NOT FROM THE FATHER BUT FROM THE WORLD. THE WORLD AND ITS DESIRES PASS AWAY, BUT WHOEVER DOES THE WILL OF GOD LIVES FOREVER.
1 JOHN 2:16-17

How sad it is when a person spends years as a Christian, but isn't changed by the message of Christ. Sadly, there are still people today who follow in Judas' footsteps rather than Jesus' footsteps. Judas was blinded by cares of this world, by money, by greed, by judging rather than accepting Jesus' message. His leadership legacy is one of warning. Will you let Jesus transform your perspective?

PRAYER

Lord, I lay down my will, my perspective on what is important, my earthly set of priorities, and how I think life is to be lived, how I should lead. Free me from what blinds me. Open my eyes; show me what matters to You. I pray in Jesus' Name, Amen.

A LIFE-CHANGING ENCOUNTER: NATHANAEL

THEN NATHANAEL DECLARED, "RABBI, YOU ARE THE SON OF GOD; YOU ARE THE KING OF ISRAEL."
JOHN 1:49

Nathanael's life changed the day his friend Philip came to tell him about Jesus. Nathanael's response to both Philip and Jesus was initially one of skepticism. When Nathanael went to check out Philip's message, Jesus gave Nathanael answers that satisfied his skeptical nature. What questions are you bringing to Jesus so that He can turn your skepticism into faith?

PRAYER

Jesus, there are situations where I question whether Your call to servant leadership will really work. I can't believe that serving others will make any difference. I want a Plan B. But like Philip and Nathanael, I believe that You know what You are talking about, and so I trust that following You as a servant leader is the right thing to do. Show me how to live and lead in Your Name, Jesus, Amen.

_____

_____

_____

_____

_____

_____

_____

_____

_____

 # A LIFE-CHANGING ENCOUNTER: PAUL

THEN [PAUL] ASKED, "WHO ARE YOU, LORD?" "I AM JESUS, WHOM YOU ARE PERSECUTING," THE LORD REPLIED. "NOW GET UP AND STAND ON YOUR FEET. I HAVE APPEARED TO YOU TO APPOINT YOU AS A SERVANT AND AS A WITNESS OF WHAT YOU HAVE SEEN AND WILL SEE OF ME."
ACTS 26:15-16

Before his encounter with the risen Christ, Paul already exhibited an exemplary zeal and commitment to pursuing leadership excellence according to the world's standards. He had the highest education and credentials. He networked with the top names of his day. He was achieving all of his goals but none of God's. Meeting Jesus changed everything in Paul's life. He was never the same. What about you?

PRAYER

Jesus, change me. Change my vision of the future; change my goals, my values, and my purpose in life so that I align with You. Don't leave me like You found me. Make me a servant and witness to You, the risen Lord, in whose Name I pray, Amen.

_____
_____
_____
_____
_____
_____
_____
_____

A PROMISE FULFILLED

NOW THE LORD WAS GRACIOUS TO SARAH AS HE HAD SAID, AND THE LORD DID FOR SARAH WHAT HE HAD PROMISED. SARAH BECAME PREGNANT AND BORE A SON TO ABRAHAM IN HIS OLD AGE, AT THE VERY TIME GOD HAD PROMISED HIM. ABRAHAM GAVE THE NAME ISAAC TO THE SON SARAH BORE HIM.
GENESIS 21:1-3

Twenty-five years after God called Abraham, Isaac was born. Twenty-five years of learning to live by faith. Abraham and Sarah journeyed with God from their home in Mesopotamia to the Promised Land, but more importantly, they learned of God's mercy, forgiveness, and grace. Where has God taken you in your journey of faith?

PRAYER

O Lord, You are the promise-fulfilling God of Abraham, who calls me to journey by faith in Your promises! Thank You for calling me; thank You for showing me mercy, forgiveness, and grace as I learn what it means to live by faith. I trust You to fulfill Your promises as I walk with You day by day. In Jesus' Name I pray, Amen.

_____

_____

_____

_____

_____

_____

_____

_____

_____

COURAGE UNDER PRESSURE

I THANK AND PRAISE YOU, GOD OF MY ANCESTORS: YOU HAVE GIVEN ME WISDOM AND POWER, YOU HAVE MADE KNOWN TO ME WHAT WE ASKED OF YOU, YOU HAVE MADE KNOWN TO US THE DREAM OF THE KING.
DANIEL 2:23

Daniel and his friends found themselves about to suffer the consequences for other people's failure. Instead of lashing out, blaming others, or complaining about the injustice, Daniel sought to understand what was going on and asked to be allowed to do something about it. In doing so, he saved his own life and that of others. How do you respond to injustice? What does this response reveal about you as a leader?

PRAYER
Lord, I praise You for meeting Daniel and his friends in their hour of need. Thank You for giving me opportunities to show faith and courage under pressure, and for pouring out Your wisdom when I call to You. May You be glorified in my life, as You were in Daniel's life. In Jesus' Name I pray, Amen.

🩶 EXALTING GOD ONLY

THE KING SAID TO DANIEL, "SURELY YOUR GOD IS THE GOD OF GODS AND THE LORD OF KINGS AND A REVEALER OF MYSTERIES, FOR YOU WERE ABLE TO REVEAL THIS MYSTERY."

DANIEL 2:47

All that we have and are comes from God. Our natural abilities, our opportunities, all our spiritual blessings and power, any insight we possess, our salvation, our life, and our breath itself. Everything that we have is a gift from God. Daniel knew this well, and he was quick to give glory to God privately and publicly. As a result, God's name was exalted by a foreign king. How will you give God glory today?

PRAYER

God, may my life and witness always point to You. You are the source of every good gift. Every talent I have comes from You. Please use me today to reveal Your greatness to those around me. May Your name be lifted up and exalted. In Jesus' Name I pray, Amen.

FANNING THE FLAME

WHEN APOLLOS WANTED TO GO TO ACHAIA, THE BROTHERS AND SISTERS ENCOURAGED HIM AND WROTE TO THE DISCIPLES THERE TO WELCOME HIM. WHEN HE ARRIVED, HE WAS A GREAT HELP TO THOSE WHO BY GRACE HAD BELIEVED.

ACTS 18:27

What are you doing to encourage the transformational work Jesus wants to do in and through others? People long to know that God has a purpose for them. They want to make a difference. They long to know that their lives count. Living for Jesus invests life with eternal purpose. Who are you encouraging to live for God?

PRAYER

Lord, You call all of us to be servant leaders. Your specific call for others may or may not align with my own, yet all of us need to be obedient to serve where, when, and how You direct us. Help me to be a supporter and an encourager to others today. I pray in Jesus' Name, Amen.

_____
_____
_____
_____
_____
_____
_____
_____

 FRESH ENERGY

HE GIVES STRENGTH TO THE WEARY AND INCREASES THE POWER OF THE WEAK. EVEN YOUTHS GROW TIRED AND WEARY, AND YOUNG MEN STUMBLE AND FALL; BUT THOSE WHO HOPE IN THE LORD WILL RENEW THEIR STRENGTH. THEY WILL SOAR ON WINGS LIKE EAGLES; THEY WILL RUN AND NOT GROW WEARY, THEY WILL WALK AND NOT BE FAINT.
ISAIAH 40:29-31

Where do you need fresh energy and renewed hope? Where do you feel like you've given your all and have nothing left to give? Perhaps you've poured yourself into someone else, and you don't know how else to help them. God holds out His hand to those who need His touch. Will you take it today?

PRAYER
Oh, Lord, I need You today. I need You every day. You give me the strength to rise again. I draw strength from Your Spirit and from Your Word. I am renewed by hope in You, and I move forward in Jesus' Name, Amen.

_____
_____
_____
_____
_____
_____
_____
_____
_____

 HEART CHECK: COMPARISON

FOR ALL HAVE SINNED AND FALL SHORT OF THE GLORY OF GOD, AND ALL ARE JUSTIFIED FREELY BY HIS GRACE THROUGH THE REDEMPTION THAT CAME BY CHRIST JESUS.
ROMANS 3:23-24

With whom are you tempted to compare yourself? Comparison sneaks into our perspective subtly, quietly. One minute we're compassionate and understanding, and the next minute we're glad that we're not the ones needing help. Pride slips in, and we find ourselves judging others instead of supporting and encouraging them. To lead like Jesus is to gratefully and freely be justified by grace alone and offer that grace to others. Who will experience grace through you today?

PRAYER

Lord Jesus, thank you for redeeming us and justifying us freely by Your grace. Stop me short when I take my eyes off of my own need for grace and begin to compare myself with others. May I offer grace instead of judgment today. I pray in Jesus' Name, Amen.

 HOW DO THEY KNOW?

AS YOU GO, PROCLAIM THIS MESSAGE: "THE KINGDOM OF HEAVEN HAS COME NEAR."
MATTHEW 10:7

How do other people know that you have been with Jesus? How will they know the difference Jesus wants to make in their lives if they can't see the difference He is making in your life? The work Jesus is doing in your life needs to become visible, so that others can catch the vision of leading like Jesus. The world is waiting to see the message of Jesus brought to life. Who will see and hear His message through you today?

PRAYER
Lord Jesus, thank You for sending people who lived and proclaimed a new way of living and leading. May the good news that there is a different way, a life-giving way of living and leading, take root in my heart and mind and flow out through my actions, attitudes, and words. I pray in Jesus' Name, Amen.

 IT'S ALL ABOUT HEART

NOW SOME TEACHERS OF THE LAW WERE SITTING THERE, THINKING TO THEMSELVES, "WHY DOES THIS FELLOW TALK LIKE THAT? HE'S BLASPHEMING! WHO CAN FORGIVE SINS BUT GOD ALONE?" IMMEDIATELY JESUS KNEW IN HIS SPIRIT THAT THIS WAS WHAT THEY WERE THINKING IN THEIR HEARTS, AND HE SAID TO THEM, "WHY ARE YOU THINKING THESE THINGS?"
MARK 2:6-8

Jesus saw into the hearts of individuals. He saw the paralyzed man's deep need for forgiveness, as well as the unbelief in the hearts of the teachers of the law. Rather than focusing on external behavior changes, He focused on the heart as the starting point for transformation. What does Jesus see when He looks into your heart?

PRAYER

Jesus, look into my heart. Bring Your transformational power to bear at the point where I need it most. Challenge my unbelief, forgive my sin, and transform my heart and mind so that I can selflessly serve in Jesus' Name. Amen.

JESUS IS FOR YOU

[RIGHTEOUS FATHER,] I HAVE MADE YOU KNOWN TO THEM, AND WILL CONTINUE TO MAKE YOU KNOWN IN ORDER THAT THE LOVE YOU HAVE FOR ME MAY BE IN THEM AND THAT I MYSELF MAY BE IN THEM.
JOHN 17:26

What difference does it make to know that Jesus is for you? To know that He wants you to succeed in what He has called you to do even more than you do? How you use your leadership roles and opportunities matter to Him and to eternity. Look to Him today. He cares. He is for you. He will lead you forward.

PRAYER
Jesus, thank You for not leaving me alone to do what You have called me to do. Thank You for being for me, for praying for me, for being here with me as I move into this day, for empowering me through Your Spirit. What a difference You make in my life! Today, I live, lead, and pray in Jesus' Name, Amen.

_____

_____

_____

_____

_____

_____

_____

_____

_____

LEADING LIKE JESUS

WHEN HE WAS IN THE HOUSE, HE ASKED THEM, "WHAT WERE YOU ARGUING ABOUT ON THE ROAD?" BUT THEY KEPT QUIET BECAUSE ON THE WAY THEY HAD ARGUED ABOUT WHO WAS THE GREATEST. SITTING DOWN, JESUS CALLED THE TWELVE AND SAID, "ANYONE WHO WANTS TO BE FIRST MUST BE THE VERY LAST, AND THE SERVANT OF ALL."
MARK 9:33-35

When the topic of authority, position, and leadership came up among Jesus' disciples, He quickly addressed it. He knew that they were being influenced by the world's view of leadership and that it was causing division instead of unity among them. What results are you seeing from your leadership perspective? How does your leadership point of view align with His?

PRAYER

Jesus, I am ready to learn from You. I need Your perspective on life and leadership. Thank You for exposing my pride and correcting me when I need it. I want to be like You. I pray in Jesus' Name, Amen.

LIFE-IMPACTING INFLUENCE

DON'T LET ANYONE LOOK DOWN ON YOU BECAUSE YOU ARE YOUNG, BUT SET AN EXAMPLE FOR THE BELIEVERS IN SPEECH, IN CONDUCT, IN LOVE, IN FAITH AND IN PURITY.
1 TIMOTHY 4:12

Whose influence has had the most profound impact in your life? Whose names come to mind? What did these people do that made such an impact on you? Was their influence positive or negative? What can you emulate in their example? What do you need to learn? What are you passing on to others?

PRAYER
Lord, thank You for the people You've placed in my life, those from whom I have learned what it means to live, love, and lead like Jesus. I realize that I am called to pass on what they have taught me, and so I also thank You for those whom You have given me to influence. May I be an example they can follow. In Jesus' Name I pray, Amen.

_____

_____

_____

_____

_____

_____

_____

_____

_____

MAKING GOD KNOWN

NO ONE HAS EVER SEEN GOD, BUT THE ONE AND ONLY SON, WHO IS HIMSELF GOD AND IS IN CLOSEST RELATIONSHIP WITH THE FATHER, HAS MADE HIM KNOWN.

JOHN 1:18 (NLT)

Jesus came to earth to make God known. His life was lived for one purpose: revealing the love of the Father so that people could find eternal life. His relationship with God sustained Him in every circumstance. When people came into Jesus' presence, they knew that they were in the presence of God. How is God transforming your purpose in life so that you also are able to make God known?

PRAYER

God, thank You for revealing Yourself through Your Son. As your child, I too want to reveal You to the world. As I find my purpose for living in you today, as I seek You through Word and Spirit, flow through me and use me to make You known. I ask in Jesus' Name, Amen.

 # ONE LIFE

SHE DID WHAT SHE COULD. SHE POURED PERFUME ON MY BODY BEFOREHAND TO PREPARE FOR MY BURIAL.

MARK 14:8

It can be easy to forget the difference one person's life can make. Yet the world today is different because of countless disciples who said yes to Jesus' call to follow and be transformed. People like Mary, who anointed Jesus, pouring out her love for Him, even though others didn't understand. Jesus accepted her sacrifice of love. What difference will your life make to Jesus today?

PRAYER

Jesus, You are worth more to me than my words can express. You are worth more to me than my reputation or any sacrifice that I can make. You have transformed my life, and I want to pour my life out in love and service to You, to do what I can to bless You, and to be a blessing to others in Your name. In Jesus' Name I pray, Amen.

_____

_____

_____

_____

_____

_____

_____

_____

RESISTING THE POWER PLAY

...THESE ARE THE ONES I LOOK ON WITH FAVOR: THOSE WHO ARE HUMBLE AND CONTRITE IN SPIRIT, AND WHO TREMBLE AT MY WORD.
ISAIAH 66:2

There will be times when we face the temptation to force change through display of power. Things aren't going as quickly as we would like, people aren't listening to us, and we are tempted to take matters into our own hands. Power plays are shortcuts that ignore God's leadership principles. Where are you tempted to try to lead in your own power? What is the risk in following God's way instead?

PRAYER

Father, I confess that sometimes I am tempted to take shortcuts, to create change in my own power, through my own words, abilities, or actions. Remind me that I am always wise to seek Your plan and Your way. Transform my thinking, attitudes, and actions to reflect Your leadership principles. I pray in Jesus' Name, Amen.

_____

_____

_____

_____

_____

_____

_____

_____

_____

SEEING THE BIGGER PICTURE

DO YOU NOT KNOW? HAVE YOU NOT HEARD? THE LORD IS THE EVERLASTING GOD, THE CREATOR OF THE ENDS OF THE EARTH. HE WILL NOT GROW TIRED OR WEARY, AND HIS UNDERSTANDING NO ONE CAN FATHOM.

ISAIAH 40:28

At times, our individual leadership challenges can overwhelm us. As challenges loom large, our perspective shrinks. Slowly, we begin to believe that our limited perspective is the only thing that matters. We forget that God is at work. We forget who He is. We forget to call on Him. Where do you need to step back and seek God today?

PRAYER

Lord, everlasting God who spoke the universe into being, I worship You today. Forgive my tendency to edge You out as I look at life and the circumstances facing me. I exalt You, the God of all history, all people, places and events who is always leading the way forward. Increase my strength and faith, I pray in Jesus' Name, Amen.

THE GOD WHO SEES ME

SHE GAVE THIS NAME TO THE LORD WHO SPOKE TO HER: "YOU ARE THE GOD WHO SEES ME," FOR SHE SAID, "I HAVE NOW SEEN THE ONE WHO SEES ME."
GENESIS 16:13

Hagar found herself in desperate circumstances. Running, on her own, trapped in the grip of pride and fear, despairing in her loneliness and hopelessness, she had given up. At this low point of her life, the Lord found her, clarified her identity and direction, and spoke words that restored her. Where do you need God's intervention to restore your hope?

PRAYER

Lord, the God who sees me, thank You for coming to me in the midst of the challenges that surround me. Thank You for calling me by name, for reminding me that I serve You, and for helping me to clarify Your vision and purpose for me. Thank You for speaking words of hope to me through Scripture. Give me strength to live for You, in Jesus' Name I pray, Amen.

THE RIGHT KIND OF DIFFERENT

IT HAS GIVEN ME GREAT JOY TO FIND SOME OF YOUR CHILDREN WALKING IN THE TRUTH, JUST AS THE FATHER COMMANDED US.
2 JOHN 4

Jesus calls us to be different from the world. He calls us out of the world while leaving us in the world. He calls us to understand when we are misunderstood, to love when we are hated, to freely give all that we have received. He calls us to be courageous when fear surrounds us, to speak out when others are silent, and to trust God's ways instead of the world's ways. How is He calling you to be different today?

PRAYER
Lord Jesus, I praise You for living a life of truth, a life that stood out from the world, a life that revealed the Father to those around you. I want to live like You today in light of the difference You have made in my life. In Jesus' Name I pray, Amen.

TO BE LIKE JESUS

...GOD IS LOVE. WHOEVER LIVES IN LOVE LIVES IN GOD, AND GOD IN THEM. THIS IS HOW LOVE IS MADE COMPLETE AMONG US SO THAT WE WILL HAVE CONFIDENCE ON THE DAY OF JUDGMENT: IN THIS WORLD WE ARE LIKE JESUS.

1 JOHN 4:16-17

Jesus modeled servant leadership for His disciples. He was very clear about his leadership point of view: *This is how you are to lead and how you are not to lead. This is why your way will not work. This is my way. Follow my example.* He modeled love and respect for people, especially the hurting and outcast. He was committed to His relationship with God, training His followers, and serving sacrificially. How will you follow in His footsteps today?

PRAYER

Jesus, thank You for leaving me a practical role model to model my life and leadership after. I want to be like You. Open my eyes to how I can follow You more closely today. I ask in Jesus' Name, Amen.

WHAT DO YOU NEED TO KNOW?

THE MOCKER SEEKS WISDOM AND FINDS NONE, BUT KNOWLEDGE COMES EASILY TO THE DISCERNING.
PROVERBS 14:6

Knowledge is the first step toward change. Learning what Scripture teaches about leadership in order to gain an understanding of His leadership point of view is the place to start. As we humbly consider how we live out Jesus' servant leader mandate, He can show us where we need to realign ourselves with His way of thinking and leading. What leadership challenges do you face today? What new knowledge or fresh insight do you need Him to give you?

PRAYER

Lord, I need Your insight first into my own life and leadership. Then I need Your insight into the leadership challenges in front of me. Help me discern how to apply what you are teaching me, so that I can align with what You are doing in the lives of others. I ask this in Jesus' Name, Amen.

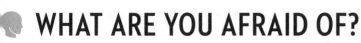 # WHAT ARE YOU AFRAID OF?

THE FEAR OF THE LORD IS THE BEGINNING OF WISDOM, AND KNOWLEDGE OF THE HOLY ONE IS UNDERSTANDING.
PROVERBS 9:10

What are you afraid of? Are you afraid of failing? Are you afraid of not being good enough? Are you afraid that God is displeased with you because you struggle with fear? Fear can be debilitating when we fear the wrong thing. But the fear of the Lord is a different story. To fear Him is to begin to live in wisdom and lead with His power. The object of your fear makes all the difference!

PRAYER

Lord, I bow before You, the Almighty Creator, the Wisdom of the Ages, and I worship You. I lay myself, with all my fears, abilities, and strength, before You. Cleanse me from ungodly fear. Clear my heart and focus my thoughts so that I can be used in Your service. In Jesus' Name, Amen.

WHEN THE STAKES ARE HIGH

THEN DANIEL RETURNED TO HIS HOUSE AND EXPLAINED THE MATTER TO HIS FRIENDS HANANIAH, MISHAEL AND AZARIAH. HE URGED THEM TO PLEAD FOR MERCY FROM THE GOD OF HEAVEN CONCERNING THIS MYSTERY, SO THAT HE AND HIS FRIENDS MIGHT NOT BE EXECUTED WITH THE REST OF THE WISE MEN OF BABYLON.

DANIEL 2:17-18

Is prayer your natural response in crisis? When Daniel and his friends' lives were at stake, along with those of others, they called out to God. They needed wisdom, they needed mercy, and they needed God to move on their behalf. They prayed not just for themselves but for all who would be affected. What do you pray about? How do you need God to intervene? Who do you ask to pray with you?

PRAYER

Lord, like Daniel, I know that You hear and answer prayer. Pour out Your wisdom and mercy. Move on our behalf, we pray in Jesus' Name, Amen.

WHEN WISHING ISN'T ENOUGH

THEN JESUS TOLD HIS DISCIPLES A PARABLE TO SHOW THEM THAT THEY SHOULD ALWAYS PRAY AND NOT GIVE UP.
LUKE 18:1

Certain results are accomplished only by intentional, focused prayer. Actually, Jesus said that at times both prayer and fasting are required. Leading like Jesus means not just wishing that things would change, but seeking God for the change He wants to bring about and the role He has for us to play in leading change. What are you praying about today?

PRAYER

Lord Jesus, I see the importance of prayer in Your life, and I listen as You teach Your disciples to pray. I am emboldened to keep asking You for what I need as a servant leader. I believe that You long to hear me ask You what You want to do and how You want to use me. So I pray today, and I wait to hear what You will say as I pray in Jesus' Name, Amen.

WHO DO THEY SEE?

...UNTIL WE ALL REACH UNITY IN THE FAITH AND IN THE KNOWLEDGE OF THE SON OF GOD AND BECOME MATURE, ATTAINING TO THE WHOLE MEASURE OF THE FULLNESS OF CHRIST.
EPHESIANS 4:13

When people look at you, do they see Jesus? When they are with you, are they aware of having been in His presence? When you lead them, does your example influence them to think, act, and become more Christ-like? Jesus' relationship with the Father permeated all His life and relationships. How does God want to transform you to be more like Jesus today?

PRAYER

Father, I know that You want me to become mature, so that Jesus is revealed through my actions. Shape me to be more like Jesus today so that others have a chance to see what a mature Christian looks like, and better yet, so that they see Jesus. I ask in Jesus' Name, Amen.

_____
_____
_____
_____
_____
_____
_____
_____
_____
_____

WHO IS WATCHING YOU?

FOLLOW MY EXAMPLE, AS I FOLLOW THE EXAMPLE OF CHRIST.
1 CORINTHIANS 11:1

We sometimes forget that eyes are watching us. Children look to us as their role models, learning what it means to be a mother, a father, or simply an adult. Co-workers look at our example of integrity and responsibility in the workplace. Brothers and sisters in Christ want to have someone whose lives will point them to Jesus. Leaders look for role models that will help them become more influential. Who is watching you? Will they see a person who lives, loves, and leads like Jesus?

PRAYER

Jesus, thank You that it wasn't just about words to You; You lived the message, becoming an example for us. Like Paul, I want to follow Your example so that my life says to others, "This is how you live like Jesus; this is how you love like Jesus; this is how you lead like Jesus." I pray in Your Name, Jesus, Amen.

💜 A NEW BEGINNING

WHEN THE LORD SAW THAT HE HAD GONE OVER TO LOOK, GOD CALLED TO HIM FROM WITHIN THE BUSH, "MOSES! MOSES!" AND MOSES SAID, "HERE I AM." "DO NOT COME ANY CLOSER," GOD SAID. "TAKE OFF YOUR SANDALS, FOR THE PLACE WHERE YOU ARE STANDING IS HOLY GROUND." THEN HE SAID, "I AM THE GOD OF YOUR FATHER, THE GOD OF ABRAHAM, THE GOD OF ISAAC AND THE GOD OF JACOB." AT THIS, MOSES HID HIS FACE, BECAUSE HE WAS AFRAID TO LOOK AT GOD.
EXODUS 3:4-6

Moses' early attempts to lead from a worldly perspective led to exile. Years later, when God called him through the burning bush experience, memories of past failure still haunted him and threatened to undermine his confidence in God. What failures keep you from responding to God's call?

PRAYER
Lord, I hear You call my name. Don't let pride, fear or past failure keep me from responding to You. Give me humility and confidence to lead like Jesus, in whose Name I pray, Amen.

_____

_____

_____

_____

_____

_____

_____

_____

_____

AN UNEXPECTED ANSWER

DO NOT BE AFRAID, ZECHARIAH; YOUR PRAYER HAS BEEN HEARD. YOUR WIFE ELIZABETH WILL BEAR YOU A SON, AND YOU ARE TO CALL HIM JOHN. HE WILL BE A JOY AND DELIGHT TO YOU, AND MANY WILL REJOICE BECAUSE OF HIS BIRTH, FOR HE WILL BE GREAT IN THE SIGHT OF THE LORD. ... AND HE WILL BE FILLED WITH THE HOLY SPIRIT EVEN BEFORE HE IS BORN. HE WILL BRING BACK MANY OF THE PEOPLE OF ISRAEL TO THE LORD THEIR GOD."
LUKE 1:13-16

Elizabeth and Zechariah had been praying for a child for so long that they didn't really expect the Lord to answer. When He did answer, they discovered that His timing was perfect, and an encouragement to them and others. What longing do you trust God to fulfill?

PRAYER
Lord, I trust You with the longings of my heart. I will keep seeking You. Take my prayers and answer them in a way that brings You glory. I ask in Jesus' Name, Amen.

_____

_____

_____

_____

_____

_____

_____

_____

_____

♥ BE STRONG AND COURAGEOUS

"HAVE I NOT COMMANDED YOU? BE STRONG AND COURAGEOUS. DO NOT BE AFRAID; DO NOT BE DISCOURAGED, FOR THE LORD YOUR GOD WILL BE WITH YOU WHEREVER YOU GO."
JOSHUA 1:9

Being a servant leader isn't for the fainthearted. Both Moses and the Lord repeatedly called Joshua to be strong and courageous. They warned him not to give into fear or discouragement but trust the Lord's presence with him, and they reminded him that the Lord would never forsake him. Where do you need to replace fear and discouragement with strength and courage?

PRAYER
Lord, thank You for the assurance of Your presence with me as I serve You and lead Your people. Help me to recognize fear and discouragement as signals to turn to You, drawing strength and courage from Your presence. Thank You for believing in me and strengthening me to lead like Jesus. I pray in Jesus' Name, Amen.

CREATING AN ATMOSPHERE OF PRAISE

BE FILLED WITH THE SPIRIT, SPEAKING TO ONE ANOTHER WITH PSALMS, HYMNS, AND SONGS FROM THE SPIRIT. SING AND MAKE MUSIC FROM YOUR HEART TO THE LORD, ALWAYS GIVING THANKS TO GOD THE FATHER FOR EVERYTHING, IN THE NAME OF OUR LORD JESUS CHRIST.
EPHESIANS 5:18-20

To be filled with the Spirit is to live all of life in light of God's presence. Praise and thanksgiving highlight His presence and activity. As we focus on God's goodness, our hearts are shaped to trust Him more, our minds are renewed, and our relationships are transformed. As you meditate on this Scripture passage, ask God how you can intentionally create an atmosphere of praise.

PRAYER

God, You are good, and Your love endures forever. Thank You for life and breath and hope. Thank You for Jesus. Thank You for Your Spirit. Thank You for the encouragement of Scripture. Thank You that I can meditate on Your goodness and choose to praise You today. In Jesus' Name, Amen.

EVERYTHING WE NEED

PRAISE BE TO THE GOD AND FATHER OF OUR LORD JESUS CHRIST, WHO HAS BLESSED US IN THE HEAVENLY REALMS WITH EVERY SPIRITUAL BLESSING IN CHRIST.
EPHESIANS 1:3

God has given us everything we need in Jesus. Peter says that we have all we need for life and godliness in God's promises (2 Peter 1:3). Paul tells us that we have every spiritual blessing in Christ (Ephesians 1:3). As leaders, Jesus has commissioned us to go in His name and authority (Matthew 28:18). What do you trust Him to supply today?

PRAYER
Lord, too often I look at myself instead of relying on who You are as I lead. Forgive me. Refocus me on who You are and all that I am and have in You. You have promised never to forsake me. You have placed me where I am for Your purposes. You have given me Your Spirit. Today, let me meditate on who You are and go in Your strength. I pray in Jesus' Name, Jesus, Amen.

_____

_____

_____

_____

_____

_____

_____

_____

FORGIVEN AND RESTORED

FOR WHAT I RECEIVED I PASSED ON TO YOU AS OF FIRST IMPORTANCE: THAT CHRIST DIED FOR OUR SINS ACCORDING TO THE SCRIPTURES, THAT HE WAS BURIED, THAT HE WAS RAISED ON THE THIRD DAY ACCORDING TO THE SCRIPTURES, AND THAT HE APPEARED TO CEPHAS [PETER], AND THEN TO THE TWELVE.

1 CORINTHIANS 15:3-5

Peter knew the power of Jesus' forgiveness. After swearing that he would never forsake Jesus, he slept through prayer and then denied and abandoned Jesus. Paul mentions, almost as an aside, Jesus' private appearance to Peter after His resurrection. What this must have meant to Peter! Have you known forgiveness this complete? How has it transformed your life?

PRAYER

Oh Jesus, thank You for forgiving me and restoring me! Thank You for Your mercy and grace. Thank You for the opportunity to show my love for You by serving others in Your Name. May I extend the forgiveness and grace You have shown me to others. I pray in Jesus' Name, Amen.

_____

_____

_____

_____

_____

_____

_____

_____

FULLY PREPARED

PETER REPLIED, "REPENT AND BE BAPTIZED, EVERY ONE OF YOU, IN THE NAME OF JESUS CHRIST FOR THE FORGIVENESS OF YOUR SINS. AND YOU WILL RECEIVE THE GIFT OF THE HOLY SPIRIT. THE PROMISE IS FOR YOU AND YOUR CHILDREN AND FOR ALL WHO ARE FAR OFF—FOR ALL WHOM THE LORD OUR GOD WILL CALL."
ACTS 2:38-39

As Peter stood to preach on the Day of Pentecost, he spoke with God-given confidence. His message was given in the power of the Holy Spirit, in full assurance that Jesus was the Messiah. Jesus had fully equipped Peter to carry on the ministry after His ascension. How are you equipping disciples to carry the message of Jesus?

PRAYER

Lord Jesus, thank You for equipping Peter and all of us to carry on Your work. What a privilege it is to be part of carrying Your message to the world. May I be as faithful in equipping new disciples as You were. In Jesus' Name I pray, Amen.

_____

_____

_____

_____

_____

_____

_____

GOD-HONORING RELATIONSHIPS

SUBMIT TO ONE ANOTHER OUT OF REVERENCE FOR CHRIST.
EPHESIANS 5:21

Scripture calls us to let the reality of our love for Christ be seen in our relationships with fellow believers. We are called minister to others according to their needs: to pray for one another, to be considerate of one another, to love one another, to exhort and encourage one another, to carry one another's burdens, to forgive one another, even to rebuke one another, if needed. The disciples practiced mutual submission, consulting one another on doctrinal issues and working through disagreements so as to honor Christ. How is your reverence for Christ reflected in relationships with those around you?

PRAYER
Lord Jesus, I want others to see that there is something different, something appealing, in the way that we Christians love one another. Help me to respect and support my brothers and sisters in Christ in visible ways as we live our lives for You. In Jesus' Name I pray, Amen.

_____

_____

_____

_____

_____

_____

_____

_____

🗣 IN CHRIST

SO IN CHRIST JESUS YOU ARE ALL CHILDREN OF GOD THROUGH FAITH, FOR ALL OF YOU WHO WERE BAPTIZED INTO CHRIST HAVE CLOTHED YOURSELVES WITH CHRIST. THERE IS NEITHER JEW NOR GENTILE, NEITHER SLAVE NOR FREE, NOR IS THERE MALE AND FEMALE, FOR YOU ARE ALL ONE IN CHRIST JESUS.
GALATIANS 3:26-28

Our position and relationships within the body of Christ are based upon who we are in Jesus. Worldly distinctions no longer define us; we are redefined as children of God, being transformed into Christ's image through His Spirit within us. How will your identity in Christ shape you today?

PRAYER
Jesus, I find my identity in You. I rest in the confidence that comes from knowing I am accepted in You. As God's child, I am free to love others in the family as brothers and sisters. May I reflect You more and more fully as I find my identity in You. In Jesus' Name I pray, Amen.

_____
_____
_____
_____
_____
_____
_____
_____
_____

↻ IN LIGHT OF HIS LOVE

THEREFORE IF YOU HAVE ANY ENCOURAGEMENT FROM BEING UNITED WITH CHRIST, IF ANY COMFORT FROM HIS LOVE, IF ANY COMMON SHARING IN THE SPIRIT, IF ANY TENDERNESS AND COMPASSION, THEN MAKE MY JOY COMPLETE BY BEING LIKE-MINDED, HAVING THE SAME LOVE, BEING ONE IN SPIRIT AND OF ONE MIND.
PHILIPPIANS 2:1-2

What benefits do you have from your relationship with Christ? A relationship with Jesus fulfills the deepest needs of our souls: the need for encouragement, comfort, identity, intimacy, acceptance, compassion, and understanding. When we invite Jesus to satisfy our innermost needs, we are free to love others as He did. How is His unconditional love transforming your relationships?

PRAYER

Jesus, thank You for your unconditional love for me. Thank You for meeting the deepest needs of my soul. Thank You for accepting me, believing in me, and encouraging me. Transform my relationships as you transform me with Your love. Teach me to love others the way You love me. I pray in Jesus' Name, Amen.

IN LIGHT OF WHO HE IS

IN YOUR RELATIONSHIPS WITH ONE ANOTHER, HAVE THE SAME MINDSET AS CHRIST JESUS: WHO, BEING IN VERY NATURE GOD, DID NOT CONSIDER EQUALITY WITH GOD SOMETHING TO BE USED TO HIS OWN ADVANTAGE; RATHER, HE MADE HIMSELF NOTHING BY TAKING THE VERY NATURE OF A SERVANT, BEING MADE IN HUMAN LIKENESS. AND BEING FOUND IN APPEARANCE AS A MAN, HE HUMBLED HIMSELF BY BECOMING OBEDIENT TO DEATH—EVEN DEATH ON A CROSS!
PHILIPPIANS 2:5-8

Jesus' life reveals the very heart and mind of God. The startling revelation is that at His very core, God is a servant. Do you share God's desire to serve? How is Jesus' presence transforming your life?

PRAYER

Jesus, as I reflect on this passage, I am humbled. I realize how much You want to transform my leadership motivations and intentions, my perspective, my attitudes and behavior. I realize how far I have to go to become like You. Thank You for Your unending patience with me. Make me like You, I pray in Jesus' Name, Amen.

_____
_____
_____
_____
_____
_____
_____
_____
_____

LEADING BY THE BOOK

KEEP THIS BOOK OF THE LAW ALWAYS ON YOUR LIPS; MEDITATE ON IT DAY AND NIGHT, SO THAT YOU MAY BE CAREFUL TO DO EVERYTHING WRITTEN IN IT. THEN YOU WILL BE PROSPEROUS AND SUCCESSFUL.
JOSHUA 1:8

The Lord had one practical piece of advice for Joshua as he began to lead God's people: Get to know Scripture. Meditate on it. Live by it. This is good advice for every leader. If you want to lead like Jesus, let the Scripture that shaped Jesus' life and leadership shape you. Make God's Word the primary influence in your thinking and decision-making. How is your leadership being shaped by Scripture?

PRAYER

Lord, I want to be successful in Your eyes. I want to do what You want me to do. I want to live and lead according to Your commands. Use Scripture to shape my leadership perspective and decision-making. I pray in Jesus' Name, Amen.

LIVE WISELY

BE VERY CAREFUL, THEN, HOW YOU LIVE—NOT AS UNWISE BUT AS WISE, MAKING THE MOST OF EVERY OPPORTUNITY, BECAUSE THE DAYS ARE EVIL. THEREFORE DO NOT BE FOOLISH, BUT UNDERSTAND WHAT THE LORD'S WILL IS.
EPHESIANS 5:15-17

Each day offers new opportunities to live, love, and lead like Jesus. New people may come into our lives; teachable moments may arise unexpectedly. Paul cautions believers to live wisely, seeking God's perspective and training ourselves so that we understand how to live life with God's purposes in mind. Are your eyes open to the opportunities God will give you to influence others today?

PRAYER

Lord, open my eyes to see the opportunities You will bring me today. Help me to live wisely; seeking to understand Your will and make the most of the opportunities You give. Prepare me through Scripture and prayer. Let me invest today for Your purposes. In Jesus' Name I pray, Amen.

NO CHANCE ENCOUNTERS

THE EUNUCH ASKED PHILIP, "TELL ME, PLEASE, WHO IS THE PROPHET TALKING ABOUT, HIMSELF OR SOMEONE ELSE?" THEN PHILIP BEGAN WITH THAT VERY PASSAGE OF SCRIPTURE AND TOLD HIM THE GOOD NEWS ABOUT JESUS.

ACTS 8:34-35

It started simply enough. Philip heard the Lord tell him to go on the road that led from Jerusalem to Gaza, so Philip went. Philip's obedience ended in an opportunity to share the good news of Jesus and baptizing a new brother in Christ. God is always orchestrating events so that we will have opportunities to witness about Jesus. Our obedience allows us to be used by Him. Where is He sending you today?

PRAYER

Lord, I trust that You are at work to draw people to Jesus. Give me sensitivity to where they are spiritually and open my eyes to the opportunities You will give me today to point others to Him. I ask in Jesus' Name, Amen.

 NO LONGER ALONE

THE WORD BECAME FLESH AND MADE HIS DWELLING AMONG US. WE HAVE SEEN HIS GLORY, THE GLORY OF THE ONE AND ONLY SON, WHO CAME FROM THE FATHER, FULL OF GRACE AND TRUTH.

JOHN 1:14

The good news of Jesus is that we are no longer alone. God has invaded our world. Through Jesus, we can be reconciled to God, find meaning and purpose in life, and enjoy true community with others. How will you take advantage of what He has given you today?

PRAYER

Jesus, You have made the way for me to live intimately with the Father. Thank You that, in You, I find the intimacy my soul desires. Thank You that I can listen to Your thoughts in Scripture and talk with You in prayer. Help me build closer relationships with my brothers and sisters in Christ as we share Your grace and truth with one another. I pray with deep gratitude for all You have done to make this possible. In Jesus' Name, I ask, Amen.

POWERFUL WORDS

I THANK MY GOD EVERY TIME I REMEMBER YOU. IN ALL MY PRAYERS FOR ALL OF YOU, I ALWAYS PRAY WITH JOY BECAUSE OF YOUR PARTNERSHIP IN THE GOSPEL FROM THE FIRST DAY UNTIL NOW, BEING CONFIDENT OF THIS, THAT HE WHO BEGAN A GOOD WORK IN YOU WILL CARRY IT ON TO COMPLETION UNTIL THE DAY OF CHRIST JESUS.

PHILIPPIANS 1:3-6

Words of encouragement build people's confidence and courage. Disappointments large and small, conflict, and lack of results are just some of the things that can rob people's energy and enthusiasm and cause them to lose sight of the vision and goal. How can you encourage others today?

PRAYER

Lord, thank You for the people who encourage me and partner with me to bring Your vision to reality. Thank You for being at work in them and in me to accomplish Your purposes. Help me to encourage others today, just as You encourage me. In Jesus' Name I pray, Amen.

 STAYING CONNECTED

SO THEN, JUST AS YOU RECEIVED CHRIST JESUS AS LORD, CONTINUE TO LIVE YOUR LIVES IN HIM, ROOTED AND BUILT UP IN HIM, STRENGTHENED IN THE FAITH AS YOU WERE TAUGHT, AND OVERFLOWING WITH THANKFULNESS.
COLOSSIANS 2:6-7

Jesus is the author, finisher, and perfecter of our faith (Hebrews 12:2), says Scripture. He is the first, the last, the beginning and the end, the same yesterday, today, and tomorrow. Life is all about being transformed into His image. The habits of solitude, meditating on Scripture, prayer, unconditional love, and supportive relationships are meant to give us staying power in our leadership journey. How are you being strengthened to lead like Jesus through these habits?

PRAYER
Lord Jesus, many things try to pull me away from continuing to live in You. Thank You for modeling habits that kept You connected to the Father. Thank You for reminding me to draw strength from practicing these habits. I pray in Jesus' Name, Amen.

THE GIFT OF PRAYER

AND THIS IS MY PRAYER: THAT YOUR LOVE MAY ABOUND MORE AND MORE IN KNOWLEDGE AND DEPTH OF INSIGHT, SO THAT YOU MAY BE ABLE TO DISCERN WHAT IS BEST AND MAY BE PURE AND BLAMELESS FOR THE DAY OF CHRIST, FILLED WITH THE FRUIT OF RIGHTEOUSNESS THAT COMES THROUGH JESUS CHRIST—TO THE GLORY AND PRAISE OF GOD.
PHILIPPIANS 1:9-11

How are you praying for those you lead? Family, friends, co-workers, ministry partners? As servant leaders, we have the privilege of bringing people into God's presence through prayer. The prayers in Scripture can guide us in praying for God's purposes to be fulfilled in their lives. Who will you pray for today?

PRAYER

Father, I pray that You will remind me to faithfully pray for the people in my life. Open my eyes to how You are at work in them. May we grow more like Jesus as we follow Him. Help us to honor and serve one another as we live and work together. I pray in Jesus' Name, Amen.

_____

_____

_____

_____

_____

_____

_____

_____

_____

 # THE WAY OF LOVE

FOLLOW GOD'S EXAMPLE, THEREFORE, AS DEARLY LOVED CHILDREN AND WALK IN THE WAY OF LOVE, JUST AS CHRIST LOVED US AND GAVE HIMSELF UP FOR US AS A FRAGRANT OFFERING AND SACRIFICE TO GOD.
EPHESIANS 5:1-2

Walking as Jesus did is walking in love. He left heaven out of love for us to show us the way to the Father. He lived among us, showing us what love for the Father looked like. He loved us, bringing healing and forgiveness and offering reconciliation with God. He restored our hope and taught us how to live in love. How will you follow His example and walk in love today?

PRAYER

Jesus, who can I love today as You loved me? I know the opportunities will be all around me. Open my eyes and show me how I can follow Your example, giving myself away as You did, and walking in love today. I pray in Jesus' Name, Amen.

_____

_____

_____

_____

_____

_____

_____

_____

 # TRANSFORMING POWER

MY MESSAGE AND MY PREACHING WERE NOT WITH WISE AND PERSUASIVE WORDS, BUT WITH A DEMONSTRATION OF THE SPIRIT'S POWER, SO THAT YOUR FAITH MIGHT NOT REST ON HUMAN WISDOM, BUT ON GOD'S POWER.
I CORINTHIANS 2:4-5

As the early disciples spoke about Jesus, the message flowed from their personal experience of being transformed by Jesus' unconditional love and forgiveness. The power of the Holy Spirit to transform ordinary people into spiritual leaders was evident in the early church. How is the Spirit's transforming power evident in your leadership?

PRAYER
Lord, I don't want my message to be just words, true though they might be. I want others to see a living, breathing example of Your Spirit's power to transform lives. May they come into contact with You, Lord Jesus, and discover the difference You can make in their lives. In Jesus' Name I pray, Amen.

 VALUING OTHERS

DO NOTHING OUT OF SELFISH AMBITION OR VAIN CONCEIT. RATHER, IN HUMILITY VALUE OTHERS ABOVE YOURSELVES, NOT LOOKING TO YOUR OWN INTERESTS BUT EACH OF YOU TO THE INTERESTS OF THE OTHERS.
PHILIPPIANS 2:3-4

When we focus on exalting God instead of exalting ourselves, we are free to value others. No longer needing to prove our worth or promote our personal interests, we can appreciate the gifts and abilities of those around us. Do you trust that God has a plan for your life? Are you able to relax in His care and provision? How can you affirm and value those around you?

PRAYER

God, thank You that I can trust You to accomplish Your purposes for me. Thank You for the ability to take my eyes off of myself and look around me, truly able to see and appreciate the gifts You have placed in others. Show me how I can encourage and support them as they follow You. I pray in Jesus' Name, Amen.

WHAT HOLDS US BACK?

AND DO NOT GRIEVE THE HOLY SPIRIT OF GOD, WITH WHOM YOU WERE SEALED FOR THE DAY OF REDEMPTION. GET RID OF ALL BITTERNESS, RAGE AND ANGER, BRAWLING AND SLANDER, ALONG WITH EVERY FORM OF MALICE. BE KIND AND COMPASSIONATE TO ONE ANOTHER, FORGIVING EACH OTHER, JUST AS IN CHRIST GOD FORGAVE YOU.
EPHESIANS 4:30-32

What keeps us from becoming the leader that God is calling you to be? Our influence with others increases in proportion to how much influence the Holy Spirit has in our lives. As we yield to Him, He will transform us into people that others trust to influence them. Where do you need to yield to Him today so that you can become more like Jesus?

PRAYER

Lord, show me where I am resisting Your Spirit. Forgive me, cleanse me, help me yield to Your transforming power. Mold me and make me into a person who lives, loves, and leads like Jesus, a person that others can trust. I pray in Jesus' Name, Amen.

 WHO AM I?

"SO NOW, GO. I AM SENDING YOU TO PHARAOH TO BRING MY PEOPLE THE ISRAELITES OUT OF EGYPT." BUT MOSES SAID TO GOD, "WHO AM I THAT I SHOULD GO TO PHARAOH AND BRING THE ISRAELITES OUT OF EGYPT?" AND GOD SAID, "I WILL BE WITH YOU."

EXODUS 3:10-12

Moses' struggle to accept God's call rings through the millennia. "Who am I?" is a question that countless people have asked. God didn't bother answering Moses' question, because He knew it was the wrong question. Ultimately, what matters is not who we are, but who God is. In light of who God is, how do you respond to His call?

PRAYER

God, when I question who I am to be answering Your call, remind me to get my eyes off myself and onto You. Thank You for calling us to be part of what You are doing. Thank You for promising to be with us. Use me, I pray. In Jesus' Name, Amen.

WORLD-CHANGERS

YOU BECAME IMITATORS OF US AND OF THE LORD, FOR YOU WELCOMED THE MESSAGE IN THE MIDST OF SEVERE SUFFERING WITH THE JOY GIVEN BY THE HOLY SPIRIT. AND SO YOU BECAME A MODEL TO ALL THE BELIEVERS IN MACEDONIA AND ACHAIA. THE LORD'S MESSAGE RANG OUT FROM YOU NOT ONLY IN MACEDONIA AND ACHAIA—YOUR FAITH IN GOD HAS BECOME KNOWN EVERYWHERE.
1 THESSALONIANS 1:6-8

Peter, John, Stephen, Paul, and other names that we know from the pages of the New Testament are just the tip of the iceberg of spiritual leaders who embraced the message of Jesus. The first century world was literally transformed by these early believers. How will your example inspire others to turn to Jesus today?

PRAYER
Lord, may I imitate the Thessalonian believers today, welcoming your message, modeling spiritual transformation for those around me, so that your message rings out loud and clear through my life and leadership. In Jesus' Name I pray, Amen.

_____
_____
_____
_____
_____
_____
_____
_____

YOU WERE ONCE, BUT NOW...

FOR YOU WERE ONCE DARKNESS, BUT NOW YOU ARE LIGHT IN THE LORD. LIVE AS CHILDREN OF LIGHT (FOR THE FRUIT OF THE LIGHT CONSISTS IN ALL GOODNESS, RIGHTEOUSNESS AND TRUTH) AND FIND OUT WHAT PLEASES THE LORD.
EPHESIANS 5:8-10

Trusting Jesus brings radical character change. Once we were ruled by selfish passions and self-indulgent pursuits; now our lives are being reoriented to God's perspective. As His Spirit transforms our minds, His truth reshapes our beliefs about life, leadership, and influence. How is He changing your thinking? How will that be reflected in your leadership today?

PRAYER
Lord, I'm reminded that while I am not yet all that I will become, You are in the business of reshaping me. I want it to be evident that You are transforming me to be like You in all goodness, righteousness, and truth. Today, may my life please You, and may I lead like Jesus, in whose Name I pray, Amen.

A LIFESTYLE OF PRAISE

I WILL EXTOL THE LORD AT ALL TIMES; HIS PRAISE WILL ALWAYS BE ON MY LIPS. I WILL GLORY IN THE LORD; LET THE AFFLICTED HEAR AND REJOICE. GLORIFY THE LORD WITH ME; LET US EXALT HIS NAME TOGETHER.
PSALM 34:1-3

What defines your life? What shapes your thinking? How is a growing awareness of God's greatness and majesty changing you? Praising God for who He is, remembering what He has done, thanking Him for His promises and great work on your behalf, and surrendering to your Creator and King will revolutionize your life.

PRAYER

Lord, You are worthy of praise! Your power, Your truth, and Your grace are transforming my life. I worship You. I find my deepest satisfaction in knowing You and making You known to others. I bow before You, lifting up my hands and heart to You. May I become known as a person who praises and glorifies You, I ask in Jesus' Name, Amen.

♥ A LOOK IN THE MIRROR

"WHY DO YOU LOOK AT THE SPECK OF SAWDUST IN YOUR BROTHER'S EYE AND PAY NO ATTENTION TO THE PLANK IN YOUR OWN EYE?"
LUKE 6:41

It can be easy to look around at others instead of looking at ourselves as leaders. Yet, truthfully, we are only able to make decisions to direct our own behavior. When was the last time you took time to examine the condition of your heart and head? How are you doing at putting into practice what you know about servant leadership? How is your practice of Jesus' habits increasing your spiritual leadership vitality?

PRAYER
Lord, I confess that when I don't take time to examine my own life, I begin examining the lives of others instead. Today, search my heart, open my eyes to what you see, and give me insight into what I personally need to be changing in order to lead like Jesus. I ask in Jesus' Name, Amen.

A VIEW ABOVE THE CLOUDS

When life's events challenge our ability to lead like Jesus, times of solitude and dialogue with God become increasingly important. Above the wind and storm, we are able to reflect on the unchanging realities of life and gain an eternal spiritual perspective on events and people, including our own role and responsibilities. The Spirit wants to use these times to renew our strength, realign our perspective, and refresh our hearts. Will you let Him do this for you?

PRAYER

O Spirit of the living God, breathe life and hope and strength into me as I draw apart to spend time with You. Reveal Your majesty! Renew, refresh, and realign my perspective; let me see life as You see it. May I reflect You wherever You send me today. I pray in Jesus' Name, Amen.

 ASKING FOR HELP

THOSE WHO TRUST IN THEMSELVES ARE FOOLS, BUT THOSE WHO WALK IN WISDOM ARE KEPT SAFE.
PROVERBS 28:26

To whom do you turn when you need help? Servant leaders look to God for help as they seek to lead like Jesus, and they also learn to depend on others. A leader exalts God by asking for help, partnering with others, giving and accepting mutual support, asking others to pray, and taking godly advice. In contrast, a self-sufficient, "know it all" attitude edges God out. The rich young ruler came to Jesus with a question, but he refused the wisdom Jesus offered. What about you? Where do you need to ask for help?

PRAYER

Jesus, keep me from being a foolish, self-sufficient leader, thinking that I have all the answers and don't need You or anyone else. Open my heart and mind to accept Your wisdom, especially when it comes through other people. Remind me to ask for help today. In Jesus' Name I pray, Amen.

_____
_____
_____
_____
_____
_____
_____
_____

 GROWTH POINTS

I PRESS ON TOWARD THE GOAL TO WIN THE PRIZE FOR WHICH GOD HAS CALLED ME HEAVENWARD IN CHRIST JESUS.

PHILIPPIANS 3:14

What are your growth points as a leader? Are you struggling to exalt God instead of edging Him out? Are you exercising authority over others or serving them? Are you demanding performance from others without meeting them at their developmental level? Are you regularly engaging in solitude, Scripture, and prayer, abiding in God's unconditional love, and pursuing trusting relationships with others?

PRAYER

Lord, it's good to stop and reflect on how I am doing as a leader and where I need to grow. Like Paul, I want to press on toward the goal, experiencing the transforming power of Your salvation and reflecting Your presence in my life. Meet me in the places where I need to grow more like Jesus. I want to be more like Him. It's in Jesus' Name I pray, Amen.

♥ IN THE FACE OF ANXIETY

CAST ALL YOUR ANXIETY ON HIM BECAUSE HE CARES FOR YOU.
1 PETER 5:7

The struggles of living and leading like Jesus can be overwhelming at times: unrelenting pressure, wrestling in prayer, hard choices that must be made, times of self-sacrifice. Peter watched Jesus prepare Himself for the cross; he watched the agony of His prayer and the nightmare of His arrest and trial. Later in life, perhaps reflecting on Jesus' time in Gethsemane, Peter urged believers to turn to God when they were experiencing anxiety.

PRAYER

God, Jesus found You sufficient in the face of anxiety and impending suffering. When I face hard times personally and as a leader, thank You for Peter's reminder to handle my anxiety like Jesus did. I don't need to pretend it doesn't exist; I need to give it all to You. I pray in Jesus' Name, Amen.

IN THE FACE OF OPPOSITION

LIVE SUCH GOOD LIVES AMONG THE PAGANS THAT, THOUGH THEY ACCUSE YOU OF DOING WRONG, THEY MAY SEE YOUR GOOD DEEDS AND GLORIFY GOD ON THE DAY HE VISITS US.

1 PETER 2:12

How do you lead like Jesus in the midst of the world's constant pressure to edge God out and exalt yourself instead? Jesus continually lived for God's approval, regardless of what others said. Like Peter, we can learn how to face opposition by watching Jesus' example and listening to Him. We can follow Peter's advice to early Christians who were being pressured and persecuted for their faith.

PRAYER

Jesus, Your example and Your words, "Not so with you" ring through the centuries, as do Peter's words. When I am experiencing pressure to conform to the world's beliefs and practices, strengthen me to live and lead for God's approval, exalting Him only. In Jesus' Name I pray, Amen.

_____

_____

_____

_____

_____

_____

_____

_____

🗣 IS IT WORTH IT?

HE SAYS, "I WILL DECLARE YOUR NAME TO MY BROTHERS AND SISTERS; IN THE ASSEMBLY I WILL SING YOUR PRAISES."AND AGAIN, "I WILL PUT MY TRUST IN HIM."AND AGAIN HE SAYS, "HERE AM I, AND THE CHILDREN GOD HAS GIVEN ME."
HEBREWS 2:12-13

Is it worth it to lead like Jesus? Leading like Jesus requires the same self-sacrificial attitude that He exemplified. It requires commitment to the Father's vision and values, compassion for others, and willingness to humbly follow God's plan, not the world's vision of leading. Jesus would say that the results are worth it. What about you?

PRAYER

Jesus, thank You for believing we were worth it. Thank You for resisting Satan's temptation to buy into the world's values and do it the easy way. Thank You for loving God and us enough to show us how to live and lead like You. In Jesus' Name I pray, Amen.

♥ IT ALL BEGINS WITH GRACE

FOR IT IS BY GRACE YOU HAVE BEEN SAVED, THROUGH FAITH—AND THIS IS NOT FROM YOURSELVES, IT IS THE GIFT OF GOD.

EPHESIANS 2:8

It all begins with grace—grace poured out freely and fully through Jesus into the lives of His followers. Forgiven, healed, transformed, and sustained by grace, we are enabled to pour out this same grace into the lives of those around us. The world is hungry for grace, although they may not be able to name it. For whom will you bring the blessing of grace today?

PRAYER

Lord, receiving Your grace has been the greatest experience of my life - overflowing, filling my whole being, overwhelming my pain, forgiving my sin, healing my hurt, encouraging my heart, breathing life into my soul, and actively remaking me in the image of Jesus. Thank You! May I be an agent of grace today, like Jesus, in whose Name I pray, Amen.

_____
_____
_____
_____
_____
_____
_____
_____

KNOWING HIM

HIS DIVINE POWER HAS GIVEN US EVERYTHING WE NEED FOR A GODLY LIFE THROUGH OUR KNOWLEDGE OF HIM WHO CALLED US BY HIS OWN GLORY AND GOODNESS.
2 PETER 1:3

How well do you know Jesus? Simon Peter initially resisted his brother Andrew's invitation to meet Jesus before accepting Jesus' call to follow Him. As he learned who Jesus was and learned more about who he himself was in relation to Jesus, he was transformed. After Pentecost, Peter became a powerful spiritual leader. Late in life he wrote the words above.

PRAYER
Jesus, I want to be transformed like Peter was, captured by Your love, taught by You, and empowered to live and lead like You. Thank You for being more than powerful enough to transform me into Your image as I come to know You more and more deeply. Thank You for calling me. I want to know You more. I humbly pray in Jesus' Name, Amen.

ONE STEP AT A TIME

THEY WERE LOOKING INTENTLY UP INTO THE SKY AS HE WAS GOING, WHEN SUDDENLY TWO MEN DRESSED IN WHITE STOOD BESIDE THEM. "MEN OF GALILEE," THEY SAID, "WHY DO YOU STAND HERE LOOKING INTO THE SKY? THIS SAME JESUS, WHO HAS BEEN TAKEN FROM YOU INTO HEAVEN, WILL COME BACK IN THE SAME WAY YOU HAVE SEEN HIM GO INTO HEAVEN."
ACTS 1:10-11

As Jesus prepared to return to heaven after His resurrection, the disciples eagerly asked about the next step in God's plan. Even though Jesus had already given them their mission and told them their next step, as we so often do, they ran ahead of Him in their thinking. What has God told you to do to make disciples?

PRAYER

Lord, when I, like the disciples, ask You about things I don't need to know yet, remind me to faithfully do the things You have already revealed. I want You to find me faithfully serving You when You return. I pray in this in Jesus' Name, Amen.

 TO BE HOLY

**JUST AS HE WHO CALLED YOU IS HOLY, SO BE HOLY IN ALL YOU DO;
FOR IT IS WRITTEN: "BE HOLY, BECAUSE I AM HOLY."**
1 PETER 1:15-16

Holiness, "other-ness" - this is the essence of God's character. He is holy,
separate from us, and set apart. Jesus calls us to be holy, to be mature, to
allow our relationship with Him to so permeate our lives that it overflows in
love for God and others as we lead like Jesus. How different are you from
the world you live in? How will you exhibit God's nature to those around
you today?

PRAYER

*Jesus, I want to be holy, set apart, just as You were holy and lived a life
set apart to God's purposes, a life defined by love for God and others.
Thank You for setting me apart through Your Spirit living within me.
Live and love through me today, I ask in Jesus' Name, Amen.*

WHAT DO YOU DO?

FOR WE ARE CO-WORKERS IN GOD'S SERVICE; YOU ARE GOD'S FIELD, GOD'S BUILDING. BY THE GRACE GOD HAS GIVEN ME, I LAID A FOUNDATION AS A WISE BUILDER, AND SOMEONE ELSE IS BUILDING ON IT. BUT EACH ONE SHOULD BUILD WITH CARE.
1 CORINTHIANS 3:9-10

How do you respond when people ask you what you do? Is your response task-oriented, vision-focused, or people-oriented? God's vision is to establish His kingdom, accomplishing tasks through servant leaders that involve and influence people. Whatever you do, whatever your role, servant leadership is the way you inject eternal significance into your daily activities and relationships. What do you do?

PRAYER

Lord, help me to remember that I am Your co-worker, enlisted into Your service, for Your purposes, according to Your plan. Thank You for giving me a role to play in what You are doing in the world. Remind me that what I do and how I do it matters to You and to others. In Jesus' Name I pray, Amen.

💜 WHEN JESUS IS LIFTED UP

THEREFORE GOD EXALTED HIM TO THE HIGHEST PLACE AND GAVE HIM THE NAME THAT IS ABOVE EVERY NAME, THAT AT THE NAME OF JESUS EVERY KNEE SHOULD BOW, IN HEAVEN AND ON EARTH AND UNDER THE EARTH, AND EVERY TONGUE ACKNOWLEDGE THAT JESUS CHRIST IS LORD, TO THE GLORY OF GOD THE FATHER.
PHILIPPIANS 2:9-11

It's all about Jesus - Jesus, whose name is synonymous with grace, whose life is an outflow of the Father's love - Jesus, who lived for the Father's glory and the benefit of others - Jesus, who poured His life into loving and leading others into relationship with the Father. How will you live to exalt Jesus today?

PRAYER

Jesus, You are worthy to be exalted. You saved us, You ascended to the right hand of the Father, where You intercede for us, and You are coming again. May You be exalted in my life and leadership today. In Jesus' Name I pray, Amen.

WHEN LEADING IS MESSY

I KEEP MY EYES ALWAYS ON THE LORD. WITH HIM AT MY RIGHT HAND, I WILL NOT BE SHAKEN.

PSALM 16:8

Have you considered the messiness of Jesus' leadership style? Rather than simply imposing His God-given vision and values on others, Jesus worked, walked, and lived with ordinary people. By sharing His life with them and meeting them at their point of need, He taught them by example and through experience. Serving, leading, and influencing people was messy and time-consuming for Jesus, just as it is for us. Remember though: We don't walk alone; Jesus walks with us.

PRAYER

Lord Jesus, thank You for walking with me through the ups and downs of learning to lead like You. When it gets messy, when interruptions come, when I fail, when people resist the vision I believe You've given me, remind me that You are with me and focus my eyes on You. I pray in Jesus' Name, Amen.

TITLE	VERSE	PAGE #

HEART

💜 🫶 ✋ 🔄 **APPENDICE**

TITLE	VERSE	PAGE #

APPENDICE

TITLE	VERSE	PAGE #

 **APPENDICE**

TITLE	VERSE	PAGE #

HEAD

APPENDICE

TITLE	VERSE	PAGE #

♥ 🗨 ✋ ↻ **APPENDICE**

TITLE	VERSE	PAGE #

TITLE	VERSE	PAGE #

HANDS

HABITS

♥ 💬 ✋ ↻ **APPENDICE**

LOOKING FOR YOUR
NEXT STEPS?

CEO or teacher, pastor or parent, shopkeeper or student—if you desire to impact the lives of others by leading like Jesus, we invite you to join the LLJ movement and expand your leadership abilities. Lead Like Jesus offers leadership-building resources for teens and young adults as well as for seasoned executives, all with the goal of demonstrating God's love for people while helping them change the way they live, love, and lead.

The following products are available for purchase at
www.LeadLikeJesus.com

LEAD LIKE JESUS

SIGN UP TO RECEIVE THE
E-DEVOTION

If you've enjoyed this devotional, you can receive a new one three times a week in your inbox. These brief, insightful and challenging reflections will help you lead more like Jesus. Sign up at www.LeadLikeJesus.com today!

CONTINUE YOUR PERSONAL GROWTH BY PURCHASING
LLJ STUDY GUIDES

Containing personal reflections, memory verses, prayers, activities and guidelines for creating your own leadership plan, these study guides contain lessons for anyone who aspires to lead like Jesus.

ENGAGE THE NEXT GENERATION THROUGH
STUDENT RESOURCES

Learning to lead like Jesus is an ongoing pursuit. LLJ materials for students are designed to foster life-changing leadership habits and develop skills early that will last a lifetime.

PARTICIPATE IN A HIGH-IMPACT WORKSHOP—
ATTEND AN ENCOUNTER

An interactive program, Encounter helps leaders create positive change in both their personal and professional relationships.

INCREASE YOUR PERSONAL GROWTH THROUGH
ACCELERATE™

Accelerate combines written content, video and powerful questions to foster continued growth as a LLJ leader. An online program delivered daily and built to move at a speed that's right for you.

LEAD LIKE JESUS

WE HAVE ALL SEEN LEADERS, IN CORPORATE AMERICA, EXPLOIT PRIVILEGES OF POSITION BRINGING RUIN TO EMPLOYEES AND INVESTORS.

Meanwhile citizens of under-developed countries languish in poverty and hopelessness in a leadership vacuum. At the same time all across the country, the witness and ministry of churches are compromised and stymied by a crisis of integrity in their leaders. In stark contrast to the failures and foibles of 21st Century leadership stands the perfect leadership role model – **Jesus of Nazareth.**

Lead Like Jesus, a 501 (c)(3) organization, co-founded in 1999, by *Ken Blanchard*, co-author of *The One Minute Manager*, and his longtime friend, *Phil Hodges* imagines a world in which leaders serve rather than rule, a world in which they give rather than take. We imagine leaders who seek to produce results from service and sacrifice rather than from power and position. We recognize this only happens as leaders adopt Jesus as their leadership role model and grow in His likeness.

We exist to help leaders of all shapes, sizes, ages and aspirations to explore and express the leadership principles Jesus lived. To that end we are both humbled and honored to be entrusted with the stewardship of this vision - 7B souls served daily by the impact of people leading like Jesus.

In **Matthew 20**, Jesus expressed His view of leadership in His Not So With You mandate. This principle is a driving force of *Lead Like Jesus*.

For more information on *Lead Like Jesus* or it's programs, services and events, contact: **www.LeadLikeJesus.com**